Send Yourself Roses

KATHLEEN TURNER

AND GLORIA FELDT

Send Yourself Roses

My Life, Loves and Leading Roles

headline
springboard

First published in 2008
by HEADLINE SPRINGBOARD

An imprint of Headline Publishing Group

Reprinted February 2008

4

Cataloguing in Publication Data is available from the British Library

Hardback 978 0 7553 1 7059
Trade paperback 978 0 7553 1 7332

Typeset in Latin 725BT by Avon DataSet Ltd,
Bidford on Avon, Warwickshire

Printed and bound in Great Britain by
Clays Ltd, St Ives plc

Headline's policy is to use papers that are natural, renewable and
recyclable products and made from wood grown in sustainable forests.
The logging and manufacturing processes are expected to conform to the
environmental regulations of the country of origin.

HEADLINE PUBLISHING GROUP
An Hachette Livre UK Company
338 Euston Road
London NW1 3BH

www.headline.co.uk

Contents

Chapter One

The best role is always ahead

I am exhausted. Wonderfully, joyfully exhausted, and filled with such extraordinary happiness and gratitude.

Those were my feelings after the two closing London performances of *Who's Afraid of Virginia Woolf?* on May 13, 2006.

People ask, 'How can you do that – two grueling three-and-a-half-hour performances one right after the other?' The four of us actors – Bill Irwin as George, Mireille Enos as Honey, David Harbour as Nick, and me as Martha – joked that it's actually one six-act play on days when there are two shows, since we're all on stage during most of the show. I liken the energy and the skill this takes to being an Olympic athlete. Which is quite a feat for someone whose feet have sacrificed most of their toe bones to rheumatoid arthritis. That's why I padded around the stage in those funny soft little slippers.

I never feel tired when I'm onstage. Offstage before and after, I wonder how the hell I did it. But onstage, it just doesn't happen. The exhaustion doesn't hit me until the very, very end when I, or rather Martha, is on the floor and George asks, 'Are you all right?' and Martha says, 'Yes . . . *No*.' Then I can allow myself to feel the body pains, to feel the mental pain, to feel the heart pain, of the character.

There's a moment in the curtain call after we've all taken the first bow together. Bill and I step back and Mireille and David take their bow. Then Bill and I step forward to take ours. The sound crescendos; it comes in this huge wave. It feels as though it pushes me back physically. It's such an amazing feeling that it takes my breath away. And I just start to beam. I feel so grateful, so grateful, to us, to them, to me, to God, that we have this incredible experience in our lives. All of us: the audience, cast, and crew. Even the critics – everyone says it's the first time the London theater critics have all agreed and given rave reviews to any play. The audiences jumped; they were on their feet applauding us almost every night. It has been a tremendous, absolutely amazing reward for the effort we have all put out and, yes, somewhat of a redemption for me.

I look out at the audience and return the waves of their love and appreciation with a full heart.

When I first read this play in college, I knew I wanted to play Martha someday. I was thrilled by Martha's recklessness, how she has no thought of consequences. Like the way she slices through George, contrasting his inadequacies in sharpest detail to her own 'necessary greater strength.' She's dangerous as hell but also very exciting and rather endearing.

Or at least I was convinced *I* could make her endearing. Even back then, I was sure I had the skill to make audiences love the characters I played. Heavens, I was twenty, and I believed I could do anything and that Martha would be a fitting challenge for me when I turned fifty. I always kept this idea in my mind.

Fearlessness at twenty springs from not knowing what challenges lie ahead. Fearlessness at fifty comes from having wrestled with life's challenges and learned from them.

Many challenges good and bad, steps I've deliberately planned or opportunistically seized, choices I've made, risks I've taken, came between the idea and the reality of playing Martha. Each of them helped to form me, to teach me, to prepare me.

The right moment to tell my story

People say to me all the time, 'Oh, you're such a regular person.' And I wonder, *As opposed to what? An artificial construct?*

Just before I left New York for the London run of *Virginia*, this book started – as many good things do – over tamales, jicama salad, and a margarita (light salt) at Zarela, a favorite Mexican restaurant. Gloria, who has been a good friend since we worked together at Planned Parenthood Federation of America – she as its president and CEO and I as chair of its Board of Advocates – said she wanted to write my biography. She told me I had a lot to say. I was rather embarrassed at first by the thought of that much emphasis on myself. It seemed too egotistical.

Then I thought about something I'd heard, that the object of our lives is the growth of our souls. And I feel that my soul is finally in a place where I can contribute. This particular moment in my life is a good time to take stock of all that. So I said I would like to be the practical, regular person that I am, and share my life lessons that might be of service to others. Finally we both figured out that I couldn't share my lessons very well without telling my story too.

I feel about this book like I feel about my acting roles. *Send Yourself Roses* is my truth as I see it. But every story has many truths. Take from mine whatever you will.

I do have stories to tell, and I believe in the power of sharing them. Many come from my film and stage work. I'll explore how my roles have broken new ground for women, how they've spanned sexuality from a femme fatale to a woman playing a man playing a woman. I want to share my passion for service. And I've had personal tragedies, rocky relationships, out-of-control drinking, and snarky critics to contend with. I've come back against all odds from a debilitating illness and being told I'd be in a wheelchair for the rest of my life, to which I said, 'Go fuck yourself.' I've experienced the joy of motherhood and the sadness of infertility, a happy marriage that eventually became a necessary separation. I've learned from it all.

But what you know isn't enough, babe: what counts is how you use it going forward.

I like where I am now and what I have achieved. I'm doing the best work of my life. I can see all that has come before: the obstacles overcome, the risks I've taken, the choices I've made, the great, great opportunities I've had, and the lessons about life, love, and leading roles that these experiences have taught me.

I don't want to be twenty again. I'm having that creative surge women often get when we pass fifty. I feel at the top of my personal and professional life.

So I'll take it from the top. Not the beginning, but now, smack in the middle of my life, or so I expect, since the women in my family have good longevity. It's the perfect vantage point to look back at what I've done so far and to look forward to see exciting possibilities I might create for my future – and those that might come my way.

The freedom to go on

I gave myself a special treat the day after *Who's Afraid of Virginia Woolf?* closed in London. I checked into the Lanesborough. It's a beautiful spa hotel, with wonderful service, near Hyde Park. I booked a facial and a massage in my room. I went to the hotel, washed my face, put on a robe, and that was it for the rest of the night. I didn't go back out; I didn't put on makeup or get dressed again. I watched a movie, had dinner in the room, read a book.

I melted into the bed. Maybe the exhaustion sharpened my perceptions because I felt so vulnerable to my feelings. They poured out of me, as though I'd removed my skin with my stage makeup.

I feel different, better, about my personal life as well as my professional life. So much confidence comes simply because I have reached this very good age. Women my age today are forging new ground. Society stops defining us by our reproductive capacity, sexual attractiveness, or other traditional measures, so we become liberated from stereotype. We are freed to grow into our full selves.

I couldn't have allowed myself to feel so positive in the past. When I was at the height of my film career, I didn't have the kind of respect I now have from the theatrical community. I hadn't yet proved that I have the chops for the stage. But now I have a stature I've never before enjoyed.

Virginia Woolf herself observed that when her Aunt Mary left her enough money to live on, her financial independence meant she 'need not hate' or 'flatter any man.'[1] She said this was of even more value to her freedom and autonomy than the right to vote.

True enough. I feel fortunate to be in a generation of women who have had the opportunity to support ourselves and be in control of our own finances – with or without Aunt Mary – throughout our adult lives. Our mothers might have defined themselves as working wives if they had careers outside the home. We have been working *women*. And I think we're much more interesting after we've been out in the world, even if we've been a bit battered by it from time to time. No, we're more interesting *because* we've taken our knocks and learned from them.

I feel optimistic about my life today because I've taken chances over the years. I've taken my own dreams seriously enough to act on them. I've accepted opportunities that have come my way without having to plan or plot for them. But I also have a long-term idea of what I want, and then I take chances on doing the things that seem to fit my talents when they come along. I take chances that move me toward my goals.

That openness to fortuity would drive other people mad. They'll say, 'Okay, what will Kathleen be doing this time next year?' Well, I don't know. I don't know what I'll be doing. Maybe it's not written yet, or maybe I'll feel like doing something else for a while. I have learned to wait until the choice becomes inevitable. I used to drive my soon-to-be-ex-husband, Jay, rather crazy because he'd always want to know the shape of the time to come. And I could never give him that.

I was brought up not to think too much of myself – that wonderful WASP tradition. So it knocks me out when an actor I respect – for example, Donald Sutherland or Dame Judi Dench – comes up after the show and says, 'That was one of the most extraordinary performances I have ever seen.' I don't know what to say. It is just staggering to me. I've admired their work for so long, it's difficult to think they accept me as one of them.

So I say, 'Thank you.' I'm much too polite to reject a compliment like that – my God. It's a thrilling thought; it makes me smile out loud. And it does change things.

Acting is the study of human behavior, but you don't have to be an actor to share these experiences. And there's absolutely no end to the study, because every year you learn more, you build on the information, the understanding you've achieved. This study of human behavior is just fascinating to me. And to find the qualities or the elements that strike chords within me and others is endlessly interesting.

Soaking in the elegant tub at the Lanesborough Spa, I looked back at all these things that came before in my life. I looked forward to my future with the excitement of embarking on a new stage of life. I felt the satisfaction now . . . and the freedom to go on from here.

And then I got up at six the next morning to catch my flight back to New York.

Kathleen Turner is a verb

I'm happy to be back in my city. I've been identified more and more with New York over the last few years, though I've been here since I drove here from Baltimore, straight out of the

University of Maryland, in 1977. I'd skipped the graduation ceremonies and told them to send my diploma to my mother in Missouri because I was going on to my future. I had a whole hundred dollars in my pocket, and I thought I was rich.

There are so many things I love about New York: I leave my apartment early to walk over to the gym, about seven-thirty a.m. The same garbage men are there who have seen me since I moved in to that apartment. They know I've had two knee operations since then, so they're used to seeing me with a cane or crutches or walker. They ask, 'How's it goin', how ya doin', how's your leg? You don't have a cane – this is great.' I say, 'I'm healing, everything's terrific.' Then I walk on up toward Broadway, and while I'm waiting at the light, the 104 bus stops. I take that line often because it goes up and down from the theater district. The driver swings open the door; he goes, 'Yo, Turner, you're lookin' good. How ya doin'?' I say, 'I'm doing great, thank you.' And I'm thinking, *Okay, garbage men love me, bus drivers love me* – it's just fantastic. New York is like a small town, because people, all kinds of people, are so friendly and it makes me feel like they're proud of me.

Being back home, routines become comfortingly normal again. I like the little things. I like grocery shopping. I like going to the pharmacy; the pharmacist is my friend. He's known me for ten years. These are the same stores I've been going to year after year after year. Makes me feel at home. I like planning meals and cooking for family and friends and for myself. I *do not* like cleaning. I'll vacuum if I have to, but that's about it. I don't like people fussing about me, though. All this business about having a car standing by for when you might need it is just another person to take responsibility for. I'd rather go out and

THE BEST ROLE IS ALWAYS AHEAD

get my own taxi and not have anybody else tied up in it. I think that's a real waste of my energy, and I don't want people handling my life, always knowing where I'm going, what I'm doing. It's none of their business. In fact, I'm downright stubborn about that. Stay out of it – I'll handle it, thank you. Please, for heaven's sake, I'm a New Yorker.

From my bedroom I can see both the sparkling Hudson River and the lights of the city. I wake up every morning to this beautiful light on the buildings and I think of what a magnificent accomplishment New York is. Since 9/11, my connection to the city has become even deeper. I think people associate me with New York more strongly too because of my involvement with the 9/11 rescue and cleanup efforts. I felt it was my responsibility to do what I could. I actually flagged down a fire truck and convinced the firemen I could be of use. So they took me to where I could help organize the clothing for the rescue workers, and I made myself available to speak to the media when they needed me to tell people what supplies and volunteers were needed.

As soon as I got back home from London, I started on a new fitness program. I had gotten out of shape and gained weight there, where I didn't have my normal workout regimen. The eternal struggle, you know. It gets to be more of a challenge each decade. I call my trainer 'my little Italian Nazi.' Her name is Suzie Amatuzi. The new program is an incredible workout. I've only been doing it four days and I already feel like I'm 50 per cent back.

'I already feel like I'm 50 per cent back.' Now, that's a real Turnerism! I waste no time.

And I had no time to waste even if I'd wanted to. It's been a rapid-fire week since I returned, between spending time with my daughter, Rachel, catching up with friends and the charitable organizations I support, and slipping back into my household routine in my apartment. I love having an apartment where I can see so many facets of the city I love. The busier rooms – my office and the living room – are all in the west part of the apartment, with the calmness of the river affecting them. My grandmother's deep blue parlor rug is in my living room. It was just like new when I got it because she never let anyone into her parlor, but I use it constantly.

After Jay and I separated and he moved out last year, I had the walls painted colors, some that excite me, some that give me a peaceful feeling. I delight in the vibrant blue, gold, and red furnishings of my slightly chaotic apartment.

It's always slightly chaotic with a teenager in the house. The minute I got back to New York, my daughter got sick. Usually when I finish a long run or a big job, I break down and get sick. But I haven't this time and I think it's because my kid needed me every day. When she gets well, I know I'll go under.

'You know, kid,' I said to Rachel this morning, 'you are really busting my chops here. Every day it's something.' And she goes, 'Well, it's not my fault.' I said, 'Well, no, it's not your fault. You got sick. And then you twisted your knee. But you know what – I've been waiting on you for days now. Taking care of you. Making your food. Bringing you water. Honestly. Getting you to the doctors, getting the doctors to you.'

It was a funny thing, though. Last night she said, 'I can't believe how painful this knee is. Next time you say your knee hurts, I'm going to do anything you want.' I said, 'Yeah, sure, thanks, kid. That'll be a cold day in – August.' But I know she means it. She's a great kid: bright, funny. She has a good sense of humor. It's a marvel to me that we have raised such a great young woman and that she's so ready to be launched into the world.

My shrink told me she wants me to start dating soon. I'm not ready for that yet, even though Jay and I have been legally separated – after twenty-one years of marriage – since before I left for London in January. But then, I haven't had sex since last August. Geez, so maybe I should think about this.

I have spent the week making the rounds to see all of my many doctors. My family doctor, Bert, is a wonderful, blunt, rather nasty-minded guy I've been going to for years. Always giving me trouble. He said to me, 'So, you're over fifty now, huh? Well, let me ask you something. You've done everything you set out to do with your life, right? You've had an international career, you're highly respected, you have a wonderful kid, you have had a long marriage. But you've got another fifty years ahead of you. What the hell are you going to do now?'

At first my heart just plummeted: 'I've done everything I set out to do? That's crazy. And I don't know what I'm going to do next. So there!' But then Bert said something rather wise: 'So now, honey, it's not about proving anything. It's about the quality of your life.' And I thought, *Yeah. Yeah, that I can live with*. There will always be an element of having to prove things because I have the need to constantly prove myself, even if only *to* myself. But truly, it is about the quality of my life from here on out. I don't need to prove anything to anyone else. This realization is very liberating, very exhilarating.

Taking risks, making choices, looking forward

Soon I'm going to do a TV role in Los Angeles, one written for me in the sitcom *Nip/Tuck*, about plastic surgery. I will play a very successful phone sex operator – no, excuse me, she regards herself as a phone sex *artist* – Cindy Plumb, who 'can make you come in English, Spanish, Japanese, or Mandarin. You may be alone, but you're not on your own.' But alas, Cindy's voice is getting lower as she gets older and her clients don't like that. So to get back her girlish voice, she is seeking a vocal cord lift. It's a comedy, of course, yet it sets me to thinking about how voice is such an apt metaphor for women in this world.

And then I'm going to a spa in California for two weeks to really zero in on the body work. 'Listen, honey, you might have to travel with me this summer,' I tell Gloria, who is trying to corral me to work on this book. 'Come with me to the spa; we can get a lot of work done there.' Gloria says, 'Sure we will.'

I'll also try my hand at directing at the Williamstown Theater Festival later in the summer to build my experience as a director. But I like not knowing everything that will happen next in my life even though I have many strong ideas about what I want to do. I like taking chances. Risk is what life is about to me. The main thing is, I don't like to repeat my successes.

Jay and I will be selling our beach house in Amagansett, toward the eastern end of Long Island. Until then, Rachel will want to be there off and on. Her idea of a great time is to play guitar all day. I have to drive her to her appointments this week because of her knee. She's not supposed to drive. So that will knock out the massage I'd planned. Well, all right.

When I'm gone, Rachel can stay with Jay. Or he'll stay with

her at my place and I'll come back to dog hair all over the place and broken dishes. Jay got the dog. He asked me if I would mind. I said, 'Are you kidding? Take him!'

Rachel will be going away to college this fall. I'll be back in time to help her choose things to take, pack up, and move to school. I'd love to do that. And then I get to clean out her room. Oh, God, you wouldn't believe this room. It's appalling. I said, 'Anything you leave – it's gone.'

Sometime after I take Rachel to college, I'll go check out Italy to see if I want to live there part of the year. I'd like to have an outpost in Europe, where they have far greater respect for older actresses than in the United States, not to mention better roles. And I'll teach my course at New York University, which I call 'Practical Acting: Shut Up and Do It!'

After I have worked so hard to get here, I find it wonderful and amusing at the same time that it seems to me as if it took a long time to become known and accepted as an actor. But to the outside world it seems as if it happened all of a sudden.

For in acting as in life, there is no real test with a scorecard of your ability, of your skill. If you write, if you paint, if you play music, there's a definitive sort of test. You have to be able to master the instrument or produce a product. You can't follow a score unless you know how to play that violin or trombone. But there's no such criteria that so easily defines the capability or the skill of an actor. I mean, somebody likes you, somebody doesn't. It's all very subjective – so anybody can say he or she is an actor, and many do. This makes many actors doubt their own absolute ability and their own real worth.

You gain confidence from the doing of it, as you successfully communicate through your acting time after time after time with your audience. And you learn how to give yourself affirmations for the work that is meaningful to you, despite what others might think or say. That's the kind of confidence I've been feeling since we opened *Virginia Woolf* in New York. I can finally accept that I am extraordinarily skilled at this job. I have earned my place.

But I do wish I had half the sense of security in my private life as I have in my professional life about my choices and priorities. When I'm acting, I know with certainty whether an action is right or wrong: Is that the right tone of voice? Is that the right gesture? Is that the right emphasis on the thought? Am I building the character successfully in terms of the movement of the story? I can be absolutely sure that, yep, that's perfect. Leave that just as it is.

And then I can come offstage and not know how to talk to my child. Should I have a firm voice here or should I use an understanding one? Do I put my foot down or do I let it go?

When I make decisions for a character, things are always very clear to me. When I make decisions for myself, my personal life, I often don't feel sure at all.

Except about this: The best role is always ahead.

Chapter Two

Every step is forward

Soon after I returned from London, I went to the luncheon that is always given before the Tony Awards for the nominees and other people involved in theater. It was held at the Rainbow Room high above Rockefeller Center. There is no press so it's very relaxed. Oh, it was such fun to see so many actors and old friends and colleagues that I hadn't seen in ages since I'd been out of the country for the past five months.

Bill Irwin rightfully won the Tony last year for his portrayal of George in *Who's Afraid of Virginia Woolf?* in New York. So this year he got to announce all the nominated leading and supporting actresses. And I announced all the male categories. Bill and I did our routine: I said, 'All right, your turn, Bill,' and he said, 'Yes, dear.' So we were still carrying on with our George and Martha routine, and we had a very good time with it.

I did not go to the Tony Awards themselves, though. They called me up two days before the event and said, 'We need you to present something.' Evidently they were having trouble getting people to come. At the luncheon I was standing in for Cherry Jones, who won best leading actress last year, because she wasn't able to be there, which was fine. It was a bit of a nod to me since I was nominated but didn't win.

But calling me up Friday morning to ask me to do the big televised awards show on Sunday – well, I thought that was rather rude. I was insulted, actually. If they wanted me, why hadn't they asked me two weeks ago at the luncheon? Or before that? They knew how to reach me in London. They knew when the event was and what my dates were. So when they asked me with just two days' notice, I said, 'A little late, isn't it? It's just a little late! No, I will not. No. I think I'm going to be having a massage at that time.'

Someone asked me whether I was angry that I didn't get the Tony last year for my performance as Martha even though the pre-Tony buzz predicted I would win. Cherry won it for *Doubt*, and what she did when she went up to accept the award was quite stunning. She said that Kathleen Turner was the most amazing actress in her role as Martha. God knows she didn't need to do that. I wrote her a letter thanking her for her graciousness.

I've had lots of nominations – Golden Globes, BAFTAs, Oscars – and I've won some awards. It would be nice to have that little Tony statue. But I have the certificates of nomination framed in my office. They're a pretty good recognition. After all, Cherry got the Tony, but I got the role.

It's more fun to play a bad girl

I went about getting the role of Martha step by step, because I found her character so compelling from the very first time I read the play. I suppose I chose age fifty as my goal with the idea that she would be past childbearing age. Because the truth is, the play is not really a tragedy unless you know that Martha will never be able to have a child. If she's young enough that it would be possible for her still to hope for a child, then her character is not as deeply tragic as it could, should be. So I had fifty set in my mind. In this day and age, we think in terms of in vitro and other variations on the usual way of becoming pregnant. And we value women for attributes other than motherhood. But I think about Martha in 1960, when the play was set. Life was so different for women then, so much more restricted.

She is intelligent, ambitious, energetic. As she confesses, she worships her father, who was the president of the university. She so desires to please him. Her father has crippled her by not seeing who she is or what she has to offer. She had briefly married 'the lawn mower,' as they referred to the gardener at the boarding school she attended; that made her a damaged person to her father. If it were today, she could have aspired to be a university president herself, or to some other career of her choosing. That would have given her life a whole new purpose, a whole new meaning. But it's 1960, so her ambitions had to be channeled, funneled, achieved by a man – her father before she was married and thereafter, her husband.

As much as she and George love each other and always have, it's been a terrible disappointment to her that he has shared none of her ambitions and certainly will not be the heir to her

17

father's presidency. After twenty-five years, George is still an associate professor. You have to work hard to fail that much.

And without children, what does she have? She gets to be on committees of faculty wives, to have a spring Easter egg hunt or a Christmas party or crap like that, which means nothing to her. She doesn't have any standing other than as her father's daughter or as her husband's wife. She's not a mother, can't be a baby maker, so she doesn't have that title of respect. Today, we women tend to have more options, not fewer, as we get older. Martha had almost none as she approached her fifties. This time of life that to me is so freeing, to Martha must have been terribly stifling.

So she sits in the empty house day after day and she starts drinking. Which I think many would do, frankly, in that situation. I think I would if I were sitting around with all that ability but no way to see that I could do something fruitful with it, or do something that used my abilities or challenged my mind. It would be dreadful. Anyone would feel defeated and might overeat or drink or do drugs.

Perhaps some exceptional women would have found another private outlet such as writing that they could control on their own. But I think that would be the exception, and that they would have been seen as abnormal by the rest of society. Martha chafes at the irrational boundaries, but not in a political way. Her behavior has no boundaries. She has no limits physically or vocally. She just throws herself around without any thought as to the proper behavior.

Poor woman, I started out feeling very angry with her and quite disgusted, and I thought, *Oh, stop it! Pull yourself together – this is rubbish*. But then more and more I began to empathize with her. This happens to me often with characters, since I play so many awful ones. They turn out to be more interesting than the good girls. You always know what a good girl is going to do. You never know what a bad girl is going to do. It's much more fun.

I didn't see the whole film and I've never seen a stage production of *Who's Afraid of Virginia Woolf?* Knowing always that I wanted to do Martha, I would never willingly want to have someone else's performance in my head. But in my readings of it, I always thought it was extremely funny. I saw big laughs. I never understood why no one spoke of it that way. I like a hard-edged humor, and that's definitely *Virginia Woolf* to me. The little I saw of the Richard Burton–Elizabeth Taylor film I disliked immensely, but I think that's because it was performed with acceptance of the culture of the time rather than a questioning of it. It seemed to me that their George and Martha were just two drunks screaming at each other and tearing each other apart for a night. I didn't understand this at all. Because my perception reading the play had been so very different.

With most characters, I find I go through stages where I truly dislike them, and then I start to find the reasons for their behavior – then I start to have sympathy for them and then empathy, and then I feel they're totally justified. Somebody says, 'How could she do that?'

Because she had to, okay?

And I *had* to play Martha.

Jumping into the fear

Fear tries to overtake me when I am between jobs. I had just finished the Broadway run of *The Graduate* and was looking anxiously to what I would do next. I am inclined to try to overcome fear by jumping right into its face, to do that which I am afraid of doing. I decided to ask directly for what I wanted most – to play Martha.

By the time I was forty-eight, I was on a comfortable standing with most of the major Broadway producers. I'd done enough work that was very good so I could speak with any of them if I wanted to. I set out to get the role I'd been coveting since I was twenty.

Liz McCann has been Edward Albee's producer for years. He doesn't allow anyone else to produce his plays. So I had to get to Liz. Fortunately, she's a great friend of the Nederlanders', who own theaters in which Albee's plays have been produced, and Jimmy Nederlander Jr. is a great friend of mine. I asked Jimmy and his fiancée, Margo MacNabb, also a dear friend, to set up a dinner with Liz and Jay and me. Just social, you know.

During the course of the evening, I told Liz that I wanted *Virginia Woolf*. 'I want Martha,' I said. And Liz said, 'Well, I don't think that's going to happen.' Edward had not allowed the play to be performed in New York since 1975. Liz told me he didn't express any desire to do it; he'd had some readings over the last few years with other actresses but had not approved any of them. And career-wise, he was still writing new plays. *The Goat* had come out that year. He didn't want to be known just for his old material. All of which was completely understandable.

I pressed on. 'Yes, but you have no idea how well I would do this. I really need – no, you really need me to do this.' 'No, no, no, no' was her response.

I kept after Liz for weeks after that. *I want to talk to Edward. I want to meet with Edward. I want to see him*. Finally she set up a lunch and the three of us got together. This was before the presidential election in 2004. Edward and I are on the same side politically, and we share a great number of concerns. It was a very interesting, challenging conversation over lunch. The man is absolutely brilliant. We never even got to the play; we just talked politics and everything that goes with that. But I'm told that I *became* Martha during the course of the lunch.

Finally, as we were leaving the restaurant, Edward said, 'All right, what do you want?' I said, 'I want to read Martha.'

When I met with Edward after that, I said, 'Look, I'm funny and we'll get a funny George. I think the dark humor in the play has never been realized.' He said, 'Oh, you don't?' I said, 'No, I don't think anybody's seen it created as the comedy it could and should be.' He was skeptical but said, 'Oh, fine, right.'

So what did I want, he asked again. Again I said I wanted a reading. We agreed to put together the reading.

Then we started desperately thinking of who we would get as George. Bill Irwin's name came up and I thought, *Oh, that's brilliant*. He is a great comedian and an inspired clown, and talk about your timing – that boy has got it. Yeah, he's got it. He has the clear, clear intelligence that needs to be demonstrated by George. And he'd just played in Albee's *The Goat; or, Who Is Sylvia?* in London for a time. I thought, *Oh, this is a stunning idea*. There were many other leading actors who wanted this reading, but once Bill's name came up, that was it for me. I said, 'Yes, we've got to get him in here.'

Next I took the extra step to make sure my own reading would be the best it could possibly be. I got together with Anthony Page, the very talented British director who has done many of Albee's plays, and he worked with us before we did the reading. Anthony later said he thought I looked like Martha, strong and somewhat plain, and unpretentious, as though I'd really lived. Ha! Is that a compliment? At any rate, working with Anthony in advance of the reading was a real plus in my preparation.

When we did our read-through, Edward was there along with the director, the producers, and a number of other people. Edward started laughing soon after we began. And let me tell you something: he doesn't laugh easily.

Now, everyone can see that in this production, there are huge laughs throughout the first act, every three or four lines. In the second act, there are fewer, and the third act, fewer still. But even in the most difficult parts, Albee sets up big laughs that previous productions have not generally made the most of. Even at the very end, when Martha says, 'Show me the telegram,' and George says, 'I ate it.' My God, it's a shock laugh, yes. But the physical action of laughing releases a great deal of tension in everyone. It allows you as an actor to build the tension back up again and to keep the audience with you.

That humor is a part of the characters' deep, deep hurt. They make each other laugh and they make each other laugh at themselves. Martha tries something and doesn't pull it off, George caps her, and she appreciates his effort. It's cool. It's part of their relationship. Honestly, I never understood why people didn't understand how funny this was.

At the end of the reading of the first act, Edward came over to me and he said he hadn't seen anything like it since Uta Hagen performed the role. And I said, 'Well, thank you. We have two more acts to go. Hold on, baby.'

In the break between the first and second act, everybody was just beaming. We were like Cheshire cats. We finished the reading around two in the afternoon. I went home thinking, *It'll probably be weeks before we have a decision on whether or not this will be a go*. And I was soon to turn my witching age of fifty!

They called at five-thirty that same afternoon and said, 'So, do you want it?' I said, 'What do you mean, do I want it? What, are you crazy? What the hell have I been saying for the last two years?'

I got the role of Martha just before I turned fifty.

And then I was really scared. I thought, *Oh my God – is there a real plan here? It's not all random? All these steps I took really made it happen?* No, I do not think it is random. My friends would say I 'Kathleen Turnered' it. I can't seem to keep from taking action when I want to get something done, even if I am afraid.

I literally got the shakes once I knew I had Martha. I was terrified that I wouldn't be able to pull off all my boasts. It was a huge undertaking. A huge test.

My last show on Broadway had been *The Graduate*, which was commercially a huge success but the critics were very tough on the play. Tough on me personally too. Ben Brantley, the *New York Times* theater critic, called the play 'weary' and my performance as Mrs. Robinson 'little more than a stunt,' more appropriate for *Xena: Warrior Princess* than the Broadway stage.[2]

And of course there had been many other jokes about my twenty seconds of nudity onstage. Maureen Lipman, the brilliant British writer, actress, and comedienne, was doing a one-woman show when I was doing *The Graduate* in London. She sent a letter to one of the newspapers saying that she would be performing her show in glasses and socks so that one may see what a real forty-something-year-old woman looks like. And then she wrote me this note: 'My ticket sales went down.' The whole thing was a joke. My great friend Maggie Smith was doing Alan Bennett's play *Lady in the Van* at the time, and she said to Alan, 'Kathleen's doing such wonderful business over there, I'm thinking that perhaps in the end scene when the lady rises, we should do that in the nude.' She said there was this long pause. And she said, 'Alan, I'm joking. I'd look like a Ubangi.' It was very funny. Women, you know, don't take this as seriously as men. At least, actresses don't.

But I knew I had some tall mountains to climb to be given a fair evaluation as Martha.

The Graduate, 2000–2002

Drifting college graduate Benjamin becomes trapped in an affair with the older Mrs. Robinson. To complicate matters, Ben then falls in love with her daughter, Elaine.

Adapted and directed by Terry Johnson
Produced by John Reid and Sacha Brooks

Kathleen Turner as Mrs. Robinson
Jason Biggs as Benjamin
Alicia Silverstone as Elaine

Mrs. Robinson: *Would you like me to seduce you?*

Getting myself back

But if I hadn't done *The Graduate*, I could never have done *Who's Afraid of Virginia Woolf?*

One of the problems of having started my career as a younger beautiful woman known for sexuality – a woman whose characters have been sexy, I should say – is that there's an inherent dismissal of her as an individual. It probably extends to beautiful young men, but certainly to young, beautiful women. There's a sense of these women being quite interchangeable, not unique or individually necessary.

These days I face a different hurdle: People assume a woman my age is not supposed to be attractive or sexually appealing. I get very tired of that and relish opportunities to counteract it. Playing the role of Mrs. Robinson, who in her midforties seduces a young man less than half her age, was one of those stereotype-busting choices. But it had a deeper personal meaning to me too.

I started performing in *The Graduate* at forty-five. Performed it at forty-six in London. We brought it to New York when I was forty-eight. I don't think people in the audience doubted that Mrs. Robinson was capable of seducing Benjamin or that she had the allure, the power, and the sexuality to entrap this much younger man. That's greatly a matter of having the confidence and projecting that confidence to others.

Appearing nude on film was not easy when I was twenty-six in *Body Heat*; it was even harder when I was forty-six in *The Graduate*, on the stage, which is more up close and personal than film. After my middle-aged nude scene, though, I unexpectedly got letters from women saying, 'I have not undressed in front of my husband in ten years and I'm going to tonight.' Or, 'I have not looked in the mirror at my body and you gave me permission.'

These affirmations from other women were especially touching to me because when I began *The Graduate* I'd just come through a period when I felt a great loss of confidence, when my rheumatoid arthritis hit me hard and I literally couldn't walk or do any of the things I was so used to doing. It used to be that if I said to my body, 'Leap across the room now,' it would leap instantly. I don't know how I did it, but I did it. I hadn't realized how much my confidence was based on my physicality. On my ability to make my body do whatever I wanted it to do.

I was so consumed, not just by thinking about what I could and couldn't do, but also by handling the pain, the continual, chronic pain. I didn't realize how pain colored my whole world and how depressive it was. Before I was finally able to control my RA with proper medications, I truly had thought that my attractiveness and my ability to be attractive to men was gone, was lost. So for me to come back and do *The Graduate* was an affirmation to myself. I had my body back. *I* was back.

But I still had some other important body work to do to be ready to play Martha. Rheumatoid arthritis eats up your joints. I knew I had to have my right knee replaced in order to physically do the play. And once that was really clear to me – because you don't want to rush into things like replacing joints in your body – I immediately had the surgery. I had only about eight weeks to rehab and get back into shape to do the play.

And I did it. I did it. The surgery probably saved my left knee too because neither of them was very good. Martha could wear cushy padded slippers to cope with the pain in my feet, but she had to be very physical in the fight scenes and her body language throughout the play. It wouldn't have been fair if I'd been unable to go on because of the pain. So I had to have the surgery. But that added a great deal of stress to the already intense stress of taking on Martha.

Who's Afraid of Virginia Woolf?, 2004–2007

Married couple Martha and George drunkenly spar in front of a younger couple. Their savage battle of wits unravels and reveals a couple who provide each other not only unending misery, but unending happiness.

Written by Edward Albee
Directed by Anthony Page
Produced by Elizabeth Ireland McCann, Daryl Roth, Terry Allen Kramer, Scott Rudin, Roger Berlind, James L. Nederlander, and Nick Simunek

Bill Irwin as George
Kathleen Turner as Martha
Mireille Enos as Honey (New York and London)
Kathleen Early as Honey (U.S. tour)
David Harbour as Nick (New York and London)
David Furr as Nick (U.S. tour)

Martha: *I'm loud and I'm vulgar, and I wear the pants in the house because somebody's got to, but I am not a monster. I'm not.*

And so when *Virginia* opened in New York to great reviews, and when Edward Albee wrote me a very kind note, which I had framed, telling me I made him happy to be a playwright, and when the critic Ben Brantley apologized in print for underestimating me, for assuming that because I'd made the choice of playing Mrs. Robinson before, I wouldn't be capable of playing Martha now, I wept.[3]

Oh, yes, this felt far better than winning a Tony ever could. Brantley saw exactly the points I wanted people to see, saw that I had been able to communicate with the audience exactly what I had intended. Even better, he really saw Martha:

At 50, this actress can look ravishing and ravaged, by turns. In the second act, she is as predatorily sexy as she was in the movie 'Body Heat.' But in the third and last act she looks old, bereft, stripped of all erotic flourish.

When she sits at the center of the stage quietly reciting a litany of the reasons she loves her dearly despised husband, you feel she has peeled back each layer of her skin to reveal what George describes as the marrow of a person. I was fortunate enough to have seen Uta Hagen, who created Martha, reprise the role in a staged reading in 1999, and I didn't think I would ever be able to see 'Virginia Woolf' again without thinking of Ms. Hagen.

But watching Ms. Turner in that last act, fully clothed but more naked than she ever was in 'The Graduate,' I didn't see the specter of Ms. Hagen. All I saw was Ms. Turner. No, let's be fair. All I saw was Martha.

Aah, I thought to myself, *well, now*. People can say, 'Maybe she was cute or sexy and she took her clothes off then,' but they'd have to add, 'Just look at what she can do now.'

Who's afraid of the next role?

I used to think I had the stage line drawn absolutely – now I'm onstage, now I'm off – but I've been informed by friends and family over the years that that's not exactly true. Sometimes it is hard to separate from being Martha during the rest of my day offstage. This character has such personality . . . so much intensity. I know that if I find myself playing a role such as I did in *Indiscretions*, of a weakened, vulnerable, self-pitying character night after night after night, I feel less capable. I feel: 'Now, would you do this for me, please?' And, 'Well, you can't expect me to handle that.'

When I am playing someone like Martha, who is so brash and bold, I might laugh louder. I embarrass my daughter more. Rachel will say, 'You're so loud, Mom!' I don't sound loud to me, but there are certain characteristics that, because you have to slip right back into them every day at seven o'clock, are more easily triggered throughout the day. I try to be aware of it. If something sparked my anger, especially when I was doing Martha, 'Hold it,' I'd try to stop and ask: 'Is this something I'm actually angry about? Or is this one of her kick-off points, one of her buttons that got pushed?' I don't carry out the agenda of my characters in my life. Just their mannerisms.

Still, I had an increasingly ominous feeling in my personal life, especially in my marriage: I felt worse about myself inside my own home than I did outside of it. It came to a head during *Virginia Woolf* here in New York but was not caused by it. Just the opposite; my professional life gave me the balance I needed to get through the personal crisis that had been brewing for some time.

I knew I was doing great work. I mean life-changing work, both for myself and for the people who came to the show. It was an incredibly demanding role and schedule. Meanwhile, I'm getting up at seven o'clock every morning with my kid to get her off to school. I'm running the apartment, the house, making sure there's food. Trying to juggle all of my responsibilities and, I think, doing it well. While I was hearing from friends and professional colleagues day after day what an extraordinary talent I have and what an admirable person I am, I would go home and feel so belittled and so undercut. I felt as if I were two different people altogether. I couldn't reconcile the two views. They didn't seem as though they could be the same person: the person inside the home who was told that she's an awful, ungiving, uncaring person and the one outside who seemed to be so incredibly capable. I felt like I was split in two.

In many actors and I know in myself, there's a great fear of failure. Every time I take another role, it carries with it the possibility that I might fail, and publicly at that. You're right out there for all to see, baby. Yet without that degree of risk, you don't grow enough. So I don't mind the thought of failing, but I have an insecurity about it. God knows, this insecurity is not something only actors experience. I suppose most people have that feeling about taking on new roles, new jobs, new challenges.

And I think insecurity can lead to a sort of self-destructiveness, so that you're no longer just taking risks in order to grow but you're getting hooked on the rush of it and you start to undermine yourself. That's when you see really dangerous behavior, like people who go out and party all night knowing they've got two shows the next day. And I certainly have my bouts of self-destructiveness. But in the end, I'm pretty solid and stable.

Some of that comes from what has always been inside of me, and some of it comes from the circumstances I've been forced to deal with in my life. So when I did finally get to the point at which I could believe that I really was these positive things people outside my home were telling me I was, that's when I said, 'Okay, it's time to take a risk.' And that's when Jay and I decided to separate.

I'm glad that we came to that decision. Because I like the person that people say is wonderful and great and talented. I think I'll stay her. And I want my life to get larger, not smaller. Now that I have fewer home responsibilities, I'd like to explore more choices. I won't be sitting in the background, waiting for somebody to need me. I'll be taking a fresh look at the future and contemplating the great roles that lie ahead. The author Gail Sheehy[4] calls this age the 'feisty fifties' and Suzanne Braun Levine's saltier description of the 'fuck-you fifties' is just how I feel.[5] I am like so many women who have fulfilled their career responsibilities and their child-rearing responsibilities, are able to be financially independent, and now at midlife are choosing to change their careers or to start new businesses or to reinvent themselves in other ways. Maybe not reinvent, because that sounds as if we weren't satisfied with what we had, but rather to expand our lives.

Because in truth, everything that brought us to this point in our lives is valuable to the next part. Every step really is forward. We learn as much from mistakes and setbacks as from successes. Not all of my steps have been as dramatic as those I took to persuade Edward Albee to revive *Virginia Woolf* with me as

Martha. But each and every step has been important.

Thinking back, though I knew I wanted to play Martha from an early age, the path to that goal was not obvious, not assured when I was a twenty-year-old aspiring actress. There were many twists and turns as I took steps forward, much life to be lived and much to be learned.

In fact, early in my life, it wasn't even a given that I'd be an actor. I encountered strong resistance from the man who mattered most in my childhood: my father.

Chapter Three

Let your passion embrace your talent

$\mathcal{I}$'m the third of four children, and the only one of us born in the United States. My parents were in Antwerp, Belgium, when my mother conceived me. My father, Richard Turner, was in the Foreign Service, in the consulate, and due to be moved in the near future. My mom, Patsy Magee Turner, decided to come back to the United States and have me in her hometown of Springfield, Missouri, where her parents, Gladys and Russell Magee, had a farm just outside the city.

I was a very large baby – what a surprise – more than nine pounds. The summer I was born, 1954, turned out to be Missouri's hottest on record. Mom says they kept me naked with a fan blowing over water to keep me hydrated so I would not die.

My grandfather – we called him Daddy Russ and I loved him so much – raised turkeys and chickens. There's a great story in the family about a truckers' strike around the time I was born. They had no way to get the chickens to market. The chickens, however, didn't know this. As chickens would, they kept growing up, going for it, and laying those eggs. Daddy Russ raced around the huge chicken coop that held 15,000 chickens, yelling, 'Get the roosters, get the roosters!' They had to do something with all those eggs. Grandmother tried freezing them. That didn't seem to work. They ate eggs with everything. Finally they set up a farm stand on the street, piled it with eggs, and put up a sign that said, 'Take 'em!'

My father wasn't relieved from his Belgian post when he was supposed to be, so he couldn't get back to see me till I was several months old. Such was life in the diplomatic corps. But I had a happy and adventurous childhood. My parents made our many moves seem like a great adventure to me.

Finding my talent early

We were soon posted to Windsor, Ontario, in Canada. My mother tells me that when I was four, we were home in Missouri to see her parents for Christmas. I stood in the middle of a department store where she was shopping for gifts and started singing Christmas carols, saying, 'Well, look at me!' to the shoppers.

I started nursery school in Windsor. It was in a church, and every morning we'd troop up onto a platform and sing 'God Save the Queen.' I learned that song very well, as did most young Canadians. Then Dad was transferred to Havana, Cuba. He went off to Washington, DC, to do an intensive Spanish study first. Mom took us kids to Missouri for those months and put me in nursery school there. One morning early on, the teacher started to play a familiar song. I stood up and started to sing 'God Save the Queen' at the top of my voice. At which point her hands came crashing down on the piano and she said, 'Not in this country, we don't!' Well, it's the same tune, so how was I to know it was 'My Country 'Tis of Thee'? But this episode didn't dampen my enthusiasm for performing.

Evidently I was a little hyperactive as a child. I went up to the front of the plane flying us to Cuba and started pushing the cockpit, saying, 'Go, go, go!' Impatient even then.

In Cuba, our house was a beautiful classic Spanish villa with interior rooms that opened onto a large garden. We had two huge Weimaraners, Oro and Plata. We kids were small enough that we could actually ride around on the dogs – if they were in a good mood. It was great. I was in *preprimaria*, kindergarten. We had to wear terrible heavy wool uniforms, tan shirts and brown skirts. I developed my dislike for uniforms then and there.

I had not yet learned to speak Spanish, though I eventually became fluent. The teacher would write a big red zero on my page with a fat red marking pen. I was definitely flunking *preprimaria*. And then the revolution came. It didn't change things at first because Castro was out in the countryside. He wasn't in Havana till the very end, but he had many of the intelligentsia, the middle class, on his side because Batista was truly a terribly corrupt dictator who favored the very rich and governed accordingly. But Batista was supported by the U.S. government. So when Castro finally took power in 1959, things changed a great deal. Cubans who worked for American families were threatened, so suddenly no one would work with us or for us.

One day I came home from school and said to Mother, 'Mom, Castro gave me candy.' She said, 'What are you talking about?' I said, 'The teacher told us to close our eyes and pray to God for candy. We did. She said, "Open your eyes." There was no candy. Then she said, "Close your eyes and pray to Castro for candy." We did and when we opened our eyes again, there was candy. The teacher asked, "Who loves you, God or Castro?" '

That was the last day I went to school in Cuba. Mother did not allow us kids to go back. I find it remarkable, looking back, how early they started this program of propaganda and brainwashing the children.

And that was just the beginning. When we dialed the phone, before the call was picked up there was always a recording saying, 'Castro is our savior, Castro is our liberator.' I saw my mother once standing in the living room screaming, 'Castro is a bastard! Castro is an asshole!' I thought, *Good Lord, can this be my mother, who is so self-contained most of the time?*

Strange things started to happen around the house. Suddenly there were tarantulas, and Dad kept a machete close to his bed. A tarantula came into my room. I yelled and Dad came running in with the machete and cut off the tarantula's long furry legs as it scrambled around. The tarantula died, but those legs kept twitching. It's still a vivid image in my mind. Then our dogs were found dead on the patio. They'd been fed poisoned meat.

Some people might think this Indiana Jones-like existence was a bit much for children to absorb. I found it exciting. It didn't even occur to me at my age that there was any plan going on here. My sister, Susan, who was enough older than me to understand more about it, found it considerably more upsetting.

But I felt very secure that my parents would make everything turn out to have a happy ending.

The U.S. government shipped the embassy's women and children to Clearwater Beach, Florida. The men stayed in Havana until all U.S. relations were broken with Cuba. It was my father's job to close the embassy and get the remaining staff out. Everyone knew that the Cubans on the staff, who had been loyal and stayed with the embassy, would face possible imprisonment and certain punishment after the Americans left. So when the officers were due to fly out, the staff supposedly escorted the officers to the airport to wish them farewell, but the officers loaded the plane with the staff and their families and sent them out first. Then, of course, the Cubans had to allow another plane to take our officers out.

I was in Miami a few years ago with Jay's band, the Suits, for a gig at a newly opened Stephen Talkhouse, the Amagansett location of which had been very supportive of Jay's band. After Hurricane Andrew, the area was so devastated that they were trying to raise funds and we said we'd help. A young man came backstage and said, 'I have to thank your father for my life. I was one year old and my mother had no papers for me. Your father took a piece of paper and wrote and sealed it with the embassy seal. They let me into Florida with my family. She's always spoken of how Dick Turner allowed the family to come to the U.S. together.' What a wonderful thing to hear years later – how brave and compassionate my father was.

Dad would not have told me about anything like this because he considered it just his job. He didn't wear his heart on his sleeve. He was very Victorian, very proper. And he was not demonstrative with any of us children. There was no doubt how much he loved us and how he would protect us. But I do remember, when I was very young, getting on his lap and saying, 'I'm not getting off until you hug me.' My brothers and sister wouldn't do this. But I needed for him to show his love. And I got it. He hugged me and laughed about my insistence, and only then did I get off his lap and go off to play.

My mom and us four kids lived in Florida during my first-grade year while we were waiting for my father to get out of Cuba, and when he did, he was sent to work in the State Department in Washington, DC, for two years. We were happy to be back together in a nice old house on Flint Drive in Bethesda, Maryland. Dad drove in to the State Department in DC every day. So we saw a lot of him, which was really great.

The cold war was the hot topic. We had to do bomb drills at my elementary school. They gave us five minutes to get home to our basements or bomb shelters. The school and the parents worked together on this: the school would call a drill at a certain time and we'd run like hell home, where our parents would be clocking us. This was supposed to save us from atomic bombs from Cuba or the Russian missile crisis. But the kids just thought it was great fun because we got to cut through everybody's yard and jump over fences.

One day, when I was in second grade, I was coming out of school when somebody said, 'The president is dead – President Kennedy has been shot.' I said, 'Oh, don't be silly – that was President Lincoln.' I got home, and Mom was leaning over the ironing board, just sobbing, tears running down her face, her eyes glued to the TV. My mother was a very stoic woman so it scared the hell out of us kids to see her so distraught. We knew something very serious had happened. But we didn't realize what a moment in history this was – kids never do, do they? It wasn't till years later that I realized our country's innocence was lost that day and that the assassination would change us as a nation forever.

As for me, throughout my still innocent mid-elementary school years, I remained quite the tomboy. Once when there was a class photo scheduled, Mother put curlers in my hair to try to improve my appearance. When she took them out, I was so appalled to see myself in curls that I crawled under my bed. There were metal chicken wire-like springs under the mattress. I hooked my fingers into those wires. My parents kept pulling me and pulling me but I wouldn't come out until they let me douse my head in water and get rid of those dreadful curls.

They couldn't get me into dresses; they couldn't get me down from the trees. I was always beating up boys because I was a better fighter than they were. When I played Ping-Pong against boys, my mother said, 'Why don't you let them win?' I said, 'Why? *Why?*' That didn't make any sense to me at all. Still doesn't.

Then we got the word that we were moving to Saudi Arabia. We would live in Rihad, the only place in Saudi Arabia where foreigners were allowed to have residences. The kids would have to go to boarding school in Europe after we finished elementary school. Mom was worried about the family being separated.

I was old enough to help with the packing and I knew the routine. Mom had her system where we would cut letters out of that tacky paper you use to line drawers and label the boxes and furniture belonging to each room so the packers would know where to put everything in the new house. We pasted these letters on the chairs and tables and beds.

Suddenly we were informed that we weren't going to Saudi

Arabia; we were going to Venezuela instead. I suppose this was because my father spoke Spanish. Mom was relieved because the children wouldn't have to leave home to continue school.

Caracas, in those days, was beautiful. Now it's terribly polluted and smoky. It's a valley just two miles wide but maybe twelve miles long – a rift in the mountains. We flew in at night. I remember thinking how beautiful all the twinkly lights on the mountains were. We landed in La Guaira, which is the port on the other side of the coastal mountains, and drove over the mountains into Caracas.

We woke up the next morning and saw that all those beautiful twinkly lights were *ranchitos* – slum dwellings thrown together with corrugated iron, and plywood. Every rainy season, many homes were washed down the hills and many people died. The lights twinkled because the residents had to steal electricity since the city services didn't extend to them, and so the electrical power wasn't constant.

There was always an element of unrest and anti-American-ism. But the worst that usually happened was that they'd break into the houses of American families and spray paint the walls with the initials of their revolutionary movement, and maybe tie somebody up, but nobody got killed. It was just a fact of life for us.

Our school was called Campo Alegre, meaning 'happy meadow.' Because we were so restricted and there was no public transportation, there was no way we kids could get around on our own; we had to have an adult drive us everywhere. So there were clubs where the kids hung out – a tennis club, a swimming club. Almost all the international student body was children of highly placed American businessmen.

LET YOUR PASSION EMBRACE YOUR TALENT

First lady ambassador to the moon

At Campo Alegre, I once again had to wear uniforms, which never sat well with me. So I started a campaign to get rid of them. We got it changed so we could wear skirts of our own choice, though jeans were still out. I began to learn that my actions could make a difference. Apparently my classmates noticed certain of my characteristics too. My eighth grade class's prediction was that I would be 'the first lady ambassador to the moon.'

It is my family's tradition and the embassy's tradition that the women start at a very early age to do compassionate work in the community. When I was about eleven, I started volunteering at an orthopedic hospital. By now I was speaking Spanish extremely well. I would make up little bags of candies and toys, and I had a ward assigned to me. Every Thursday I would go and bring the children candy and read books to them. There was a prevalent practice in South America called *limosna* in which the parents took a child, preferably a very attractive child, and they broke an arm or a leg and didn't allow it to heal back right, so the child looked crippled. Then they used the child to beg. Sometimes this was the entire family's income, what this beautiful child would bring in by begging.

Once a year or so the health department would go through town, sweep up all these children, rebreak and set their broken bones, put the children in the hospital, then hand them back to their family. When I started working at the hospital, I met a beautiful little girl who was in a body cast from her stomach down. Her legs had been broken. She was almost healed when I first saw her. Six months later she came back with exactly the same injuries and got exactly the same treatment – another three or four months on her back in a body cast. I went home and I said to my mother, 'I can't do it. I just can't do it anymore. I can't pretend that these kids are going to be all right or that my bringing them candy makes any difference.' So I stopped. But despite this unsettling first experience, volunteering and service became for me a bedrock value that stays with me to this day.

Since we lived near the top of a little hill and there was a park with a playground at the very top, I decided I would earn money that summer by having a playgroup. I'd take kids for a few hours so the mothers could go off to do things. I was able to buy my first watch that way. We didn't have much money and there was constant, constant awareness of where the money was going, why, what we had, and whether this was more important than that to buy. The lack of money was a real strain on my parents' relationship – it's the only thing I remember them having fights about. So I didn't ask for a watch. I found a way to earn the money or do without.

I don't remember what kind of watch it was. But it's what I wanted and I worked for it and I got it.

Then came the big earthquake. The night it struck, my parents were outside of town at an event. Caracas has a history of earthquakes. Every child in school learns about a very famous one in the 1800s, when it struck during a religious procession, so all the people were out in the streets. The story goes that the streets opened up and swallowed the people. Then in an aftershock the streets closed. For days cries from people trapped in the earth could be heard. But that was in 1812. They weren't exactly able to get out the bulldozers, you know. Every child in Venezuela knew these stories.

When this earthquake hit us, it was the most extraordinary sensation. We rushed out of the house, my two brothers and me. The noise was shocking, frightening. It was as if we were being passed by a train on either side and an airplane overhead. Then we saw one of our cars go down the driveway and start down the hill. A crack was running up the side of the house. We were holding on to each other, screaming and trying to understand. When the earth isn't stable, you have nowhere to go. It's not like you have another choice.

My sister was trapped in an apartment where she was baby-sitting. My father and the father of the children Susan was babysitting drove into the city at full speed. When they couldn't go any farther because of fallen buildings and debris, they jumped out, ran to the building where Susan and the children were, got up the stairs using their cigarette lighters, and got them out. The next day, that building went down in an aftershock.

We children were all terrified. But I couldn't imagine my father allowing any of us to die. It was simply impossible. Wherever we were in the world and whatever trouble we got into, he'd get us out. We just knew this. So none of us thought that my sister might die. Still, I had never felt so vulnerable in my life. I had never felt so helpless. This was too much adventure even for me.

The earthquake was such a viscerally frightening memory that it stayed with me even after we left Venezuela. In London, where I was living a few years later, I remember walking down the street with a young man who I hoped would be my boyfriend, when I started to feel and hear a similar vibration and noise. I picked the poor guy up, threw him into a doorway, and jumped in after him. Well, the movement was the Underground. But I didn't think. I just acted.

He did not become my boyfriend.

My parents' choices

My father was always a real protector to me. Because he grew up in China, where he was raised by his missionary grandfather and two very Victorian maiden aunts, he had an extremely black-and-white, clear-cut view of right and wrong: perfect behavior, respect for elders, rules for everything. He was absolutely adamant about his convictions.

Dad had trouble sometimes with his personal relationships. He was stiff, really quite shy. And he would get terribly formal when he was uncomfortable. People read that as having a superior attitude. His career suffered as a result.

He hadn't joined the Foreign Service in the usual way. You usually went to Georgetown University, took your degree, and were hired into the State Department. He was hired into the State Department in China when the Americans liberated China from the Japanese; he was a son of a prominent family and was trilingual, speaking both Mandarin and Cantonese. But he had never gone to the university. I think that made him feel insecure, as though he wasn't as qualified as he should have been.

He always worried about being promoted. There was an unwritten rule that if you were not promoted as an officer within so many years, you transferred over to the Foreign Service staff. It's not quite the same job or the same prestige as an officer has. At one point he came back to our house in

Caracas after he'd gone to the embassy to find out about the promotion list. I was upstairs looking over the walkway, waiting to see his face when he came in. My mother must have been standing on the porch, because Dad came halfway up the walk. He looked up when he saw her and he gave a smile that was so sad. So sad, so apologetic. And my mother said, 'Oh, don't worry.' Fortunately, the next year, he did get the promotion. Mother had a bottle of red cooking wine in the fridge, which she promptly pulled out to make a celebratory toast. In her haste, she dropped the bottle on her toe and the toe broke. She had to go to bed in great pain. We all laughed about this afterward, but at the time it wasn't very funny.

Mother was brought up in Warrensburg, Missouri, the third generation of college-educated women. She was taught and she taught us good manners. She was a terrific mother. She did her full share of embassy wife functions, but she was always there for her children. She was quite strict in many ways, too – she grew up during the Depression, when money and food were in short supply. She can remember eating melted fat on bread as her evening meal. But she had charm. She was gracious, innately gracious. *Is* innately gracious. She has an excellent way of putting people at ease and drawing them out. She has social skills my father lacked. But they both had a special strength and courage. I think they made a very good team.

I was about to turn thirteen when we left Caracas. I left behind my first boyfriend, Dario Gonzalez. His family was Cuban. Young boys and girls were not allowed any time alone together. We were always chaperoned. His parents picked me up once to go to his house for dinner. His mother looked at me and said (in contrast to the Florida woman who was so grateful for my father's intervention), 'Turner, Turner . . . is your father embassy?'

I said, 'Yes, my father is at the embassy.' 'Consul?' 'Yes.'

'Two weeks,' she huffed, 'I waited in a line in Havana. Two weeks I waited. I was the next one and he closed the window and he said, "I'm sorry, relations have broken." We said, "No, no, one more. One more visa." And he said, "You know I cannot do it. We have broken off diplomatic relations with Cuba."'

Dario and I were thinking, *Oh God, oh God, oh God.*

She got over it and it was a pleasant evening. But of all the goddamn boyfriends I could have in the world, I pick the one whose mother got the window shut in front of her face by my father.

Well, you just have to, don't you?

The whole family would come back to the States every two or three years. Dad had to be debriefed in Washington and we'd go to Missouri to have summers with my grandparents. Their farm was a fantastic place for the kids. That big old chicken coop, now unused, was cleaned out and made into a bunk room for the four of us. We had a fridge out there with our own soft drinks and snacks and a bathroom and our bunk beds. We would run around the fields all night. The adults had no idea. And I'll tell you, after we had been so locked up in Venezuela, this freedom was heavenly. We had a nice creek where we'd go catch crawfish. We'd have huge July Fourth picnics out in the fields, and we always made our own ice cream. Daddy Russ had a big brick oven built out there for barbecues. Oh, God, it was great. It was every kid's dream of summer. We didn't put on shoes for months; we ran around like mad. We just had a great time.

We did have to do some work. We picked peaches and plums; usually we had left by the time the apples came in. But we had to dig the vegetable garden and weed it. We'd have contests over who could dig up the biggest potato or carrot. And when Daddy Russ mowed the fields, we would make huge grass forts and organize fights, pelting each other with spoiled fruit. I'm ashamed to say, usually it would be my older brother, Andrew, and me, because we were only eighteen months apart and always very close, against my older sister, Susan, and my younger brother, David, which was completely unfair because they were totally unathletic and couldn't defend themselves.

My grandparents were terrific people. Very practical, down-to-earth. Daddy Russ was an engineer and a truck driver during World War I. He was in the U.S. Army Air Corps, as they called it then. He told me once that when the influenza was sweeping the troops over in France and Spain, he and some of his company holed up in a chateau, found the wine cellar, and stayed drunk for two weeks. He said, 'Now here are the lessons: Number one, you got so much alcohol in your blood, you don't get sick. Number two, if you did get sick, you wouldn't feel it.' They never did get influenza.

Those summers were so wonderful. We'd come back to New York by boat, a lovely little liner called the *Grace Lines*. I ran around all over the ship. Luckily my parents got a little seasick, so they didn't know where we were or what we were doing. Once when we were in New York, we went to Radio City Music Hall. We saw *The Glass Bottom Boat* with Doris Day. It was thrilling. I still love that movie.

Our parents created special ceremonies to mark our many moves so that they felt like celebrations and not disruptions. Each of us kids would get a new traveling outfit, which we couldn't wear until we got on the boat or plane. When we moved to Venezuela, I got a blue knit dress with a low waistband and a pleated skirt. I thought I was so chic. I wore the outfit long past when it fit me.

Because of how my parents handled the moves, I was never afraid of going to a new place. I looked at it as an opportunity for new adventures. I fantasized about whom I would meet and who I could be or what we might live like when I got there. I'm sure this was good training for my future, but at the time it was pure fun.

Still, my grandparents' farm held the most special place in my heart. I would say to my grandfather every time we had to leave to go back to our posting or on to a new one, 'I can't stand it, I can't go to [wherever]. I can't wait to come back here next time. I don't want to go.' He'd look at me and he'd say, 'Well, you just have to, don't you?'

That became a mantra in my life. *Well, you just have to, don't you?* I can't stand this; I'm in too much pain. *Well, you just have to, don't you?* I mean really, truly, I think that's been one of the truest life lessons I've ever received. Doesn't work on Rachel, though. I say, 'Well, you just have to, don't you?' And she says, 'No.' I ask, 'What alternative do you have?' 'I don't know,' she says.

My uncle, Robert Magee, MD, and his wife lived not far away. He used to go quail hunting, so we got to eat the quail, which we thought was quite a delicacy. For a farewell breakfast when we were going back to Caracas, my grandmother made deep-fried quail and biscuits and gravy. I just loved it. I always associated this meal with special occasions. So one summer years later, when I was about to go off on location to do a film and I wanted to make something really special for Jay, I made this same breakfast for him. He took one disgusted look and said, 'What the hell is this? You can't eat these little quail!' City boy, you know.

Awakening to my passions

I craved independence so desperately. I chafed under the constrictions of our life in Venezuela. So I was glad when after five years in Caracas we moved to London. My father was consul at the embassy. The first day, Andy and I found a large Tube station near where we were living. We said, 'Bye,' got on the Underground, and rode for hours and hours, every direction. Just to be fuck free, to move about on our own, was so wonderful.

By then I was in the ninth grade. We kids were beginning to learn a little about the facts of life. We had a family ritual. We always, always went into their bedroom to say good night if we'd gotten home from something late or if we were just going to bed at any time. That was a family thing. But when the door was closed we knew we couldn't go in. In London, the door was closed a lot, which I thought was great. I had no idea what was going on. I just thought it must be great fun. I guess because of this I've always thought that sex was healthy, was good. Beyond that, I was blissfully ignorant about sex during my high school years.

My junior year, the American School moved into a new building in St. John's Wood. They were trying out a new educational system with open pods, and the classrooms all opened on to a central area. The teachers hated it because you could hear everything everyone was doing. The curriculum was geared so that students would finish all the basic work requirements by Wednesday afternoon. Then we'd have two days to do our own projects. If you could get ten or twelve students to agree on a course, the school would provide the teacher for it. In a school of four hundred we had fifty-two English courses, on Chaucer, on Shakespeare, anything we could dream up. They only did that for about a year, because most kids just took the two days off and didn't pursue extra study. I, however, was having a ball learning on my own. To me, this freedom was so invigorating and so lively. *Excuse me, I have to go to Stratford now to study. Bye.*

When I was about thirteen, I was taken to see a play – I think it was *Mame* with Angela Lansbury. That was when it hit me: *I could actually make my living this way, by acting on the stage.*

The start of real acting for me began during high school in London. There were seven of us who were sort of a theater mafia. We produced, directed, acted, chose the plays, got one teacher fired and another one hired. Took over the theater department altogether. It was great fun.

My senior year, I audited classes in drama at the Central School in hopes of going there after high school. My parents did not want me to do this. My father *really* did not want me to do this. To him, being an actor was barely one step up from being a streetwalker. We argued often and ferociously about my growing passion for acting.

We had monumental fights about politics too during those days of the Vietnam War. Dad's view was that if you're an American citizen, you never allow anyone outside the country to hear you disparage your country. Ex-pats, as citizens living abroad are called, are generally fiercely patriotic.

But these were the days of marches to the U.S. embassy opposing the war. My little cadre of seven agitators decided we would organize such a march. When I told my father, his reaction was, 'No, you aren't. No, you won't.' And I retorted, 'Yes, yes, I am doing this.' Much anger and shouting later, Dad said, 'Promise me one thing: Don't go stand in front of the embassy.' I said, 'All right. That's a compromise I can live with.' So I waited on Oxford Street when my friends went and yelled at the embassy. Then I joined them when they came back and we walked on to Hyde Park Corner.

I still believe there is always a diplomatic aspect to confrontation.

I owned the world

It was such an open life. We kids could jump on a ferry and go to Amsterdam for the weekend. My father had a sort of adopted great-aunt in the Herrensgrat, a remarkable woman who'd been in China with his family. We'd go knock on her door unannounced and she'd say, 'Who's there?' We'd say, 'Dickie's daughter and Dickie's son,' and she'd be delighted and say, 'Oh, come in, come in and have some tea.'

Another day, we'd go to Paris. Our theater company would train with other international schools. And I was captain of our volleyball team; we won the young English championship my senior year. So we'd go to Frankfurt, to Brussels, and all over the continent for tournaments. It seemed to me we were citizens of the world and the whole world was mine.

My sister and brothers and I have always been very hardworking on our schoolwork. This was terribly important to my father, particularly because he didn't have a university degree. He made us all promise we would take degrees, no matter what work we chose to do. And we all have. We're all Dr. Turners, in fact. Susan is a doctor of urban policy and sociology. Andy's a doctor of psychology and is now the director of the WWAMI medical education program at the University of Idaho and Washington State University, and assistant dean of the University of Washington Medical School. My younger brother, David, has a doctorate in political science and computer administration. I have a doctorate in literature, but it's honorary. I did call up my siblings when it was offered to me and asked if they would mind terribly if I accepted this honorary degree. They said they felt I had done all the work necessary to accept legitimately. Which I thought was very sweet of them.

My sister, Susan, is a lovely woman but terribly shy. I think that's been a problem for her all her life. She hates confrontation, is afraid of creating a situation in which things will come to a head. And then for some reason she got my father's mother's family's height genes. She's about five feet tall. It's a contrast because the rest of us are quite tall.

My older brother, Andy, and I have always been athletic. My younger brother, David, God bless him, wasn't, but then he had asthma as a child and so I think he didn't start running around and being crazy at the same young age the rest of us did.

Andy and I were very close as children, though Susan says we frightened her with our constant fighting and screaming and even beating each other up physically. And then Andy and I changed; we grew apart for many years. But we've come back together now that we're older and I think much wiser. He's a real stick in the mud, though. Oh, he is a stick in the mud, even though he's a lot mellower now.

David is in New Zealand, where he is Director of Research and Modelling at the New Zealand Ministry of Justice. He has one daughter, a sweet girl named Molly. Sounds like a total Kiwi. All those long, long *e*'s. Very funny. But I am getting ahead of myself . . .

The world changes in a flash

One June day during my last year of high school, Dad, David, and I were alone at home. Mother was in Germany at a conference for the day. She was the volunteer head of TOFS, Troops on Foreign Soil, for the Girl Scouts. Andy and Susan were in the States in college. They were to come back in a couple of days to spend the summer with us in England.

My father and I had one of the most tremendous of our frequent arguments. I wanted to go to Stratford-on-Avon to see the acting and stay over with friends. Dad told me not to go, but I said I was going anyway and stormed off in my usual manner. I called home that night and told them I was in Stratford. In my family, we always called when we arrived at our destination and when we returned to our hometown.

I took the train back to London as planned the next morning. I called from the station when I arrived in London. Mother answered and said, 'Get in a cab and come home.' Now, we didn't have much money, and taking a cab rather than using the Underground or the bus was an unusual extravagance. I asked,

'What do you mean? I don't have any money.' She said, 'Just get a cab. Get here right away.'

I got home to find the house filled with people from the embassy. What the hell was going on?

I walked in through the front door, and I saw my father's chair with his jacket on it right where he'd taken it off when he came home, just like he always did. His pipe was by his chair near the book he'd been reading. Mom was in the kitchen, fussing about finding food for the people.

No one had told me anything. So I walked around feeling something must be terribly wrong but mystified as to why all these people were there. Then this sanctimonious woman came up to me and said, 'I know you must think as I do what a blessed relief it is that he's with God in heaven.' Next thing I knew my arm was drawn back and she was about to lose her teeth, when the consul general grabbed my arm and hustled me off to the kitchen.

That's where Mother finally told me Dad had died.

We had a nice back garden that went straight back from the house and then turned to the right with hedges in a sort of L shape. My father's rose garden was way in the back. He wanted the place to look perfect when my brother and sister got home from college.

He was mowing the lawn and had turned the corner into that back section, which couldn't be seen from the house. So Mom didn't notice anything at first. Then she called for him, and when he didn't reply she went back and found him lying dead on the ground.

Dad had had a coronary thrombosis. He was probably dead before he hit the ground – 'falling down dead,' they called it.

By the time I got to the house, the body had been taken away.

Well, I had no time. I had no time. The house was filled with people. Mother wanted me to help with making food for them. She was finding refuge in the only place she could, in taking care of other people. I found David upstairs. He was absolutely stalwart. We dealt with everybody and got people to start leaving. Somebody said, 'Your mother has to take these – they're Valium.' I said to Mother, 'Yes, you must take this.' She said, 'I'm not taking it unless you take it.'

I said, 'No, no, I'm not.' I was seventeen and I hadn't even had a moment alone to sit down and realize that my father had died. The minute I'd walked in the door there were all these people in my home, and I was still reeling. I wanted my wits about me to absorb it all.

I got Mom to take the Valium and lie down. David and I began cleaning up. Suddenly we heard my mother bolt awake with a loud cry. She had realized my brother and sister were due to fly back from college. She didn't want them to be alone on the plane knowing their father had died. But of course they would call ahead before they got on the plane. She wanted me to answer the phone and tell them only that we'd be at Heathrow to meet them, to make no mention of Dad's death. She wanted me to pretend that nothing had happened. This was *not* a role I wanted to play.

For a long time I wasn't sure I could forgive Mom for that, because it hurt so badly to know that I was lying and to be unable to share my grief with Susan and Andy. There I was for two distraught days until we went to meet Susan and Andy at Heathrow. We told them in the car home that Dad had died. As soon as we got home, I went up to my room and closed and locked the door. I didn't want to come out; I didn't want to talk to anybody. Isolating myself was the cause of the greatest rift between Andy and me, because he thought I was being selfish. But my God, I'd been living with the situation for two days without any time to myself. I was angry and scared and so confused. I thought, *Okay, now I can hand it over to them so I can go sit by my window and try to understand what the fuck is going on.*

What I didn't tell my mother or anyone was that I was convinced Dad had died angry with me because of the argument we had just before I stormed out to go to Stratford. I couldn't bring myself to talk about this guilt. But it stayed with me and gnawed at me.

Mom, of course, was racked. Dad had wanted to be cremated but Mom would not allow it. She demanded an autopsy. And she wanted to go see the body. Well, none of my siblings agreed to do this, but we felt it was impossible to let Mom go alone. The mortician had put makeup on him, flesh-tone makeup. His hands were folded on his chest but clearly they'd gotten him after rigor mortis had occurred, because you could see they had broken the fingers to make them bend. It was the most appalling, appalling thing. I mean, the makeup alone was such an invasion of his self.

It was a typical London day: rainy, gray, lousy. We kids had gotten Mom through seeing Dad's body, but it had been enormously traumatic. I was truly at the end of my emotional rope. She got into the car. Just at that moment, I was overwhelmed by a feeling that I couldn't stand being with her anymore – I was so distressed about how Dad's body had been handled. So I took the bus home. That was yet more ammunition for my brother Andy, who was seething, telling me,

'You left her. You should have stayed with us and brought her home.'

The next week I was to graduate from high school. I don't remember taking my exams, though evidently I did. The family all went to the graduation ceremony. Mother was still really out of it. That year they announced the Honor Society at graduation rather than earlier in the year as they usually did. Susan and Andy had both been in the Honor Society and Dad was very proud of that. I, frankly, wasn't trying for it and didn't think I'd get it. Well, when they announced at the graduation ceremony that I was now a member of the Honor Society, all I can remember is starting to laugh, just hoots and hollers. I was thinking, *Right – one week too late, assholes! Just one week earlier*, one week earlier, *and he would have known*. Oh my stars and garters, I made an awful scene.

My family thought I was out of my mind, which of course I was. But nevertheless you don't behave that way in public. They had to hustle me out of there. I still think it's so ironically funny. But then, I've always had a sick sense of humor.

Mom had a memorial service in London with Dad's coworkers, and then she decided to have another service and the burial back in Missouri. Now, we couldn't afford two trips back, so she had the body preserved until we were ready to leave London for good several weeks later. We flew the coffin home with us. Dad was buried and Mom will have the plot next to his. It seemed to me this was going on forever, prolonging our agony. It was like he couldn't be buried enough or memorialized enough.

I'll tell you: I'm getting cremated, baby. That's it. If somebody doesn't like it, that's too bad. They will not inherit unless they cremate me, okay? I mean, my God, lugging a fucking body around the world, for heaven's sake! It was awful. But it wasn't my choice. It wasn't my right to criticize, either. I think it gave Mom peace. She goes to the cemetery regularly. We planted yew trees and in the fall there are brilliant, beautiful red maples all over. It gives her what she needs: closure, comfort. And that's good. That's good.

But I don't need to go to a graveyard to feel near my father. I talk to him every time I go onstage.

Chapter Four

See your moment and seize it, honey

My whole world died with my father.

He was an absolute rock, for all of us. I had always known a sense of security. Not just personal, family security – I literally felt secure in the world. I knew if I was in Russia, Africa, anywhere, and I had a problem or need, all I had to do was get to a U.S. embassy and say, 'I'm Dick Turner's daughter. You have to help me.' The wires would flash, the phone calls would fly, and someone would say, 'Yes, we'll take care of you.'

When Dad died, the door to that world slammed in my face. The State Department gave us just one month to pack up and leave England. Mother was in such shock and pain. She had to deal immediately with surprises like learning her credit card was canceled because the person who paid the bills was dead. It was 1972, after all, and women generally couldn't get credit cards in their own name, especially when, like Mom, they hadn't been working for pay. You can bet I filed that little kernel of truth away, and it influenced my financial choices later in life.

How the hell could we pack up a house, get out of England, and come back to America without access to the money we needed to make such a quick transition? Oh, it was terrible. I was so scared, so angry, so desperately sad.

Well, we just had to, didn't we?

Soon we were plunked down in Springfield, where we could live with my grandparents until Mom sorted things out. She was so unhappy, so lost. There was no joy anywhere. Any memory I had of having wonderful times in Missouri by then was long gone. Grandmother and Daddy Russ no longer had the farm I'd so loved in my childhood days. I didn't feel like a child anymore anyway. I drove out to where the farm had been one day. Whoever bought it had razed the farmhouse. They left the old stone fireplace standing, and that was it. It was gone, torn asunder just like our life.

We were all desperately unhappy and our unhappiness intensified our exasperation about the many sudden changes in our lives.

Andy and Susan were both away in college. David, my younger brother, started high school in Missouri, and I enrolled at Southwest Missouri State University at Springfield. I moved into the dorm for the fall semester. David was the one I felt the sorriest for. He's so smart, always has been, but he was a little geeky. He was never a jock, was never athletic. So he was bullied and treated badly by the other kids.

My high school education in England had been the

equivalent of the first year of college here. I asked the university if I could test out of freshman year. They said no.

I felt as isolated as I've ever been in my life, truly isolated in a way I didn't know you could be. It seemed to me that I had nothing to share with people my age. None of them had ever traveled abroad. I was stunned by the lack of connection to the rest of the world. Before the Internet or CNN, I couldn't even get much news from outside of Missouri, certainly nothing about Europe or the rest of the world. To my mind, I'd lost being *part* of the world. It sucked, big-time.

I had a return ticket to London. I'd sleep with it under my pillow and I'd think, *I'll get back there someday.* But I couldn't leave my mother and brother. There was nothing, absolutely nothing to do except to keep going, pursue my acting, and try to do what I could for Mom and David.

By this time, I had fully awakened to my passion for acting. I knew acting was unquestionably the unique gift I could contribute to the world. I silently wrestled with my secret guilt about the argument my father and I had just before he died. But I never considered abandoning my acting, not even once.

Nothing but failure could ever have stopped me from allowing my passion to embrace my talent. Only if I had become convinced that I was not a good actor would I have considered another direction for my life. If I left the audiences untouched, if I had not managed to find the core of communication that is acting, if I was clearly not doing my job well by my standards, then maybe my father's opposition to my career would have weighed more heavily than my own commitment to what I was by then sure I was meant to do with my life. And that sense of purpose helped to sustain me through the most difficult times.

Still, after classes I would go back to my dorm room and feel so fucking lost. I'd brought my recording of Tchaikovsky's First Piano Concerto in B-Flat Minor with me from England. It's one of my favorite pieces ever. I'd play it over and over and I would think, *There is more. There is more. There is simply more. If someone can write this music and play it so beautifully, I know there is more. It might not be here, but it's out there somewhere.*

It was up to me to regain the larger world that I longed for with such intensity. I vowed I *would* get it back.

But where to start? I didn't know where to turn or whom to ask. In my family you do not fail. Not only do you not fail, but you don't let others see how difficult it is. It was unthinkable to ask for help. Maybe you got help sneakily: 'I'm having a little trouble with this idea. What do you think?' But you didn't ask straight out for help. And I didn't even realize I needed help. I thought I had to handle it on my own, or – or what? Be disgraced? Be less than I should be? Be – I don't know what.

I've been criticized for not being vulnerable enough as an actor. Well, it's probably true, or at least was true until recent years. For so long, vulnerability meant weakness to me. It meant inability. So I'd find ways around appearing vulnerable, using humor or other tactics. Allowing myself to be vulnerable in front of thousands of people or even my close friends and family was simply not an option for me. Couldn't admit it, couldn't see it, couldn't do it.

Yet deep inside, I yearned for my father's help and guidance. I was missing out on something profoundly important, and I knew it.

My father in heaven, or within me

I started speaking to my father before I would go onstage because it was reassuring. I was in unknown territory, and it gave me a touch of comfort to feel a connection someplace from my previous life.

The first time I spoke to him in this way was when I was playing Bananas in John Guare's *The House of Blue Leaves*, early in my college career. She has a fantastic monologue about driving her old green Buick she calls 'the Green Latrine' into Manhattan. In the middle of Times Square, she sees Jackie O on one corner, Cardinal Spellman on another, and Bob Hope and Lyndon Johnson on the other two corners, and she gets them all into her car. It's a great half-mad, half-gleeful, half-tragic – that's too many halves but it's true to the tragic wackiness of this play – monologue.

Before the curtain goes up for any performance, I always go onto the stage to check props and the set. I never want to find an essential prop missing in the midst of a performance.

I was on the stage checking things out and thinking about how Bananas was so vulnerable, so afraid. I appealed to my father to give me the courage to be this vulnerable woman. I'm so terrified to show weakness. But I knew it would not have been good acting otherwise, and above all I wanted to act well. I asked my father to help me show Bananas's vulnerability. And he did.

My ritual ever since is to stand onstage behind the curtain before it goes up and say, 'Father' – at that point I don't just mean him, I'm thinking in a larger spiritual sense – but then I say, 'Dad, help me to use my mind and my spirit and my heart to give.'

Whether there is an afterlife or not, I don't know, but I know I carry my father within me. And I believe there is a little awareness, a tangible connection. Whether I give it to him or he gives it to me doesn't matter. It always makes me smile when I feel it. Some nights I see his older face telling me matter-of-factly, 'All right, Kathleen, do the job.' Other nights I see him as he was in pictures when he was very young, laughing, and I'll think, *Ooh, it's a good night. We're going to have a lot of fun tonight.* Honestly, I think he knows. I think he sees. It would be such a damn shame if he didn't. Because he never knew any of us kids as adults. And he never saw me onstage as a real actor.

At times my heart ached knowing he and I would never have a chance to resolve the conflict between his disdain for acting and my absolute conviction that acting is my unique talent and I had to choose to embrace it. But deep in my heart I felt my father's most powerful lesson animating me. He had taught me by his example that living with integrity means I have to be true to my convictions just as he was to his.

Dad was always there as a strong positive force in my life, but his disapproval was equally intense. Like the time he drove my mother to my high school to watch one of my performances. He wouldn't come in to see the play because that would have violated his principles. But he wouldn't abandon his daughter, either. Instead, he sat in the car outside the school during the entire program.

Inside the theater, I pictured vividly how his hands must have been clenched on the steering wheel while he waited. Mom went out at intermission and reported to him, 'She's doing well.' She laughed when she told me about this, and I thought it was rather funny too at the time. It was just Dad, and how he was.

Now that I am a parent, I understand how it could be that even when he disagreed with his willful daughter's choices, Dad was always there, waiting in the car.

Whether it was my father's spirit or fate at work, my life was about to take a new turn.

When my Southwestern Missouri theater group performed *The House of Blue Leaves* in Kansas City, the famous director Herbert Blau – one of the founders of Lincoln Center in New York and American Conservatory Theater in San Francisco – was in the audience that evening. He was about to become chair of the arts department at the University of Maryland in Baltimore. After the play, Blau asked me if I would come to Baltimore for my last year of college. Working with him and his company was a fantastic opportunity. I was thrilled to be invited, and there was no question that I wanted to go.

Now I had my mother to contend with.

Mom was furious that I wanted to move to Baltimore. She and I had a big fight about it. She said I was being selfish to leave. I finally said to her, 'I am not your daughter anymore. I am a woman, and unless you can treat me as one, we cannot go on.' I packed my bags, got into my gold 1968 Oldsmobile Delta 88, which I'd bought for three hundred dollars, and drove away.

But I'd learned an indelible lesson from my father's death, and after I cooled down a bit I turned the car around and drove back home. Never again would I part in anger from someone I love. I had to talk it out with Mom, even though I knew that would not change my plans in the long run. And it turned out that she had been more frightened than angry. She wrote to me later saying she hoped one day I would understand how frightening it is for a parent not to understand her child's wants and needs. She felt it was her responsibility to keep me safe, which she could not do from across the country. Mom had her doubts, too, about my choice to pursue acting. She pointed out to me that my siblings were all going into professions that work for the betterment of individuals and communities and said she thought I only wanted to be important. That stung me so hard. I made a bet with her that through my acting I would have a greater impact on the world than any of them. 'Give me twenty years,' I said, 'and you'll see.'

I went on to Baltimore for my senior year.

The first couple of nights I slept in my car because I didn't have any place else to stay. Then I found a basement apartment I could afford. I lived on crackers, peanut butter, and iced tea mix because I didn't have any money even though my mom had relented and was helping me with my tuition.

The theater experience in Baltimore was quite thrilling. We created the Experimental Theater Festival, the first of its kind. We didn't sleep for about three weeks because there was so much to be done. We had twelve performing spaces and I was in charge of the box office. I don't know how I did it. I don't know how anybody did it. But we hosted people from all over the world, whole companies and single artists, and it was a huge success. I met an interesting and diverse group of people.

With the kindness of time, the fog of my father's death began to clear.

New York life

The school year ended and I went directly to New York. I'd planned to share an apartment with a girl from the theater department who was living in the East Eighties. It was a railroad flat, meaning that each room linked to the next. The bathtub was in the kitchen, with a table on top of the bathtub for kitchen use. The toilet was in the hallway. The problem was that her boyfriend, with whom she had supposedly split up, moved back in. There was no privacy and the place was too small for three. So I talked my way into another little apartment not far from there.

My first day in New York, I went to a temporary employment agency. They put me at a travel agency that specialized in booking people to and from Israel. I guess the little old man who ran it thought I knew what I was doing, because he took off on vacation after I'd been there two weeks. Customers were yelling at me in Yiddish and Hebrew; this WASP from Missouri didn't know what the hell they were saying or what they wanted. As soon as the owner got back, I said, 'Sorry, I have to leave.' I tried a number of other temporary jobs, then went the usual route for aspiring actors and became a waitress. The tips were good, and I could be available to audition during the day.

I got an agent fairly quickly. Once a month or so, this one agency I'd heard about held auditions. Actors would go in and do four short pieces for them so they could take a look. I did my four little monologues – a tragedy, a comedy, a classic, a modern. After I finished, I said, 'Thank you very much for your time' and started to leave.

My soon-to-be-agent, David Guc, who turned out to be also my soon-to-be-significant-other, immediately said, 'Would you sign with us?' Surprised, I asked, 'You want me to sign now?' 'Yes.'

They gave me a standard union contract. But being my

determined-not-to-be-fleeced-by-these-big-city-boys self, I took it to a lawyer. I paid fifty bucks I didn't have to spare only to be told it was a standard union contract. Oh. Thank you. Yeah, I knew that.

My New York acting debut came quickly, but wasn't very dramatic. I auditioned for an off-off-Broadway play called *Mr. T* by Michael Zetler. The part had been cast but the actress dropped out and they were desperately recasting because the play was opening in ten days. Michael says that he and the director, Bob Zuckerman, looked at each other and said, 'If she wants it, she has it.' I said, 'I want it.' I was off and running.

After that, I played in *Gemini* at the Little Theater on Broadway. I played the rich white 'the world is just how Daddy said it would be' college girl who can't handle the fact that her boyfriend is gay. In the first scene of the second act, she is whiny and insensitive, revealing herself as a spoiled bitch. I kept rehearsing and working on it, but I just couldn't get this scene right. One night on the stage during a show, it came to me that I was sabotaging my own performance because I so wanted the audience to like me and not to think that I was anything like that girl! Whoa! I had two choices: to be liked or to be a good actress. I chose acting.

About the same time, I got a role on the NBC soap opera *The Doctors*. At twenty-two, you can keep the kind of schedule I had. I'd show up at the TV studio at seven o'clock in the morning, work till five, grab some sushi for a quick dinner, and be at the theater by six to go onstage at eight. Week after week after week. It was just crazy. No more, honey, but back then I could do it.

The work on this soap opera was so awful. They had a team of writers who apparently didn't talk to each other. One day I'd have a script in which the woman can barely speak English – 'I wanna and I gonna and I dunno' – and the next day a script that said, 'Well, the delicious irony, my sister, is that chronology has nothing to do with it.' What? Trying to reconcile these inconsistencies was impossible. So I went to the producer and said, 'Let me play the role as a drunk because it's the only way I can explain this woman's flip-flops of character.' He said, 'Sure,' and that's how my character, whose name was Nola, became an alcoholic and a comic irony villainess. I made her a very popular character, I might add.

But I had to get out of there. My contract was for two years. After eighteen months, the producer left. I used his leaving to break my contract. They told me they'd sue me. I reminded them that if they sued me, they couldn't recast the character and keep the story line going. So it was more profitable for them to simply recast the character. They let me out of the contract.

Turned out, I'd learned a great deal from the soap opera. There, you're given the script the day before, and you have to make your acting choices immediately and make them work on camera. This can lead to bad acting, because you start to think that the first choice is always the right choice, which is simply untrue. But the luxury you have in theater, of exploring for weeks what your choice will be, is not possible in TV. So my soap opera experience was good training for film work.

Seeing the opportunity

All my early ambitions through high school and college were to be a huge stage actor. I didn't think about film at all. My fantasies were of roses at the stage door. Film happened to me.

But that's because when the moment came, I saw the opportunity and was willing to seize it.

The beginning did not look auspicious. *Body Heat* auditions in New York were being cast by two partners, both men. They refused to see me. This was not surprising. I had no film experience, and we're talking about a lead role in a major studio film. Also, I'd had a previous audition with them for another part, at which I'd had the gall to challenge them when they dismissed me. I hadn't been able to help myself, so certain was I that I could do the role. 'All right,' I'd said to them, 'what do you want? What is it that you want? Why don't you tell me and I'll show you that.' My little fit didn't sit very well with these guys.

But in the proverbial twist, what I thought was a curse turned out to be a blessing. The grande dame of casting directors Marion Doherty had trained three women protégées named Wally, Julie, and Gretchen. Gretchen and Julie were in New York and Wally Nicita was in L.A. Unbeknownst to me, the three of them had spotted me somewhere and had made a bet as to which one would cast me in my first major film role.

About three months later I went to L.A. to screen test for a different film. Wally heard I was there and called me in to read for her as Matty Walker. I dressed up – high heels, a tight dress, and makeup – and I read for her. Afterward, she said, 'Don't move, just stay right where you are, I'll be back within half an hour.'

Wally came back with the film's director, Larry Kasdan, and Fred Gallo, the producer. She said to them, 'Sit down; Kathleen's going to read for you.' I read for them, they said, 'Thank you very much,' and I left and went back to my hotel. I got a call late that afternoon: 'Would you come back tomorrow? And show us something a little different.'

So I put on my blue jeans and white T-shirt and went back. Larry handed me the only scene in which Matty ever really talked about herself or her background. Actors never see the whole script before they read, but I am very good at cold readings, thank goodness. I lay down on the couch and read the scene, a monologue.

When I finished, they were all silent. I looked around, wondering whether I had blown it or aced it. Then Larry said, 'I never thought I would hear that out loud exactly as I hear it in my head.'

There were a couple more hurdles yet to come. Larry set up a screen test with Bill Hurt, who would be playing Ned Racine, the male lead, and then I had to do one with the Ladd Company, who would be the film's distributors. The people at Ladd understandably wanted to see what I could do since I'd never done a film before. And studios are notoriously conservative about using untested actors, always looking for a sure thing.

The Ladd office where I was to perform was all white, and I mean snow white, from the walls to the sofa to the carpet. Apparently the executives for whom I was to test had been there all day smoking, because there was an ashtray full of cigarette butts on the table. Skeptical and searching for a place to start, they asked me about my soap opera. I told them how I'd made Nola the first comic soap opera villainess by persuading the producer to let me turn her into a drunk.

'Well, then,' the executives said, 'let's see you do a drunk.' I started by throwing my script onto the table. I was so nervous, I forgot all about the full ashtray. Oh, God, all those ashes and butts went flying around this pristine white room. Horrified, I fell down onto the floor and started cleaning the mess up, groping for the dozens of cigarette butts while apologizing and mumbling about how embarrassed I was. But they assumed I was still acting and apparently they thought it was pretty good acting at that.

I got the part. Wally told me later that she won a lot of money. I thought it was very appropriate that a woman had cast me in my first major film role. I liked that.

Body Heat, 1981

In the steamy Florida heat, the sultry Matty talks local lawyer and lover Ned Racine into murdering her wealthy husband.

Directed by Lawrence Kasdan
Produced by Fred T. Gallo and George Lucas

William Hurt as Ned Racine
Kathleen Turner as Matty Walker

Matty: *You aren't too smart. I like that in a man.*

. . . And seizing it

I loved Matty Walker from the start. I do not care for victims, and Matty was clearly not waiting for anyone else to rescue her. She was a woman well aware of the tools she had been given – the abilities to attract and manipulate men. The emptiness inside her came very much from the knowledge that she had not achieved anything on her own. And I am convinced that at the end of the film, Matty may have gained the riches she desired but has realized that she lost the ability to trust in love.

Anyone watching the film has to believe her, just as Bill's character has to believe that she is sincere the whole time. But at the same time she has to leave little clues: a tone of voice that wasn't quite right or a word or a look or a turn of the head. Something subtle you don't notice when you're watching the first time. But when you get toward the end of the film and the exposure comes, you must be able to realize looking back that those clues were there. Matty appeared so sincere. Yet in retrospect, you recognize a character who was capable and showed you, could you have but seen it at the time, that she was manipulating everyone all along.

Bringing people along with you through that process is what makes acting an art. It's why I can read a speech and you'll understand my every thought and get my excitement or disappointment, yet someone else can read the exact same words and not only do you not feel anything but you don't even get what it's about.

I believe all the knowledge I need for my character is in the script. I work with that thought in mind, and I develop the character, hopefully with the director, but sometimes just following my own instincts. If I play a fifty-dollar whore on Hollywood Boulevard, I'm not going to go out and walk the street to see what it's like being a cheap whore in Hollywood – thank you, no. I will use my imagination, and what knowledge I've been given in the script. I'm definitely not a 'method' actor. I take the script and mark an arc of these crucial moments in the story. Within that arc, the crucial moments are the bases that I have got to land on to push the story in the right direction.

In films, I try to make sure the camera gives enough credit to these bases, because if the audience doesn't catch them, the story cannot progress in a compelling way. I'll say to the director, 'This is a very important thing. I'd really like you to consider a tight shot on this.' Or, 'Set this shot up for me with the camera emphasis here.'

Having Larry Kasdan as my first film director was an extraordinary stroke of luck. I learned much of this from him. I loved Larry. I could have been *in love* with him. If he hadn't been married with kids, I might have just jumped on the boy. He has a terrible, terrible voice – one of the worst voices I've ever heard. Like Joan Rivers's: grating, off-putting, like fingernails on a chalkboard. He reminded me of a Hobbit. But he's a cute little guy, very smart and funny. He's significantly shorter than I am with curly brown hair. But he was so passionate about the film, and I found his boyish excitement incredibly appealing. He had written for major films – *Star Wars*, for one – but he hadn't directed any of his own work. He was so happy to be directing, and his excitement was infectious.

Bill, Larry, and I felt like a little club. The three of us against the industry making a film that was going to be so groundbreaking. Oh, boy. We realized we were making a film that would not just push but open the envelope in its realistic treatment of sexuality.

We spent many good days together. And good evenings, laughing with the producer, Fred Gallo. Fred is a great guy who felt his job, God bless him, was to protect us from the studio suits telling us to do this or change that. Fred intercepted everything, which was both unusual and essential to the integrity of the film.

When we started, no one expected that *Body Heat* would become as big a film as it did. The first time I read it, I had big doubts about whether we could hold the line between being dismissed as sensationalistic sex or being seen as a ground-breaking film that would change how sexuality is portrayed in film. I didn't have a problem with the explicit sexuality since I'd grown up mostly in Europe and South America free of brainwashing with the hypocritical U.S. attitudes about sex. Yes, you could say that South America is machismo and thus has exploitive attitudes toward sexuality, but it does not have our prejudice against sexuality per se. In England, there are some repressive attitudes toward emotions, but I still don't think that they deny sexuality or feel shock about it as we do here. And certainly in most of Europe they accept sexuality as a given in a way that we don't.

I was a legitimate stage actress. I knew I did not want to be labeled a porn star by my first film. It was a thin line and it could have gone either way, given the script. I could have done something safer but I took that risk, that leap of faith. I chose to do *Body Heat*.

The risk to each of us was substantial. We had to believe Larry would keep it on the right side of the line. He did. I think his brilliance was in using film noir techniques to make its dramatically new treatment of sexuality look old fashioned. Film noir has a formality and shape to it; its very familiar form enabled people to accept more readily the daring new content we were presenting.

Freezing through *Body Heat*

Just when it was decided that I would do *Body Heat*, the actors went on strike. This was June. I went back to New York, filled in on soap operas, and started waitressing again. Waiting for the strike to end, Bill and I were terrified the studio would drop the project. But it didn't. In later years, I learned that we had George Lucas, the executive producer, to thank. He refused to let it go. I'm very grateful to him for that.

We didn't get to start shooting until December. That meant we went into rehearsals around November. The studio would pay for only two weeks of rehearsal and Larry wanted four. So we worked for two weeks without salary. Despite that, I was very lucky that my first film director insisted on four weeks of rehearsal before he'd start filming. It saves immeasurably when you begin shooting because you know what you're doing and you know what your blocking is. You don't have to figure it out while 180 expensive crew people wait on you.

One of the things I love about acting is how interdependent everybody in the cast and crew is. Even if you do have some screwed-up star ego, everyone knows you ultimately can't do anything without, say, the gaffer. It keeps you grounded.

We were supposed to start shooting in the summer (*Body Heat*, right?). But by the time the strike was over in the dead of winter, it was incredibly cold, even in Florida, where we started the shooting. The actors were dressed in little T-shirts and shorts. The crew was wearing duffel coats and snow hoods. We just wanted to kill them. We relied on tricks so we didn't look cold when in fact we were freezing our butts off. We'd tense and tense and tense and tense every single muscle in our bodies;

when they said, 'Roll,' we let it go. And then we couldn't shiver because we'd held our muscles so tense. We'd put ice cubes in our mouths and spit them out when the director said, 'Roll,' so our breaths didn't come out as clouds. My mouth felt like a Popsicle all the time.

Larry, Bill, and I went to Florida to Matty's house to rehearse and find where we wanted to play scenes. It was incredibly intimate, though it's not a real intimacy, the three of us talking about choreographing the sets and working with the cinematographer on camera angles. I was only twenty-five. I didn't have that much experience, sexually, personally, and here we were clinically discussing the best way to look like you're going down and giving head. I felt very much torn in two about this – both embarrassed and excited, very professional yet totally amateur.

Larry surprised us with what he thought was a brilliant idea. He decided that to shake up our inhibitions we'd do the hardest thing first. The morning we started to film, he changed the first shot from the one we had expected to do and instead had us shoot the sex scene in the boathouse. This is the only scene with true total nudity. Every other scene, we're in the bathtub or on the bed, where there were ways to cover and hide. But not in the boathouse. The boathouse was full nudity, both front and back.

Breaking sexual barriers

So Bill and I are down in the boathouse with our robes on, meeting the crew for the first time. 'Hi, I'm Kathleen. You're the camera operator? Oh, that's wonderful. Oh, you're the focus puller? Yes, thank you. You're the gaffer. Uh-huh. Props? Nice.'

Handshakes all around. Then we take off our robes, get completely naked in front of these people we have just met, and start doing the scene. Larry legitimately thought this would break the ice. But it was so hard for me.

We choreographed the scenes and camera angles minutely so the viewer would see only what Larry and the cinematographer wanted. We rehearsed them like a dance. It's reassuring to an actor to know there won't be random camera action. It's a more secure feeling to think, *All right, I know at this point the camera is on my back, at this point it's on my face, or it's on his hand moving up my body*.

The most famous scene, the break-in through the windows when Bill grabs the chair and smashes it, was a complete fake because of how we had to film it. We were trying out a new camera process called the Steadicam. The plan was that once Bill got outside, he'd go to the left on the patio to the library and look in, cross back and look into the windows of the front door, and then cross right again to look through the windows of the door where he finally just smashes it, all this in one continual shot. Well, the camera kept fucking up.

Hour after hour I stood in that hallway, and my anticipation was building. It was certainly working for the scene, taking my emotional pitch sky-high. But this scene had to be a night shot. And even with all the film tricks in the world, we couldn't stop the sun from rising. At five-thirty in the morning, we got the shot up to Bill grabbing the chair, smashing it, and stepping in just as the sunrise gave us too much light and we had to cut.

The next night we picked up right there, when Ned grabs Matty and we start that very sexy scene in the house. Well, my goodness, it was like blue balls for all of us. 'Goddammit, I was so ready yesterday!' we quipped. We were cracking everyone up. We managed to snap back into character and finish the scene. But honest to God, it was so frustrating.

After Ned breaks in, he grabs Matty with a sense of longing so fierce and so palpable that you can't help but ache with him. This is what makes the film so strong. As I recall, we go right down onto the floor there in the hallway. There was a balcony above a central well in the house's entryway, and a camera was mounted up there, shooting us from above. That in itself was a little scary – cameras weigh hundreds of pounds and the specter of one dropping on me was disconcerting.

But more disconcerting was having all the crew on this balcony looking down over us. It made me feel as if I were in an arena, like a gladiator in a forum, with thousands of people waiting to see me get torn apart. After almost every scene that powerfully sexual, I'd go back to my trailer and cry, just sobbing and sobbing.

It wasn't that it felt degrading to do these scenes, but it felt incredibly emotionally intrusive. When I'm on camera I don't feel like it's actually me being filmed; I feel like I'm just playing the character. But when the director says, 'Cut!' I'm snapped back to being a young woman who's exposed my body to these (mostly) men. They were courteous and considerate and we had the minimum amount of crew in every set for whatever was needed. But still, my God, it was so raw.

We finished filming the parts we needed to do in Florida and went to California, where we filmed both at the Zoetrope studio and locations along the California coast. We were freezing all the while, except for in the studio, where we were so grateful to be warm. For the first time, I understood how intricate and specific film acting could be. You want a close-up shot of only your hand, with your fingers tapping? You can do that with film. It could never be seen on stage past the twelfth or fifteenth row. On the stage, you have to find a gesture that explains the same thing but is bigger and more visible. On camera, one flicker of your eyes tracking somewhere else and then snapping back is a thought. Every second in film can be a thought.

I found it so exciting to think, *All right, when I choose to look at the camera and how long I stay with that before I have to look away is one of those clues that can tell you in retrospect whether Matty means what she says or is lying.* She goes forward and then she turns back and says, 'Of course, darling.' But she has dropped a subtle hesitation that says it all. So the techniques of film acting can be absolutely brilliant. That was an exhilarating discovery to me as a first-time film actor.

Working with Bill Hurt was also enlightening. To me, Bill is an actor's actor. He was very different in those days from the way he is now. He's changed and matured. In those days he was pretty wild. He drank a great deal, did a lot of recreational drugs, loved those mushrooms. He loved women, too. I don't know how many he went through during the filming. Later on, he settled down.

Bill thinks differently from most people and he's much more 'method' in his acting than I am. He was in the role all the time. He wanted to stay in character and be called 'Ned' even offstage. So I had to talk to him about things that were in the character's experience, not necessarily in his own experience. And he insisted on keeping his mustache though the producer said it looked sleazy. Actually, Bill kept it because he thought sleaziness worked for the part.

Bill got a little teed off when I would chat with the cameraman up until the moment we were ready to act. He didn't like to joke around before the camera rolled. My way of letting off tension is to tell ridiculous jokes, have a great laugh, and then roll the camera and get to work. Bill thought I wasn't taking my acting seriously enough. He would glare at me. He said he just couldn't understand how I could switch so instantly into character and summon the emotion necessary.

Well, I don't want to be in that character until I start to act her. Staying in character when I am not on camera or onstage seems very fake to me. I really don't think about acting until I do it, and then when I do it, I do it completely.

Bill and I and sometimes Ted Danson, who was his good friend in the film and on the set and who was delightful to work with, had intense discussions about interesting topics like whether we humans are just parasites on earth. I ate those up. We'd spend an entire evening talking about questions like 'If you had a choice of how you would die, what would you choose?' I remember Bill's choice was to be sucked up into a jet engine and immediately dispersed. My choice, I think, was *not*. Or, if I must, to go in my sleep without knowing.

When we finished shooting with Bill, Larry and I and some of the crew went to Hawaii to shoot that last shot along the beach with the strange boy. It was a nice way to end, with just the cinematographer, the camera operator, the producer, Larry, and my hair and makeup people. And so it was a very small, calm ending to a film that would bring such momentous change to my life.

I still have that bathing suit. I've never worn it again, but I still have it.

Lessons in bravery and humility

The most important lesson I learned from *Body Heat* is how brave I could be. Which is essential in acting. You must put aside your fears and just fucking do it. I think I was protected by my ignorance. I did not truly understand how powerful the impact of this film would be – otherwise I probably would have run away screaming.

I wasn't very sure of my own sexuality at the time; I hadn't yet realized my own sexual power, or even acknowledged my sexuality to myself. I felt as if I were being forced into actions I didn't understand. This left me feeling terribly vulnerable, terribly shaken. The fact that I would go back to work and do whatever was on the list to be shot the next day was pretty brave.

And then I had to learn how to handle the intense attention a lead actress gets from the people she works with in a film. It's head turning to be the center of focus for months on end in that intimate little world that gets created during the making of a film.

You get more attention while you make a film than most people do in their entire lives. It's that much. It's a dichotomy: you're the reason that all those people are there. Your success in your performance leads to their success. Their good work is then part of a great or successful film. I believe very strongly in having good relations with the crew, knowing their names, knowing their jobs, asking, 'How are you doing? How's your kid today?' Everyone relies on the lead actor as a figurehead. But at the same time, you are so dependent on them to make you look good, which you know and they also know. It creates a world apart that has nothing to do with the real world.

One of the hardest things to learn is how to handle the absence of that attention when this particular little world ends. The day you wrap, that world is gone. Everybody goes back to their homes, their cities, their countries. You become completely alone in the space of one day. You might keep in touch with people for a while, but they go on location elsewhere and you go on location elsewhere, you start another world with another set of people. It's incredibly intimate and the experience is so personal. Then suddenly the intimacy gets dissolved and you're supposed to step back into real life, where you may or may not be so important.

I wasn't important at all after *Body Heat* wrapped, at least for the six months or so until it was released to the theaters. I learned that those months of filming are not life. That's all pretend, a bubble. That's Never-Never Land. I learned to keep in mind that I was going back to real life. People who resist that, who want to keep getting that unrealistic level of attention, become selfish, grasping, irresponsible people.

Ultimately you have to take care of yourself. That's the rule in life, not the exception. I suppose if you have enough millions of dollars, maybe you don't ever have to take care of yourself. But I've never been that rich. Since *Body Heat*, which paid a magnanimous $30,000, I've been well enough paid that I have not had to worry about money constantly as I did in my younger days, and that is a great gift. But I've never been able to afford, or wanted to have, a house that requires five servants, where dinner appears on the table because someone else shops, cooks, and serves. I don't even like being taken care of in that way. I know people who don't lift a finger, who don't do anything except their film roles. Their lives and their children and their finances and everything are taken over by other people. Which would leave me rather bored. I mean, what the hell would I do all day?

Fortunately, after we finished filming *Body Heat*, my practical midwestern roots made me want to take care of myself and not have others fawning over me. I came home to New York. I had no income, so I started waitressing again. Friends would say to me, 'You've been away.' 'Yeah, I was shooting a film.' 'So what's it called?' *'Body Heat.'* 'Oh, I see.' People assumed I had been off doing a porn film.

So for six months until the film got into the theaters, I was back to being an impoverished actress, waitressing, doing soaps, temporary work. Do the math, honey – I had an apartment to pay for in New York, and now one in L.A. too. But the studio didn't want me to take on any other big jobs until the film came out and we could see what the public reaction would be.

I was bored and anxious and not happy with the waiting. I tried to envision how the film's release would change my life, but I couldn't. I don't think anyone could have known before it happened.

Luckily, having grown up in the diplomatic corps, I had a good basic sense of how to behave in public. But nobody tells you how to handle sudden worldwide exposure. You may have had classes in acting, speech, movement, and dance, but nobody teaches you how to be a star.

Chapter Five

If you feel sexy, so you are

If there are no lessons in how to be a star, just imagine how little guidance you can get about how to be a sexual icon. I truly had to figure this one out on the job.

Now listen, babe, if you're looking to read about my ménage à trois here, let me warn you, I'm not telling even if there was one. And I'm not asking you about your sexual experiences, either. For some things we all deserve to have a little privacy. But sex and sexuality in general – now that's fair game. These are powerful elements of human life, the stuff that gives energy to the great dramas of the stage, the screen, and human history. It's the primal energy that continues to propel *Body Heat* so that even now, more than twenty-five years later, it always ranks in the top ten on lists of the world's sexiest movies.

I confess I didn't have a clue that such sexual power would be unleashed by *Body Heat*, the vehicle by which most Americans and people around the world first came to know Kathleen Turner. At the time I got the role of Matty in *Body Heat*, I was a skinny woman with long legs, almost no boobs, good hair – I always had really good hair – and bad teeth. In London, the dentistry was appalling, and my first six months back in the States I had six root canals. One of the studio's worries when I auditioned for *Body Heat* was that my teeth didn't look *American*. So they paid to have a fake cover made for my teeth. It was awkward because it changed my lips, and that changed my speech, the airflow and the sharpness of the consonants. I worked with it and got used to it. Still, when I look at some of the pictures in *Body Heat*, I see the different line of my upper teeth, my lips. It was uncomfortable and didn't add to my confidence, but I didn't have any choice if I wanted to play the role. They certainly weren't paying me enough to have my teeth done properly.

I didn't grow up thinking I was a beauty and still don't think I am. To my mind, I'm a good-looking American woman. I was always tremendously athletic, thank God. It gave me a well-toned if not voluptuous body. As a girl, being so athletic gave me confidence. I thought of my body as strong and capable. As I began to mature, I became aware that men found me attractive. When I got to college and was paid a great deal of attention, I thought, *Oh, okay, I got it, I look pretty good*. Still, it never occurred to me that I had sexual power per se.

In the doing of *Body Heat* I discovered the concept of using sexuality as one of my acting abilities. That was a new idea to me. In fact, many times while we were shooting, I was terrified the camera would catch me giving Bill my best smoldering, come-on-if-you-dare look – and the audience would just giggle. Bill and Larry assured me that would not happen.

Ned says Matty has a body she shouldn't be allowed to go out in. His attraction to her is so visceral that he paces like a caged leopard ensnared by Matty's sexual bait; his desire is so intense that he smashes all boundaries of social acceptability and morality. And even though Matty was conniving, leading him on to do her bidding, I actually imagine the sex Matty had with Ned was great and that she enjoyed it too. Good sex was a bonus though not the reason for doing it, because for Matty love and sex weren't the most important things. She was simply a woman using the most effective tools she had at hand in a completely calculated and amoral way to gain control over her life.

This was not a new story line in human history by any means, but the way we did it in *Body Heat* in 1981 broke sexual ground. People are fascinated by sex scenes partly because of the drama, partly as sex therapy, and partly from pure old prurient interest. Where you draw the line is a matter of judgment. *Body Heat* marked a new line of demarcation in film that I think already had begun to exist in the culture, between an era of buttoned-up sex and an era with fewer sexual boundaries.

People often ask me who among my leading men was the best kisser. It's hard to remember that looking spontaneous and steamy on the screen happens only because it has been carefully choreographed, just like a dance. Sure, actors are human and can get turned on to a certain extent. Doing is feeling. And if you start to sweat in a scene, it's probably because you *should* be sweating. (Though because of the cold weather when we filmed *Body Heat*, Bill and I had to be spritzed to simulate perspiration. *Brrr.*)

But mainly, actors are caught up in the mechanics of the choreography. The body with or without clothes is in costume. And like Matty in *Body Heat*, we actors are simply using the tools we have at hand to tell the story as best we can.

You have to work out in advance whose face is going to be more toward the camera during a kiss, whose nose will go where, is the side of the breast to be shown or the whole breast, and is that sheet in just the right place. You sit in production meetings with whole crews calculating who is to be on top of whom for how long and then counting the seconds while the camera should be rolling a tight shot on your butt. Very sensuous, isn't it?

Portraying sexuality is now just another acting tool I pull out when I need it. But I don't think of what I do when I use this tool onstage or on-screen as an integral part of who I am.

Even as Martha in *Virginia Woolf*, I needed sexuality as a tool. Neither Nick, the young professor she seduces, nor the audience starts off thinking of Martha as a particularly attractive, seductive woman – perhaps even just the opposite. But though she's using Nick and Nick is using her, you have to believe there's a possibility of a real 'let's go fuck' feeling. And I've always imagined that Martha and George had a great sex life and that was one of the things that kept them together.

There's a point when I get Nick to come over and kiss me. When I start to seduce him, I turn on a tap. I just mind-shift into fuckable. And the audience goes with me. That's all I know. It's a way of thinking.

Hell, I can even be sexy as a cartoon rabbit.

I once said something that has often been quoted and misquoted: 'You know how it is when you know you are really sexy? On nights when I feel great about myself, if I walk into a room and a man doesn't look at me, he's either dead or gay.' People tend to cut off the first part and they just take the part I applied to myself. That doesn't carry the idea I intended. To me, the point of sexuality and understanding the power of sexuality is in understanding how you feel about yourself.

This applies to all women of all ages, and to men too actually: If you feel, *Goddamn, I am sexy right now*, well then, so you are!

The difference between sex and sexuality

Sexuality as a grand theme in the human drama and *having sex* are two very different things. Let me step back a few years and explain how I learned this.

I was terribly disappointed the first time I had sex. I was a late bloomer, nineteen going on twenty and still a virgin, which seemed quite extraordinary even in those days. So I thought it was about time I figured out what the hell all this fuss was about. I saw an attractive young man, a performer who was traveling the college circuit and had come to the Southwest Missouri campus. He had a little van he traveled and lived in. I thought this was a pretty good bet for first-time sex because 1) he had a bed in his van and 2) he would be gone the next day.

After his show, we went back to his van and I suppose I seduced him. Afterward, I thought, *Well, that's not much of anything. What is all the talk about passion and how the earth moves?* It wasn't like that for me at all.

Ah, but about six months later, four of us from the Southwest Missouri State University theater department rented a rickety-rackety old house – my best friend, Cat, myself, and a guy named

Craig and his best friend, Jack. The guys had the downstairs; Cat and I had the upstairs. I started falling in love with Craig. Now the twist was, Jack started falling in love with Craig too, and Cat started falling in love with me. So things were getting a little crazy in this house. Something had to give. Cat moved out and Craig moved upstairs with me.

Well, now! I began to understand that being in love with someone is a whole different ball game than just having sex. I started to think, *Okay, this is good. I like this. I believe I will keep this in my life.*

No dummy, me, baby: I used birth control from the very first time. I had gone to the Planned Parenthood clinic in Springfield, Missouri, and got the Pill. I wasn't going to be one of those girls with an unwanted pregnancy. Not at my age.

Growing up in Europe, I had learned a very different attitude toward sex than we tend to have in the United States. Sex wasn't a forbidden topic; it wasn't some shameful hide-it-in-the-closet thing. Overseas I went to American schools where they taught us sex education, though nothing as specific as some kids get nowadays. But there was in the European culture an acceptance toward people making love that was quite aboveboard and open. I think that is the healthier way to go.

That's why I didn't have the kind of fear many young American women seem to have about going to get birth control when they anticipate they are going to become sexually active. To me it was another necessary medical treatment. Just as if I'd broken an ankle I would have gone to a clinic, if I wanted to prevent pregnancy, I would go to Planned Parenthood. It made perfect sense to me. It was a health process. And it was the responsible thing to do.

But the school year ended, Craig went his way, and I went to Baltimore.

By the time *Body Heat* filming ended, I had been living for several years with my agent, David Guc. He was great at first, and very supportive. When I was still a young and rather insecure Kathleen trying to make it in New York, just paying the rent from job to job, I said to him, 'I don't have any proper clothes for auditioning.' David said, 'You can wear jeans anywhere now, but just get a really gorgeous, expensive silk shirt. Wash it out every night if you have to – if you've got a great top, don't worry about the jeans.' So I went and bought a beautiful deep dark green, kind of a racing green, side-button silk shirt for something like a hundred dollars. I remember taking the 104 bus home, crying all the way because I was so scared about having spent so much money on a piece of clothing. Jesus. I still have that shirt. It made me feel more secure. I needed that assurance at the time because I had to put myself out there every day as I auditioned and, often, was not chosen.

But as I began to get more successful, David started criticizing me and reminding me that but for the grace of him I would be nowhere. Never mind who was actually doing the work. I was gaining confidence in my acting, yet the certainty with which I could play a role on film or onstage stood very much in contrast to the growing uncertainty I felt in my personal relationship. David had believed in me from the beginning. He taught me a great deal and I trusted his eye for acting roles that were right for me. But his increasingly cutting words became unbearable in our daily life together.

I finally said to myself, *Look, when I start to feel better about myself away from home than I do at home, I need to get out of the situation*. So I left the personal relationship with David, though he remained my agent for some years. He was a pretty good agent, so I saw no reason to change. I just didn't want to live with him anymore.

I believe the source of some of my uncertainty can be found in conflicting messages all women get in our culture. Having sex is, after all, the easy part; understanding the complexity of sexuality and its intersection with power and personality is a much more difficult challenge. It's endlessly fascinating in a script, endlessly frustrating in real life. I would soon see some of those conflicts playing out in how the world reacted to *Body Heat* and me as Matty.

Sexual iconography

The first review of *Body Heat* – and first review I ever read of a film I was in – was Janet Maslin's in the *New York Times*. Janet wrote it because Vincent Canby, the usual reviewer, was away. I picked up the review feeling optimistic because the comments I'd heard so far had been very positive. Well, the review said, 'Mr Kasdan demonstrates enough talent and thoroughness to breathe life into sections of the movie, particularly those parts that don't involve Miss Turner.'[6]

I thought, *Oh my God, that's it. I threw my heart out and it fell. I missed the other side of the canyon. Oh, shit*. I felt like I was going to throw up.

But most reviews elsewhere were good, so my stomach got back to normal. Then when Canby came back he wrote his own review in which he completely disagreed with Maslin. 'If Mr. Kasdan . . . had presented Miss Turner's Matty as a woman with, say, blindingly platinum hair,' he wrote, 'she'd be one of the most talked about new personalities in films today.'[7] And I thought, *Well, that's okay*, New York Times. *Screw you, Janet Maslin*. In the years since, she's been fine. But that was some kind of way to get a first review of a first film.

When I tried to understand the reason for the diametrically opposite reviews, I wondered if there was a male–female difference going on in reactions to the explicit sexuality. We had expected a general resistance. We knew that to some people it would seem shocking, which is crazy because near-naked females are used to sell beer and trucks, but we Americans won't acknowledge that sex is what's selling the product. The double standard is insane.

But also I think when *Body Heat* came out in 1981, some women were angered by its stereotypical manipulation of men by a woman who's so blatantly sexual. From a feminist perspective, this could be seen as degrading rather than a woman's deliberate use of her sexual power.

Ultimately both men and women came to admire Matty as I did. The men would say, 'How could you do this to a man? But damn, you got away with it.' And the women would say, 'All right, sister, you did what you set out to do.' They both admired Matty's ability to use such power as she had. Clearly, Matty had shaken up the sexual iconography, challenging the power dance that goes on between men and women off the screen, and that becomes reflected on the screen.

In an instant, I came to be seen as a distinctly sexual character in the public eye, even though it was not Kathleen Turner but Matty who had so shaken up the power dance. In the cultural script that repeats itself over and over, there were many attempts to dismiss me as nothing but the sexy persona of the character I had played, to make me not individually necessary but rather just a stereotype.

I've tried to prepare my daughter for the phenomenon I've experienced of beautiful young women being dismissed and devalued as interchangeable. I tell Rachel that if a relationship doesn't make you feel good about yourself as an individual, then it's not right. My grandmother told me once years ago that if you're ever with somebody who you find embarrasses you in public or private, you're with the wrong person. Walk away.

Rachel honestly doesn't let me talk much about sex with her. She doesn't want to talk to her mother about it: 'It's gross – how could I?' I mean, if I say something like 'God, I'm horny,' she'll say, 'Mother, please! That's disgusting!' And she's never seen *Body Heat*. She's never told me if she has, at least. But I have tried all her life to represent sex as a great, healthy joy, when you have the right partner. And I've encouraged her not to get too serious too soon. I want her to give herself time to grow up and know who she is first. It's best to enjoy the company of men as playthings until you're about twenty-nine. Then you begin to get mature enough for serious relationships and children. That doesn't mean being irresponsible in your personal life or that you shouldn't be a responsible citizen before that time. But give yourself time to ripen.

Someone asked me to compare Matty to Paris Hilton. I thought, *Jesus, most of the pop culture icons today are entirely superficial*. Do they have the right look? Are they thin enough to wear the right clothes or to be always up to the edge of fashion? It's not about their style but whatever fashion dictates – are they able to carry that off? And if they are, then that creates a certain celebrity-ness. But I have no idea what these people think or what they do during their time or how they live, other than through someone else's eyes. And I find that it makes me angry that no one ever asks these sexual icons, so-called, what their values are.

It is astonishing that the news media is so driven by who so-and-so was seen with last night or who is having whose baby. Well, to me this is not news. I don't care about those people, or at least I don't care about what they are doing in their personal lives. I don't think I'm unique in that. Nor do I think I'm unreasonable. I just don't see why I should care about their personal lives. What have they given to society that I should care about?

I am seriously unhappy about the way women are 'sold' today, through film and media. I don't think women want to be anorexic. I don't think they want, as they do in *Charlie's Angels*, to strip and lap dance – how humiliating. How hypocritical. Who determines that model of attraction? I walk around in the world every day, and I don't see anyone who looks like that. So if most of us 'people' are nothing like the Hollywood image, why do we care what a few weirdos look like? Give it up!

Okay, you could say there is a thin line between how I perceive myself, where I choose to place myself and my values in my life, and how others will take my work and interpret it. I'll just tell a few stories about how my work seems to have entered the culture and let the judgments fall where they may.

I was shooting in North Carolina when this guy came up to me. I thought he was going to give me a compliment. He said, 'Honey, there are portions of your body that are completely worn away on my tape of *Body Heat*.' Uh-huh. Funny. Funny man.

There's a rock band named Kathleen Turner Overdrive, and a group called Falco has a song called 'The Kiss of Kathleen Turner' ('Under the seven moons, I made a solemn vow / I need the kiss of Kathleen Turner right now.'). It's as though the sexual icon that is symbolized by the actress named Kathleen Turner has entered the cultural lexicon as a metaphor for that beautiful, sexually potent young woman.

And then sometimes people I've just met will ask me to say, 'You're not too smart, are you? I like that in a man.' I'll say, 'Yeah, sure.'

It took me a while not to be startled by the many examples of how *Body Heat* and the characters Bill and I played have entered the language as metaphors. In the documentary film *Enron*, the deservedly defunct company's former vice president and most courageous whistle-blower, Sherron Watkins, called Enron's voraciously greedy, fraudulent behavior a *'Body Heat* moment.' She described Ned banging on the door for Matty, so obsessed with his desire for her that his moral capacity was completely overridden, and she said, 'There's a *Body Heat* kind of angle to this where [Jeffrey] Skilling is Kathleen Turner and Andy [Fastow] is William Hurt. And in the end Andy got suckered into helping all the executives make their earnings.'[8]

There is even a newsletter written by lawyers in Washington, DC – they were like the *Body Heat* Club. They wrote continual updates on Larry, Bill, and me, our lives and our work, and they created stories about what might happen in theoretical spin-offs of *Body Heat*. I thought that was really weird, especially considering that we didn't portray lawyers very favorably in the film.

Be essential in any role you play

To understand my choice to play Matty and why I think she did become such an authentic sexual icon is to understand how I choose all my roles. It has nothing to do with the sexuality element of the character.

I choose my roles for film and stage the same way I choose my roles in life. The woman I play must be integral to the script. If the film or play will be just as good without her, then I will not play that part. I play women who are intelligent, crucial to the story, and actors rather than merely acted upon.

My character doesn't have to be the lead. But I always ask, 'If you took this character out, would you simply have a man without a girlfriend or a wife or a child without a mother? If you took me out of the script, would it make a difference? Would it change the plot and the purpose of the story?' If the answer is not a clear 'Yes!' then I'm not essential. Then they don't need me. And I don't need this role.

I never wanted to play a woman who learned nothing, who did not grow. The woman might fail in what she sets out for, but she must try. She must believe she can effect change in her life, not wait passively for someone else to rescue her.

It's the same way off-screen or offstage. The simplest measure in life to me is to take that job or that choice to move to another house or to get a better car or to do whatever it might be and ask how your life would really be changed by it. Would your life be changed so much if you bought a more expensive car? No? Then it's not essential. If your car is breaking down and you must have a new car in order to get to work, yes. It is essential. If it's not inherent to the story, then you can choose to have it for pleasure, if you want. But don't feel that it's going to satisfy your needs.

Once, when Jay and I were first married, shortly after *Romancing the Stone* came out, I had the experience that so often occurs after a successful film. Producers and directors immediately want you to do essentially the same thing again. I was approached to do *King Solomon's Mines*. Another jungle adventure, right? Angry natives and all that. My agent (still David Guc) called me up to tell me about the offer. David said, 'They want you for the role in *King Solomon's Mines*.' I said, 'Oh, please. I'll tell you what. Tell them five million dollars.' There was a pause, and he said, 'That's their first offer.' I said, 'Then tell them no. Just no, no, no. Just tell them no. I don't want to talk about it anymore – tell them no.' And I hung up.

Jay couldn't believe what he'd heard me say. 'Did you just turn down five million dollars?' he asked. I said, 'I don't want to talk about it. It didn't happen.'

Well, did you see that movie? Oh, God, was it bad. I was absolutely right. Not even a close question.

But, you see, what made me so adamant is, the role I was offered wasn't essential. The film wasn't essential. And the money wasn't essential. That was clear to me. Kind of shocked Jay, though.

No one can doubt Matty Walker was essential. She is a character who knows the future because she is the protagonist of it. She is no victim. You have to be aware of that, but at the same time you know she totally accepts that she is playing the role in her past. There are all these hints and clues the actor has to leave for the audience so that at the denouement, what happens is believable. Oh, that's brilliant stuff. That's layer upon layer upon layer of really cool stuff. That's the fun of acting.

I've played many parts with ironic humor. Not to mention sick humor. I like to be funny. I think you communicate better with humor. Humorous parts are challenging and more interesting in a lot of ways. I find it easy to connect with people over wrenching emotions, rage or fear, anger or loss. Those are gut to gut. But in comedy, in real humor, you have to go through the mind to communicate. The audience has to laugh at a concept. You're not just making them feel; you're making them *think*. Half the time the audience is laughing at themselves, because they fell for something; they thought you were going to say this and then you say that. They'll be appreciative that you fooled them. It's a real mental communication. I don't know how to describe or diagram how it's done. But it's fascinating, the way you can be in touch with people's thinking using humor, get right there in their heads – it's fabulous.

I enjoy playing roles that are a little weird and out of the mainstream, too. So it doesn't matter what kind of role it is to me, so long as the role is essential, in life or before an audience. And sometimes the audience as a group becomes smarter, more reactive, than a single individual would have been to the performance. This is something I truly treasure.

I first experienced this audience empowerment when I was playing the role of Camille in an updated version of the classic Dumas play of the same name at the Long Wharf Theater in New Haven twenty years ago. Everyone knows that at the end Camille dies of consumption and that she gives up her great love when she dies. Everybody knows she's going to die. The problem, right from the top if you are playing Camille, is *how* you will play her dying. You want to hold the audience right through the moment of her death, but how do you do that when everyone knows the ending?

I was rehearsing this part, and the directors asked repeatedly which way I was going to act out my death. I said, 'I don't know yet, I don't know yet, I don't know yet.'

Finally we opened. I came out onstage and reclined on my daybed. I was trying desperately to breathe as Camille literally, slowly, drowns. So I had labored breaths, ending with a long intake of breath. Hold it, hold it. Twenty seconds later, I exhaled ever so slowly. *Got 'em. Now, die on the inhale*. The audience inhales along with me and holds it. When that whole theater releases that breath together, when they have to let it go, oh, I am so happy. It worked beautifully.

But it only worked because Camille was essential.

Opposites attract me

I often choose my next role to be the opposite of the last one I did. The point is not to do what's easy, but to be challenged. And that's exactly what I set out to do after *Body Heat*.

I wanted a different kind of role partly because I knew I would be bored by repeating similar roles. I didn't want to repeat something I'd just done. It just wasn't interesting. And then of course it made sense to try to get in as much variety as possible right at the beginning of my career so I wouldn't be stuck in one category, especially one that would be short-lived, for the rest of my career. Think about it: the sexy *young* woman character wasn't going to last me too many years.

I knew I did not wish to repeat a Matty Walker type of character in my next role. You know damn well you're going to be typecast if you repeat the same type role. As a sexy young woman, that would have been fine for five or six years. That was not for me.

Well, when *Body Heat* came out, then there were many pseudo-*Body Heat* offers, sort of *Body Heat B* scripts with evil-seductress characters. They would have been boring because I'd just done that, besides being awful films. I wanted to impress people with other things I could do, to show a range of work rather than just one quality. So once I had decided I was not going to repeat *Body Heat*, I needed to find a way to contrast it.

Just when I was looking around for something that would show another side of me, somebody sent me *The Man with Two Brains* script. Steve Martin was the lead and Carl Reiner was directing. It seemed like a film where I could feel, *Yes, this is one that will let me make fun of Matty Walker altogether.*

When I contacted Carl to ask if they would audition me, he indicated they weren't at all sure I would be the right one for the job, seeing as how they weren't sure how funny I was. I persisted and finally got an audition. I went in and threw myself all over the room. I crawled up Steve's leg, behaved quite outrageously, and I got them laughing. And so they said, 'Yeah, okay, you can work in this.'

And oh, it was a crazy time. Carl was just amazing. He seemed to know exactly how many beats to hold for a laugh. Even though we were filming months and months away from having an audience, he would say, 'No, hold that one more breath, hold that two more beats, and let them get the laugh in there.' And I'd agree because I knew he had a magnificent sense about the comedic moment.

Dolores Benedict, my role in *The Man with Two Brains*, was an over-the-top, crawling the walls, tearing the scenery parody of the sexy Matty Walker and her intentions. It's very funny, very comedic. And Steve Martin is one of the best comics in the whole damn country. It was amazing to find myself getting to be funny with Carl and Steve.

The Man with Two Brains, 1983

Dolores is a woman with a record of marrying for money, but she gets more than she bargains for when her new brain surgeon husband falls in love with a brain without a body. ·

Directed by Carl Reiner
Produced by William E. McEuen and David V. Picker

Steve Martin as Dr. Michael Hfuhruhurr
Kathleen Turner as Dolores Benedict

Dolores: *Nobody's going to keep me from working in this town.*

Carl was great to work with and so much fun. Steve wasn't much fun even though he is so funny when he is performing. He's gotten a lot looser and nicer over time. But he was quite stiff and unfunny when he wasn't being funny in his film role. I was disappointed that I didn't have more fun with him on what was a most fun-filled script.

I've only used a body double for a sex scene once in my whole career. In *The Man with Two Brains* I was seriously offended by the scene in which my character is about to have her ass rubbed. I did not think it was funny at all. I told them to get someone else's ass to rub.

After this film, I thought, *Okay, now I've proved I'm sexy, I've proved I'm funny. All right, it's time to get back to the stage*. Because I wanted to keep my stage acting credibility as well. Then came an opportunity to play Titania and Hippolyta in *A Midsummer Night's Dream* at the Arena Stage in Washington. And I said yes to that.

I can't control which job comes along that will give me that opportunity to play a different sort of character. That's the nature of the profession. But I can set my parameters and be there to take the one that feels right when it comes.

Chapter Six

Stake your claim and make your stand

So much of my feeling of self-worth comes from my job. When I was starting out, just being able to get acting jobs consistently was very much a measure of my own feeling about myself. Later, when I wasn't working, when I couldn't get a job, when I didn't get the job I was seeking, I would feel downcast.

After I finished *The Man with Two Brains*, I was feeling a little down. The *Midsummer Night's Dream* role was brief. Money wasn't as tight as it had been at first, but still I was far from financially secure. I was between boyfriends – I'd broken it off with David but I hadn't met Jay yet. I felt kind of like a target. On the one hand, I was the hot girl in town. On the other hand, I felt as though I was perceived as just a sex symbol, somebody's trophy.

No surprise, then, that the character of Joan Wilder resonated with me right away when the script for *Romancing the Stone* came my way. Joan stands in strong contrast to both the comedic-sexy Dolores and the conniving femme fatale Matty.

Joan became one of my favorites. Of all the characters I have ever played, I relate most to her because of how she develops over time. She starts out insecure but through the doing of things she learns her power and becomes her own woman. I liken that to my own development. Joan is a good person, a smart person, and the fact that she is so completely unaware of herself in the beginning is endearing. As she meets the challenges that come along, she gains confidence and a sense of leadership. She stakes her claim and makes her stand.

She's one of my few 'nice girl' characters, but that's not why I like her. It's because despite her shyness she has the courage to become the protagonist of her own life. Her adventures in Colombia are a recapitulation of the growth that I experienced by doing *Body Heat* in spite of the fears and insecurities I had going into my first film adventure.

At the beginning of the script, Joan is a mousy writer of romantic novels, living vicariously through her characters. She hardly ever leaves her apartment. She has this belief that the world is what she dreams up in her writing. Being a novelist, after all, she can write life so it happens the way she wants it and not accept less. She won't accept that something she desires isn't going to happen – she doesn't give up. When Joan has to travel to South America to find and rescue her kidnapped sister, she becomes stranded in the jungle. Help comes in the form of Jack Colton, soldier of fortune played by Michael Douglas. After many adventures, she and Jack fall in love. Joan returns to New York without the man but with a new hit novel. Then Jack appears bearing *El Corazón* ('the heart'), the stone he had been seeking.

I felt that Joan's insecurity about herself in the beginning – feeling she's not attractive, deciding she doesn't want to go out into the world to face the possible damage or hurts that most people just roll with – was a common bond. I understood her desire to hide away. I never hid out to avoid dealing with the world, but like Joan, as I met the challenges that came along, my confidence increased and I became more secure about my own worthiness.

Originally the role of Joan's editor was shot as a man – a supercilious, misogynistic man. Poor Joan cowered even more when he told her over and over that she was writing nonsense. Her books made money for them, thank you very much, but he did not regard her as a serious writer, which translates to not being a serious woman. I was really glad when they decided to reshoot those scenes with the editor as a woman named Gloria, played by Holland Taylor, because I thought it served Joan's character better not to be quite so beaten down. I'm also grateful because that was the beginning of my long friendship with and love for Holland. She remains one of my best friends to this day.

I think my adventurousness and willingness to throw myself into things comes through in Joan. That's also something we have in common, even though at first her adventures were created in her mind rather than being real physical adventures, and she was rather bound up emotionally.

Michael Douglas produced as well as acted in *Romancing the Stone*, so he had a lot at stake in its success. He originally intended to have Debra Winger in the role of Joan, but they didn't seem to get along as well as he'd hoped. They met to discuss it at a Mexican restaurant and she bit him, or so he said.

When I went to read for the part, my reputation worked against me again. They were concerned I couldn't be dowdy enough to grow from a shy, unawakened woman into the fully sexual and assertive being Joan becomes. So I left my expensive green silk shirt at home this time. I put on old baggy sweat clothes with holes in them, no makeup, didn't wash my hair. I wandered around the set bumping into things and falling down, being clumsy and cute. They seemed to think I could pull off the role after that.

I have to admit that when we did the early shots, it was hard to be as mousy as they wanted Joan to be. I kept saying, 'Oh, couldn't I just have mascara? Could I just have the mascara, please?' No, no, no. You have to look really plain and dowdy. No mascara.

We couldn't shoot in Colombia, where the film was set, because of the drug trafficking and the danger. The security force we would have needed would have been impossibly expensive. So they had scouted locations in Mexico. I felt very comfortable there. I loved going back to Latin America. The food and the language felt like home to me. Michael thought he spoke Spanish, but he didn't really. Not to mention his accent, which is absolutely appalling. He had one bilingual assistant director. And some of the Mexican actors, such as Manuel Ojeda, didn't speak much English. So I was kept busy translating or coaching on the proper pronunciations. Both in and out of this role, I felt completely essential.

Romancing the Stone, 1984

When her sister is kidnapped, romance writer Joan Wilder finds herself in the midst of an adventure she could never have thought up. Wilder travels to Colombia, where Jack Colton becomes more than just her partner in adventure.

Directed by Robert Zemeckis
Produced by Michael Douglas

Michael Douglas as Jack T. Colton
Danny DeVito as Ralph
Kathleen Turner as Joan Wilder

Gloria: *Joanie, you are now a world-class hopeless romantic.*
Joan Wilder: *No, hopeful. Hopeful romantic.*

Romancing the Stone and Michael Douglas

The *Guardian* writer Suzie Mackenzie once compared me to Bette Davis, saying there's a strong strain of sadomasochism in our work.[9] Maybe she was referring to my stunt work in *Romancing the Stone*.

We started shooting *Romancing* in Jalapa, up in the mountains. That early sequence with the bus riding through the mountains up to the famous mudslide down the hill did pretty much happen to me in real life as it appeared on the screen. I was sitting on my makeup man's makeup case off to one side of the camera with my back up against the cliff. A mudslide poured down and buried me to my waist. I was yelling in Spanish, 'Don't pull, dig. Just dig!' Well, of course nobody listened. Everybody panicked. They frantically pulled me out of the mudslide and ripped the skin of my left shin almost all the way down the leg.

My makeup and hair people, Tom Case and Cathy Blondell, were wonderful. We were an hour and a half away from the hotel in Jalapa. They held me down in the car with ice packs on my leg till we could get to some real medical attention. For weeks after that, they had to spray that fake skin over the wound so you wouldn't see how torn up my leg was. It healed well eventually.

I hadn't known Michael before we started on *Romancing the Stone*, but we got along really well. Danny DeVito has been a part of our friendship also. Danny and Michael go back forever, to drama school together. They were always playing tricks on each other. Michael and Danny and I socialized a lot outside of the film. With *Romancing the Stone*, we were up in the mountains of Mexico without anything else around. So any entertainment and fun had to come from what we did together. Tom and Cathy stayed with us through all our films, as did some others in the crew, and Bob Zemeckis of course. The spirit of adventure caught all of us. We were adventuring by day and we were adventuring by night. I told them the one way to avoid the *turista* was to have a jalapeño and a shot of tequila every day. Well, *I* never got *turista*. That became a daily ritual.

Michael couldn't find the right gemstone for the emerald Jack was seeking. He had stones made over and over. He'd say, 'No, it's too cloudy' or 'It's not the right color.' He would find something that wasn't right with each one until they finally did get one he liked. We had many rejected 'emeralds.' So every week, whoever got banged up the worst would get a heart. I got two, the first time for the mudslide. And then there's a scene in the airplane that crashed with all the dope in it. It was always raining, always muddy where we were filming. As I was getting out of the plane, I slipped in the muck. I put my arms out to get my balance and pierced myself on the side of the plane. That earned my second *corazón*. I got away with seven or eight stitches that time.

And then in the big fight scene with Manuel Ojeda at the end, we're down rolling over and over and he hit my head really hard on the stone. Head wounds make you bleed like a stuck pig. So the blood is coursing down my neck and everybody's yelling, 'Oh my God, oh my God!' For the arm and the head injuries, I just went to the trailer on the set and a very nice local doctor sewed me up. Then I went right back out to the set.

They didn't let me swing across the gorge. We used a stunt double because the insurance couldn't cover that. But other than that, I did all my own stunts. They put me up on a high ladder with a rope. I would swing in and drop down. They built a mock of the beginning of the bridge so you could see when Joan starts to go. The problem was, they kept having to say, 'Cut – Turner, you're smiling again. You're supposed to be scared.' 'I know,' I'd say. 'I'm sorry, I'm sorry.' But I just kept laughing as I did these big swings. I was having such a good time. I love that action stuff.

Michael and Danny both have a rougher sense of humor than I do. Maybe that's a guy thing. But it quickly became apparent to them that I was needed for the film's success. And that I was a good sport whom they could ask more of than they could of many other actresses. I became accepted as one of the guys. They had no compunction about throwing me into a pool or playing their other tricks on me. Michael expected me to weather all the hardships that anybody else would. We three were kind of a gang. It was really, really fun.

From Jalapa we went to Vera Cruz, where the port was. Later, we shot in the countryside while based in Mexico City, which was nice. Michael's father, Kirk Douglas, came down for a visit and I was his dinner partner. Ever since, when I see Kirk, he calls me his Mexican date.

The production was up against the money; expenditures were overbudget. Toward the end of the film some of the 'suits' came down from the studio. Michael was afraid they'd pull the plug on us. He told me to be charming and sweet and make these guys happy. I put on my best charming and sweet act. Whatever we did worked.

For a time, I was sure I was falling in love with Michael. And I think he was falling in love with me. I was certainly inspired to portray Joan's accelerated sexual awareness by working with Michael.

Now at this point I was unattached, and Michael and Diandra, his wife at the time, were separated. So I figured it was okay, it was fair. It was a very heady time when I thought, *Oh, I'm falling bad*. Then Diandra showed up in Mexico wanting to reconcile. I saw that Michael wasn't free to pursue another relationship. We couldn't keep up the romance. But we kept our friendship. Michael always says very nice things about me . . . as well he should.

Michael and I did some very challenging scenes together. The mutual trust and the emotional connection we've always had enabled us to take on whatever hair-raising perils were necessary. The scariest scene was wading through the waterfall to get to the cave behind it. The viewer can't see this at the bottom of the footage, but the water was churning and the currents were scary. Michael and I were tied together, which meant that if one went down, we both went down. They couldn't tie us to the bank because the camera shot was long and you would have been able to see we were tied down.

It often rained so terribly hard that the roads were washed out. Michael had truckloads of gravel brought in every night. We called it 'Douglasland.' It was physically so demanding, very tiring. We both got hurt a lot. But I got more stitches than he did. He might say that's because I'm clumsier than he is. But really it's because I took more risks than he did. Oh, yeah, there's a little competition. Just a touch. Come on, wimp. Yeah. Oh, come on, Michael, I'll do it. I'll show you.

But oh, God, the laughs. And the end of the week, we'd say, 'Okay, who's got the margaritas?' And then we would just howl at what had gone on that week.

Love happens when you least expect it

Pretty soon, it didn't matter that Michael and I were not to be in a romantic relationship. We were finishing the last of the shooting on West End Avenue in Manhattan. I was looking for my next job. I had run into David's office to pick up a script, and at that moment Jay came in to pick up one of David's associates, Mary Meagher, to take her out for dinner. She introduced me to Jay.

I actually had some money now. And I wanted to get a nice

apartment. I had been living in a one-room sublet in the most western part of 57th Street. It hadn't bothered me before, because I was so seldom there. But now I felt I needed more of a home. So, because Jay was in the real estate business, Mary asked him if he could give me a hand finding a nice place to live. He sent over a list of buildings with available apartments on the West Side, where I wanted to be. I looked at a lot of apartments. I didn't like any of them.

I guess I became a challenge to Jay, and he said that one Sunday he would take me himself to go look at these spaces and point out to me what I was obviously not seeing. I said, 'Well, if you're going to be so helpful to me, then I will take you to lunch first.' We went to the Russian Tea Room and had a great lunch. I introduced him to caviar. We spent the rest of the day driving around town and looking at apartments.

Then he asked me to dinner. We just kept talking and talking and talking. Finally we went back to my little hole in the wall and kept talking. We talked about families, ambitions, dreams, who knows what else – we just never stopped. And it must have been about four o'clock in the morning or something when I finally said, 'Well, you can't stay here – you have to go.' Jay left and then the phone rang a little while later and he said, 'Why?' I said, 'Because this is weird.'

I saw him every single day that I was in New York after that. And we never ran out of things to talk about.

I got an apartment, a nice two-bedroom on 23rd Street between Sixth and Seventh. It had a fireplace and great light. I liked that; I need light. I think I spent one night there alone before Jay moved in. I said when I moved in, 'I need to feel what it's like to live here and that the apartment is mine. No offense, but I'm just going to be here alone tonight.' The next day I said, 'Well, that was stupid. Get your stuff and come on over.'

I had no credit cards at that time. I didn't believe in them. My philosophy was, if I didn't have the money to pay for it, then I would not buy it. I wasn't going to fall into the trap of actors who owe so much money that they have to take jobs they despise. I thought the solution was not to have a credit card and to deal completely in checks or cash. So although I'd never owed any money, I also had no credit rating for making major purchases. I wanted to get a TV and I took Jay with me to Macy's. He had to put the TV on his credit card, and then I paid him back in cash. Finally he convinced me to get a credit card and charge something so I could get a credit rating.

It was fun falling in love. It was New York. We were young; everything was so exciting. Jay was building quite a business and I was much in demand. We were both really happy. After four months or so, we were at the Palm Two, our favorite restaurant, on Second Avenue. It was a rainy night in April. And we had such a good time, such a sexy time. We were dipping strawberries in whipped cream and feeding each other, all that wonderful sort of thing.

As we were leaving the restaurant, Jay said, 'Well, I guess we should just get married.' And I said, 'No, no, no, no. I want a story for my grandkids. I want a proposal, I want drama.' He threw away his umbrella in the middle of Second Avenue in the rain and knelt down in his best suit and asked me to marry him. And I said, 'Yes! Get up, the light's changing – yes, yes!'

Butterfly days

I'd always said to myself that I would never marry or get too deeply involved with anyone until I knew how I would be. Marrying a girl who's trying to become an actress and marrying a woman who is a star is marrying two completely different people. So I had sworn that I would not marry while I was in the pupa stage. Until I knew whether or not I was going to be a butterfly, I wasn't going to take the responsibility that comes with sharing life with another person.

When I met and fell in love with Jay and we decided to marry, I was already Kathleen Turner. I had done *Body Heat* and *Romancing the Stone*. It was quite clear that I was a leading lady and most likely had an excellent future in the business. Which does not mean it would be easy for the guy. It just meant I knew who I was. Public recognition is an incredible confirmation of your own beliefs, your own talent. Instead of being a wannabe, you are doing it. You are this person who communicates with millions of people around the world. And it affects your personal life in ways you can't necessarily anticipate.

Almost immediately after we became engaged, I went off to do *Crimes of Passion*. This wasn't the best time for me to go on location to do a movie, but I always finish what I start. When I make a commitment, I follow through. My friends say: 'Kathleen says it, she does it.' But *Crimes* almost became the exception, presenting many obstacles, including a tough situation for me, for Jay, for our relationship. I feel to this day it was some of my best work even though I wasn't so thrilled with the film as a whole.

Ken Russell, the director, is truly a genius, but a mad,

self-sabotaging genius. And the writer of the script, who I believe also had some producing power, was easily one of the most unpleasant people I had ever worked with. He had written this woman named China Blue as a fifty-dollar whore working Hollywood Boulevard at night; he created her as a character who seemed willing to accept any kind of degradation.

During the day, she was a highly successful fashion designer named Joanna Crane. Her sense of worthlessness was reinforced by becoming China Blue. But at the same time, she proved her power by becoming sexually attractive to men. I see that confusion about sexuality in many women, and ultimately in myself. I hoped other women would see it and identify with her when she regains her sense of self.

Ken would push the story as far as he could get away with. One of the most famous scenes – and the most moving – was a beautiful one in which a dying man's wife hires China Blue. The wife can't bring herself to sleep with him, but wants him to 'feel like a man.' China Blue takes off her dress and shoes and is in her bra and panties when the man says, 'Stop, I can't do this. I love my wife. I understand, but I can't do this.' It was really so touching.

The writer wanted me to strip altogether in that scene. I said, 'Nobody's going to listen to the words with the shock of this naked woman in front of him. That's not what it's about.' What the scene was about to me is what China does next. She takes off the blond wig, which symbolizes her identity as China Blue, and tells him her real name. She gives this man the gift of her own vulnerability as he's giving his back to her. And she says he is stronger than she is because he has stopped pretending. If the scene had been done naked, it would not have been nearly as powerful.

Those kinds of battles I had to fight mostly on my own. The male co-star, Anthony Perkins, came to my trailer and said, 'I'm going to tell Ken no – I think the scene should be like you want.' I said, 'Thank you. I'll follow and we'll double-team it.' Then I went in and Ken said, 'Well, Anthony thinks you should absolutely be naked.' I said, 'I'm sorry? No, I won't.'

Ken was drinking a great deal at the time. As the days went on, things got increasingly out of hand and there was no order. It was really hard to keep it together. And Anthony had an appalling drug habit. He was doing drugs in front of everyone. You could see his heart beating a mile a minute. He had his little bottle that I was told was benzyl nitrate. We'd rehearse a scene, then before a shot when they'd say, 'Roll camera,' he'd take his bottle out and sniff it with each nostril. His face would go red and he'd burst into a sweat. And suddenly I wouldn't know which way he would go in a scene, if he was in control of himself or not. It was scary. I was quite worried about getting hurt. It was nearly impossible to work with Ken or Anthony, actually.

There's one scene where I'm dressed as a nun and Anthony is playing a priest. The game is that China confesses and begs forgiveness from him, after which she falls down to the ground in abject misery – and then raises her head, laughing in his face. Before the scene, Anthony had said to me, 'You won't be able to do that without some of this,' and tried to hand me his drugs. And I said, 'Oh yeah? Watch me, asshole.'

But I got a good laugh from the crew at the very end. It was one of the last shots. Ken said, 'Roll,' and I went, 'Wait,' and I pulled out one of Anthony's empty bottles and pretended to sniff it. The crew rolled on the ground with laughter, a good release after all they had been through.

Crimes of Passion, 1984

Sportswear designer Joanna Crane becomes the hooker China Blue by night. When a street preacher begins to hound her, one of her clients helps her and, in the process, falls in love.

Directed by Ken Russell
Produced by Donald P. Borchers, Barry Sandler, and Larry A. Thompson

Anthony Perkins as Rev. Peter Shayne
Kathleen Turner as Joanna Crane/China Blue

China Blue: *B movies have always been my inspiration.*

At one point during the filming, I got very sick. The clinic didn't open until seven-thirty or eight in the morning, so I went and shot the first couple of hours from six to eight in the morning. Then I said I had to go to the clinic. The doctor thought I had meningitis and said I should go into the hospital. I called Jay. He came out on the first plane; he was there within hours. Turned out I didn't have meningitis, thank God. It was scary. I was really sick. I started shooting again two days later. But I'll never forget that Jay jumped on a plane and got to me as fast as he could.

In the end, I just wanted to get through and finish this movie. As soon as we were done, I was on the red-eye home. I slept twenty hours straight when I got home. Jay said that if I'd slept through to twenty-four, he would have taken me to the emergency room.

When God was my special effects man

Jay and I had one of the best weddings ever. We took a big beach house and put up both families there. Jay and I stayed in a small house in the dunes. Everyone got to know each other and had a wonderful time. There was quite a cultural fusion.

One day, Gramommy and Daddy Russ wanted to buy us dinner, but they said, 'We've got such wonderful cooks right here – why should we go to a restaurant?' So they went out and bought pounds and pounds of frozen shrimp. Here we were on Long Island with fresh seafood all around and the midwesterners go buy frozen shrimp.

I'm a social Christian. It's part of the midwestern social culture. I don't agree with many of the beliefs, like who is going to heaven. Jay is Jewish. It meant a lot to his family to have a Jewish wedding, so that's what we did. Daddy Russ gave me away. He said, 'Do I have to wear one of those fancy suits?' (meaning a tuxedo). The answer was no. 'And do I have to wear one of those funny hats?' (meaning a yarmulke). The answer was yes.

I wore an antique dress that the costumer from *Crimes of Passion* found for me. It was a Victorian cotton lawn tea dress. Jay wore an off-white suit. The rabbi was from Central Synagogue in New York. He was a great guy but a little starstruck. When we went to meet with him before the wedding, he knew all about me but hardly paid attention to Jay. The wedding was to be Saturday night. The heat that day was intense. We'd set up two tents, one for eating and one for dancing. I kept pacing upstairs in the house, impatient as always and ready early as usual. My hair and makeup were done; I was all set for the wedding. I sent for Michael Kaufman, the best man, and told him to tell the rabbi, 'Let's get on with it.' Michael delivered the message. The rabbi replied, 'I'm marrying a good Jewish boy to a *shiksa*. At least she can wait until the sun goes down.' I said, 'The sun is down in Jerusalem.' But for once I had to wait.

God was my special effects man. A thick fog rolled in as soon as Jay and I said our vows. It was beautiful and it made the candles we had placed all around with paper bags over them look like halos. We had a great party. Some weddings are so stiff. Ours was the opposite – it was so much fun.

Michael was dating his wife-to-be, Sandi. Sandi had locked up the little beach cottage where Jay and I were staying and we couldn't find the key, so we couldn't get in when we left the party. Finally, Jay ripped off the screen, stuck his fist through the window, opened the door from the inside, and let us both into the cottage.

Kind of like in *Body Heat*.

The special effects did not continue indefinitely

Just before *Crimes of Passion* was released, I was offered a private screening. I said to Jay, 'Why don't we invite some people to join us?' He invited his guy friends. After we finished the screening,

I suggested that we all go get something to eat. Jay said, 'I don't think so. I think we need to be alone.'

I was perplexed, but I got into the car. Jay shut the door and confronted me: 'How could you do this to me?' I asked, 'What do you mean?' He said, 'You embarrassed me in front of all our friends.'

'You made up the guest list,' I reminded him. 'How could you do it? How could you play a whore?' he asked angrily. I said, 'What? Do you think that makes me a whore? A fifty-dollar Sunset Boulevard pickup? What are you talking about? I was acting.' I, of course, only saw the work in it. I thought I'd done some really amazing work, in fact.

Then Jay said, 'I don't want you to do anything like that again.' And I said, 'Whoa – now we have a problem here, because nobody decides on the work I am going to do except me. I'm sorry if this upsets you and I'm sorry if I didn't sufficiently prepare you' – though I did give him the script to read before I did it – 'but we're going to have to get this straight right now that you cannot tell me what I can and cannot do in my work.'

He wasn't very happy with me for a couple of days, but then he accepted it. That was pretty rough to get through, but it forced us to deal with some of the inevitable strains on our relationship.

I think who I was and the fame that went with it were very attractive to Jay. But over time, perhaps his subconscious resentment built up too. Once at an opening early in our marriage, a photographer yelled at Jay, 'Are you the new Mr Turner?' He replied, 'Yeah, I killed the others.' Which I thought was wonderful and brilliant.

The first time I went on location after our wedding, we still had just that one TV I'd bought at Macy's on his credit card. When I got back, there was a TV in every room. I asked, 'Why in God's name do you need so many TVs in this small apartment?' He said he didn't get married to live alone.

I never felt my family's well-being was threatened when I was away. They were home in safe and familiar surroundings and I was living in a hotel. So when Jay would say, 'I didn't get married to live alone,' I would reply, 'You're living at home – it seems to me the better part of the deal.' Because of course I was living alone too when I was away from home working.

Nobody can make you do bad work

There is still to some extent an implication that a woman is selfish to put her job or her career equal to being with her family. I don't think men are ever criticized because they attend to their careers or speak up for what they think they deserve. As Roseanne Barr has said, 'The thing women have yet to learn is nobody gives you power. You just take it.'[10]

How did I get a body double for my ass when I didn't like that scene in *The Man with Two Brains*? I just said, 'No. Get someone else's ass to rub if you want that scene.' There was no negotiation. Why should there be? When Ken wanted me to strip naked in *China Blue*'s scene with the husband, I said, 'No, it does not do justice to the meaning of this scene.' That's it, end of story. A man who behaved like this would be called strong, someone who knows his own mind; a woman might be called temperamental, bitchy. But no matter. Like Joan Wilder, you stake your claim and make your stand.

That's exactly what I did when Twentieth Century Fox sued me for $25 million.[11]

It's the only time I was ever sued and was quite a revelation to me. I had signed to do a sequel of *Romancing the Stone*. It was to be called *The Jewel of the Nile*. I was looking forward to it because I had so come to identify with Joan. And since she had been such a wimp at the beginning of *Romancing the Stone*, I thought it would be nice to play her as her more assertive self.

But Diane Thomas, who had written *Romancing the Stone*, hadn't been able to arrive at a mutually acceptable deal with the studio to write the sequel. So Michael Douglas and the studio hired Lawrence Koner and Mark Rosenthal to write the sequel. They sent the script to me and I hated it. It had nothing of the spirit or the humor or the adventure or the character – it was just a stunt movie. It was boring, and I didn't think it was at the same level of quality at all. So I said, 'I will not do it.' They pointed out I had a contract to do it.

I was unsure of what to do at first. Then I talked to a friend who asked me, 'Would you like to go after the big boys?' I said, 'What do you mean?' He took me to the famous attorney Roy Cohn, who asked, 'What's your case?' I said that agreeing to do a sequel is not agreeing to do a sequel of lesser quality. That I would assume the sequel would be the same quality as the original film. 'They can't make me do bad work,' I said.

Roy said, 'I love it.' I came home one day soon after that and my doorman waved a New York tabloid at me. He said 'Twenty-five mil, huh?' Startled, I said, 'What?' He said, 'Oh, Fox is suing you for twenty-five million dollars.' I said, 'They are?'

So I called Michael. He took the hard line. Michael is a wonderful friend and a terrible enemy. He said, 'You don't have any choices here.' Which made me angry. I said, 'I have the choice to do only the quality of work that I believe in.'

I guess Roy countersued them or threatened to. Because Michael asked if I would drop whatever it was if he got Diane back to rewrite the film. I said, 'Absolutely. I never said I didn't want to do the film; I just want to do a good film.'

He brought Diane back, and they got the script to me the day I was flying to Morocco. Well, I read it on the plane and so much of it was still just so fucking wrong. I worked myself into quite a fury. I didn't realize Koner and Rosenthal were sitting three rows behind me on the plane as I spouted to Jay about what appalling shit it was.

The Jewel of the Nile, 1985

In this sequel to *Romancing the Stone*, Joan and Jack are getting tired of the simple luxury life. When Joan is abducted, the ensuing adventure shakes their relationship up.

Directed by Lewis Teague
Produced by Michael Douglas

Michael Douglas as Jack Colton
Danny DeVito as Ralph
Kathleen Turner as Joan Wilder

Joan Wilder: *Exotic ports, great parties, spectacular sunsets – it's not enough!*

When I got to Morocco, Michael and I sat down in the hotel room, took apart the script, and compared the versions from Diane, the writers he originally hired, and from a script doctor he'd also brought in. We put together a script good enough that I said, 'Yes, I can do this one.' So we settled it.

But my point was still valid. Absolutely, I will do your film if I have committed to it. But why should you then force me to do a film that is to my mind inferior and would have been a failure? That would be damaging to my reputation and to yours.

I learned a very big lesson. First, I've never signed to a sequel again. Second, from that point on, I made sure I had script approval. That became part of my contract. So no one could change things or demand that I do things I hadn't agreed to.

You fight!

The Jewel of the Nile was interesting once I finally got into it. I was excited about going to Morocco. I looked forward to seeing that part of the world. I always forget that I'm going to be working sixteen to eighteen hours a day so I really don't get to see anything else when I'm on location. Jay wasn't too thrilled about going – a nice Jewish boy traveling to Morocco. He did come over a couple of times, but it wasn't the most comfortable situation for him.

The culture was a difficult one to work in. My diplomatic training again came in handy. We'd all been coached on how to avoid misunderstandings, how to not be disrespectful to the religion or cultural norms. It was emphasized that women needed to wear loose, long-sleeved clothing and keep our legs covered. No running around flaunting our limbs, they said. So we tried to comply. But it was hard to remain passive about the state of women in Moroccan society: no voting rights, no ability to travel without a man's consent. And oh, God, it was so hot. One day it was 120 degrees in the shade, literally.

We were very isolated again, so we clung to each other. We'd go to the souk together or to find something to eat because we'd get absolutely desperate for food other than lamb, which was served over and over at the hotel. There was a lot of territory to explore, and many beautiful places in Morocco. Michael would often go scouting to look at locations, so Danny and I would go with him sometimes.

One night Michael and I almost died. We were based in Fez at the beginning. The second team was in Meknes, filming the sequence with the train. One morning, Michael and I had to go to Meknes to fill in the close-ups for when we're hanging off the edge of the train. We finished and flew back to Fez, just the two of us on the little jet. The Fez airport had shut down for the night and turned off all its lights. The pilot tried to land anyway. Somehow the plane wasn't level to the ground. One of the wings touched. So he yanked us straight back up before the plane could go into a cartwheel. Michael and I held hands. I said to him, 'If you make it, tell Jay I loved him. If I make it, I'll tell your wife you loved her.' The plane swooped around again and managed to land this time, but we had been really close to death.

After we finished in Fez, we went to Ouarzazate just on the edge of the Sahara Desert. The cinematographer, the director, Michael, Danny, and I were in the governor's guesthouse. It was on the top of a little man-made hill. There was a small pool, maybe twenty feet by thirty. We would come back from the set out in the blazing desert and dive right into the pool. We'd come up shivering and blue with cold. Because even water that was so hot felt so much cooler than our body temperatures.

Some of the crew got really sick with dysentery (perhaps because we had no tequila and jalapeños here). Ugh. It was tough. One day I was driving to the set and I said, 'The hell with all this clothing. It's so hot, I'm just going to put on a T-shirt and my shorts. I won't get out of the car so no one will see me.' Well, of course that was the day the car broke down. I had to sit in that roasting car for an hour and a half before they could get another car to rescue me. I said, 'Okay, tomorrow I'll wear a long skirt, no matter what.'

At one point, we were staying in the Jamal Palais. I was in the harem's quarters. I had a room upstairs with a secret winding stair that went down to a hidden garden that was so beautiful. And there was gorgeous vividly colored tile everywhere, blues and reds and gold alongside the lush green and the fountain in the little garden. I used to feel very sneaky about going up and down the stairs, fantasizing that I was sneaking out of the harem. Jumping on the back of an Arabian stallion, perhaps, to ride away.

It was very hard to get room service, because they would hear a woman's voice and hang up. They don't take orders from women. I had to call Michael and say, 'If you want me on set this morning, you'd better get me some fucking coffee.'

Danny's wife, Rhea Pearlman, was driven mad by this discrimination. She finally marched into the kitchen herself and said, 'Get out of the way.' They were so freaked out that they actually started waiting on her. But she had a little child, Gracie, which might have made her more acceptable.

Jay came to Ouarzazate and had his thirtieth birthday there. I tried hard to make it special. The governor's guesthouse was built in a square with a courtyard in the middle that had a fountain. I had champagne flown in, and I got ahold of sparklers and put them all around the courtyard. I swooped into the courtyard before Jay, so there'd be all these celebratory things setting the scene for him when he came down. But he wasn't in a very good mood when he arrived. That was the day we shot the wedding ceremony. Jay sulked: 'Sitting on the hillside with the goats watching my wife get married to Michael Douglas isn't my idea of a good time.'

Then we had one fabulous, fabulous long weekend when Jay and I were driven to Marrakesh. When we discovered it was Ramadan, we declined to eat the lunch that had been prepared for us to take in the car, since the driver couldn't eat during the day.

Once in Marrakesh, we went to the Hotel La Mamounia, which is supposed to be one of the most beautiful in the world, and I think indeed it is. All of Marrakesh is a beautiful old brick color, brownish red-orange. La Mamounia was a palace. Our suite seemed to go on forever. Twelve people could have lived in there; there was room after room after room. It had a sculpted, stone lace look that reminded me of the Alhambra.

They left us a bottle of Laurent Perrier rose champagne. We popped the cork, poured a couple of glasses, and walked out onto the gorgeous balcony that overlooked the desert. The sun was just setting and there was a double rainbow. It was the most stunningly beautiful sight. I will never ever forget the joy we felt seeing that magnificent double rainbow over the desert. That was a lovely weekend.

And we finally got to eat, at a famous restaurant in Marrakesh. Typically, women cannot own property in Morocco. But a woman, a white woman in her seventies yet, owned this restaurant. Her mother had been chef to one of the kings. As a thank-you, he allowed her to own this house and have a business in it. She had passed it on to her daughter, who was a little wiry-haired thing. I asked her, 'Do you want to tell me just how you do this? Isn't this very, very hard for you?' She pretended to whip out a sword, and she grunted, with a determined look on her face, 'You fight, you fight, you fight, you fight.' She was just wonderful.

So for years afterward, if somebody said to me, 'Isn't it hard to do that?' I'd say, 'You fight, you fight, you fight.'

Chapter Seven

Banish the yet

I loved that Moroccan restaurant owner who said, 'You fight.' I had been intensely uncomfortable in Morocco trying to balance my diplomatic respect for another culture with my conviction that women should have an equal place in society. If I lived there, I would surely be an activist fighting for women.

Actor and *activist* come from the same root word, and I consider myself both. Early on, I was influenced by a saying of Margaret Mead – that we should never doubt that a small group of committed individuals can make a difference, and indeed it is the only thing that ever has. Yes, people get things done in groups and in movements, but there are always individuals contributing to every part of that movement or adding to its ideas. It always breaks down to someone doing something, taking action.

So I've never been as discouraged as I've heard many people say they are. I hear it even more now from younger people, a generation behind me, who say, 'Oh, what's the point? Sure, I could send some money to Darfur, but it's a corrupt government and who knows if it will ever get to the people who need it.' True, there are many difficulties and many reasons why good intentions don't work out. But that's no argument not to do it.

My basic belief is that if you don't profit from harm to anyone else, then you're all right. You're on the right track. When you perceive that your action is going to injure someone, you must avoid it. If harm does happen, you must try to mend it. My father taught me that. In the simplest words, that's the goal of living. If I can see harm coming to someone, then I won't do or I won't advocate it.

But besides doing no harm, an activist also tries to do some good.

An activist is someone who lives in a community and sees a cause that could serve to better that community. The activist gets involved. I don't agitate to cause trouble (much). I only need to know that by *taking action* I can make the world a little better. Anyone can do the same. To be an activist you have only to rid yourself of one thought: the 'what I have to give has to be really big or why bother?' thought. People have been led to believe that their contribution *can't* really be significant *yet* because they aren't old enough or famous enough or wealthy enough *yet*. That *yet* is a thief. It can rob you of your self in the moment. *Yet* means you are going to make a contribution *someday*. But each of us has so much to give right now.

Ever since I started volunteering at age eleven at the orthopedic hospital in Caracas, I absorbed the idea that service is a central theme of life and have been involved as an activist somewhere. My father once said to me that just living in a community is like paying rent, in that you have shelter and services like water and electricity but you make no improvement on the property. To improve a community, to make it better, is like buying a house. You can invest in a community by giving time or other resources toward things that need improvement. When you invest in a house or a community, you have a higher stake in its future.

That's why wherever I have been and whatever my financial circumstances, I have always budgeted time for organizations and causes I believe in, even if I could only do one small task. I put this into my calendar, just like I wrote in my class schedule back in college or my professional appointments now.

The Paul Newman effect

One day well after I had established myself as an actress, I was waiting in line to vote at my polling place. I'd brought my newspaper to read because I figured I'd be waiting for a while, and as I scanned the headlines, I overheard two women behind me talking. One said, 'I'm voting for so-and-so because Paul Newman likes him.' I thought, *Oh my, does this mean if I say, 'This is my candidate,' in public, people will be more likely to vote for him or her?* Yes, it seems they would.

Overhearing those women talk about how Paul Newman's choices influenced them made me realize that the fame and exposure I have can be used purposefully to channel attention to human needs or programs. I suppose that the most useful quality I have for organizations I support is to bring attention to the group through my activism. Well then, I had better be very careful with my activism choices and take responsibility for them, because my participation in a cause or for an issue or candidate might influence someone else's. Call it the 'Paul Newman effect.'

It's actually frightening how much attention people pay to what celebrities do. I don't believe I should cram messages down people's throat or that people *ought* to listen to me because they know me in my public role. This whole fame business works for you and very much against you. People often approach you with a sense that they already know who you are even though you've never met them, and they have usually made up their minds about you. I don't even like the word *celebrity* because, to me, celebrity is not necessarily earned. It's a very flippant term. Celebrity just means big exposure in the public eye. It doesn't discern the quality of your life or your work.

But I've come to understand that people do listen. And of course, even the selection of material and characters I play reflects my values, which in itself has an influence. Everything I do is very consistent in that way. The characters I choose to play set an example of strength even when they are flawed. And I believe acting is compassion-based. You have to be aware of other people, put yourself in their place and have the empathy to sense what is motivating them. As an actor you become more tolerant of others because you are constantly trying to examine what the other person is thinking, feeling, or needing. All this empathy is the basis for service and activism as well.

My favorite line from *Who's Afraid of Virginia Woolf?* isn't Martha's – it's George's. He says, 'You create government and art and realize they are and must be the same thing.' What that means to me is the utter centrality of service in whatever way one chooses to do it, whether it's politics, art, charities, or helping people one to one.

Actors are often accused of being activists to feed their own egos – or their publicists'. Over the years it becomes clear who is actually involved and who is simply a charity butterfly. There are many actors who have my great respect for their real involvement. And then there are actors who lend their names but don't show up. If I give my name, I will be there, or will support the endeavor in some direct way. If I'm not able to help when they need me, then I do not allow them to use my name because it will make me less valuable to them when I am needed later. It's a fine line.

I think you have to take a real stand on issues at some point, even controversial or unpopular ones if you believe in them passionately. I mean, nobody opposes Citymeals-on-Wheels or Childhelp USA, do they? I support those because they are worthy charities. But I'm also on the board of People for the American Way. I don't think this organization should be controversial, because it represents bedrock American values. But it seems to be. And to me, that makes it even more important for me to lend my name and my efforts to them. I don't view myself as confrontational or pushy; I simply feel it is necessary to stand up for my beliefs. And to get involved politically too when issues I care about are at stake. I'll work for candidates who I think will do a better job, or for issues, though I don't work for either political party.

I also enjoy speaking at fund-raisers. I write nice speeches; Hillary Clinton said I should publish my speeches. I love getting people stirred up. And I'm known for being rather blunt. Or, not euphemistic, let's say.

Sometimes I go to Washington to meet with members of Congress and lobby on issues. I'm pretty good at exercising the diplomatic aspect to confrontation. Though, I did almost sock the late Senator Strom Thurmond once. I really came so fucking close. I went with Joseph Papp, the late founder of the New York Public Theater, to Washington to lobby for the National Endowment for the Arts. Their funding was on the verge of being completely eviscerated. We were not altogether influential in making our case, because the funding was cut significantly, but at least it still exists.

We met with Senator Thurmond and his committee, explaining why we felt this was a terrible injustice. I said something I deeply believe: What we have left of the societies and civilizations that preceded us, more than any other aspect, is the arts – the paintings, plays, music, architecture. These are the legacy left us, and we must prioritize our arts accordingly, because this is what we will be leaving to the future. To say they are not a necessary part of our education and our feelings about ourselves is practically criminal to me.

So Strom Thurmond says, 'Now, little lady' – which of course pleased me no end – 'Now, little lady, I've been around here a few more years than you, wouldn't you say so, boys? Ha-ha-ha. Little lady, I've always liked blondes. Ah, well, I'm here to tell you that this funding just isn't gonna happen, honey, little lady.'

I had my arm cocked back. Thank goodness Joseph Papp grabbed my wrist and pulled it down. But I thought, *One more 'little lady' and Strom's lost his teeth*. Or his dentures or whatever the hell they were.

Usually, though, I am very measured and diplomatic. I learned courtesy and how to deal with the public long before I began doing these public events as an actor-activist. My father used to say that we were all American ambassadors abroad. Which absolutely cowed me. I thought, *Oh, God, you mean if they don't like me they're going to hate my country?* But the point is that how we behaved reflected not just on the family but also on the United States of America. That's a heavy burden, but one I have carried for so long that the transition into being a public person as an actress didn't seem all that different, just radically magnified. That knowledge and the fact that I really like people help me fulfill this responsibility that comes with the Paul Newman effect. Or maybe the Kathleen Turner effect.

What you learn or have isn't enough; what counts is how you use it

When I was in college in Maryland, I had no money to give but I volunteered a few hours a week at Planned Parenthood because they give health care in a very direct and practical way. I have gone to public schools and read to children. These are my talents. These are things I can do. I went to New York University Hospital to visit wards of men dying with AIDS. You can't overestimate what a little attention means to people. And I just feel, *Shit, why don't I do this more often? What was I waiting for?*

I like the idea of community service for everyone, on the Peace Corps model. That would be thrilling, absolutely wonderful. More and more kids take gap years from college. Sometimes they use them to get work experience; sometimes they just waste them. If colleges were to offer credit for the service done during that year by students, and if they counted the credits toward the students' degrees, it would be a great encouragement.

I tend to choose organizations that I think give practical and direct help to better people's lives, especially those that are oriented to women and children. Those are my priorities. Yours might be different, and that's great – I am just saying choose whatever appeals to you and do it. Yes, the problems of the world are huge. But that doesn't mean you can't do anything about them. Those who try to tell you that you can't make a difference are telling the biggest fucking lie in our society.

My approach is not to start with the huge ideas. Don't start thinking you have to save a million children in Africa. Start by asking, 'Is there one family I know in my town that isn't getting enough food? Maybe just for the children. If I buy two jars of peanut butter instead of one, two cartons of frozen peas instead of one, can I be of service to them?' It could be completely anonymous or given through a food bank, because you always have to worry about hurting someone's pride when you offer charity. But what's the big goddamn difference when you go to the store and you buy two cans of coffee instead of one if you can afford it? Service and activism can be as simple as that.

And what will you get from your service? You will get knowledge. Knowledge that is *not* measured by grades, or scores, or diplomas. You will get the knowledge of your own self-worth, and the good that you can do today. With your own hands and your own voice you are already an activist and you alone have the ability to make the world just a little bit better right now.

When I am home in New York, I work for Citymeals-on-

Wheels. It was founded by the food critic Gael Greene and does remarkably important work. We go to people who are essentially shut-ins and deliver a certain number of meals to them at their apartments. My adopted territory is on the West Side around the theater district. Many old people live around there – they were dancers or singers or actors who live in rent-controlled circumstances, who've had their tiny little apartments, most of them walk-ups, for maybe fifty years. They get help twice a week or so to get up and down the stairs so they can go out for necessary shopping. I think growing old is probably easier here in New York City than in a suburban situation because you don't need a car and so many things can be delivered. But everyone needs to get out now and then. Now I have a phone buddy, Muriel Fleit. I talk with her every week or so. The contact helps keep older people connected, and they have so many interesting memories to share.

The stories some of them tell – 'You wouldn't believe it to see me now but in my day, I was light on my feet' – are quite wonderful. I always want to stay and listen. Most of them haven't a clue who I am, which is rather sweet. One woman said to me, 'You know, you have such a nice voice; you should think about acting.' I said, 'I will, thank you.'

Taking on too much

My life is a constant balancing act of family, work, and service. There are times when I can do more and times when I can do less community service. When I know I am going to have a break in my work, I call up a charity and say, 'I will have these three months when I won't be working. What can I do for you in that time?' In 2004, between *The Graduate* and *Virginia Woolf*, I told Gloria that I would do one speech a month anywhere in the country for Planned Parenthood (of course I ended up doing fourteen). If I am performing in a city, I usually contact a charity beforehand and say, 'I have Monday nights off. What would you like me to do for your local affiliate?' And then there are times when I have to say, 'Look, I will be away filming or immersed in a play and I simply cannot participate during that time.'

The biggest scheduling mistake I ever made, and have never repeated, was agreeing to two films back to back with no break, *The Jewel of the Nile* and *Peggy Sue Got Married*. Well, they weren't quite supposed to be back to back, but *Jewel* ran over its schedule by more than three weeks.

Working a little extra time to finish *The Jewel of the Nile* wasn't hard duty once we left Morocco. By the end of our filming there, I really thought I was going to die if I didn't get out. I felt tired and beat up. I had lost my dimples; I couldn't even smile anymore. The place had gotten to me so badly. The poverty, what you saw on the streets, the treatment of women, the heat – it was just unbearable.

We'd had all kinds of problems doing our routine work in Morocco. For example, we'd ship the raw film to Europe to be developed, and the Moroccan officials would claim to have lost it. Now, we're talking about hundreds of thousands of dollars' worth of work. It was getting really tense and nasty.

Michael Douglas had rented a big plane to take all of us out to the South of France to shoot the scenes we needed to do there, but I was truly feeling desperate to leave. So he finished up my last scenes that had to be done in Morocco and let Holland Taylor and me fly to France ahead of the rest. Which was lucky for us, because Michael's plane wasn't allowed to leave at first.

Michael loaded everything – film, costumes, sets, crew – on this big plane and was trying to get permission to take off. Whoever he had given the requisite bribe money to had apparently not made the necessary arrangements, and the whole crew sat on the tarmac for a whole day in Ouarzazate in June before they were given permission to leave. Holland told me, as she and I flew past the coast of Morocco and out over the Mediterranean, that tears were flowing down my face. I rented a house in the South of France called Mas L'ara, in Vence, just north of Nice. Holland stayed with me, and Jay came as often as possible. The house had a pool and a lovely garden. Michael stayed at one of the fancier hotels in Nice. We all felt like we were living high.

But because of the extra time needed to finish *Jewel*, the time I would have had between films was eaten up. I was home for just a few days before I had to turn around and go back to work on the next film. That was very difficult for both Jay and me. I never took two jobs so closely back to back again. It was too destructive.

Since then, I've made sure my contracts state they will pay for my family to come on location every month and for me to fly home at least once a month. I don't believe I was ever away from Jay or from Rachel after she was born for more than two weeks at a time. And I make sure I have some good time off between jobs.

I'd try to get home to be with my family for a little extra time whenever I had the chance also. One really funny thing happened when we were shooting *Prizzi's Honor* and I saw an opportunity to get home early. As it happened, we were shooting a scene on a Friday at the Los Angeles airport. There was a three-thirty flight from LAX to New York. They wrapped up filming me that day at two-thirty. And I said, 'You know what? I'm going to be on that three-thirty flight.'

So I was off and running. I took my kit from the trailer – I had clothes at home so, hell, I didn't have to go back to the hotel for anything. I grabbed my purse, and then Jack Nicholson, who was co-starring, said to me, 'Shouldn't you call Jay first?' I said, 'No, the whole idea is it's going to be a surprise. I'm going to show up at midnight and go, "Honey, I'm home."'

Jack said, 'Well, what if he's not alone?' I said, 'What?' Jack said, 'You better call.' I said, 'I am not going to call. And he is going to be alone.'

I managed to get on the plane. Well, then of course there I was sitting there for six hours going, 'Could it possibly – no, it couldn't – could it? – No, it couldn't. No.' I got home and I crawled into bed. Jay was asleep and completely surprised: 'What?' And I said, 'Honey . . .'

But I'll never forget that 'What if he's not alone?' What do you mean, what if he's not alone? Never crossed my mind! Terrible, terrible, terrible Jack.

Prizzi and Peggy

I start to read a script and either it becomes real and I see myself doing the role or it doesn't and I don't. And if it doesn't, I'm just honestly not interested. It might be a terrific role for someone else but I wouldn't have the inspiration. I couldn't see myself doing it without that inspiration. I saw myself in *Prizzi's Honor* immediately. Who could resist such great lines about life's most important lessons? About choices: 'Does he ice her or marry her?' About the consequences of actions: 'If he's so fucking smart, how come he's so fucking dead?'

Doing *Prizzi's Honor* was rewarding for several reasons. John Huston was directing. It was his second to last film. And working with Jack Nicholson was great.

John was having a lot of trouble breathing. He had emphysema, so he had his oxygen tank at all times. You could see that when he wanted to get up and cross the room, he would count the steps in his mind, take that many breaths, and then he would go. As a result, he left many of the decisions to Jack and me. He'd say, 'Why don't you put together something and show me?'

At first I found this a little disconcerting, just because with a director like John Huston I didn't expect to have that much freedom. But then I began to love it, because I would have ideas that he could put a camera to. For example, in the first date between my character and Jack's, she's seducing him. We started with a wide two-shot, right, sitting next to each other at a restaurant table. And then as the scene progressed, we unobtrusively, almost subliminally, came closer and closer together. As I spoke I'd shift my weight and then Jack would shift his. We ended up finally touching in a tight two-shot. John put the camera on a long dolly, so as we moved together the camera moved closer and it complemented our movements.

Jack said he felt very challenged because Huston told him at the beginning of our filming that he's seen Jack break character and wink his eye at the audience, as if to say, 'Oh, I'm not really doing this. You know me.' John challenged Jack not to do that –

to commit totally to the character instead. To help him get into the character more completely, John suggested that Jack use a technique in which he stuffed a Kleenex in his upper lip, changing the way he talked and the way his face looked. Then he started to get into it. He really started to have fun. It was kind of like what Marlon Brando did in *The Godfather*, except Marlon had stuffed his lower lip.

It was Jack's idea that we start one scene with me thrown over the edge of the couch and with him obviously just getting up from having sex. I thought it was rather shocking but then I liked it. And in the bed scene, the rolling over and over was my idea. Jack wasn't that happy about it because he had a bad back. He kept saying, 'My back, my back.' We rolled over and over from one side of the bed to the other while the camera was moving along at the same speed. We called it the who's-on-top game. We got carried away; Jack almost fell off the bed, yelling as always, 'My back! My back!'

Jack was not a morning person. Not at all. His car would pull up to the set and it would look like there was only the driver in it. You'd say, 'Jack?' And his head would pop up in the backseat. He even used the drive to the set to sleep. This was great for me, because he'd say to me, 'Will you take the close-ups until ten?' 'Yes. Yes, absolutely – I'd be happy to take my close-ups early, thank you, Mr Nicholson. Because I do a lot better early than you do, let's just keep it that way.' So we suited each other. But, oh, he was fun and he was outrageous and I enjoyed working with him very much.

Prizzi's Honor, 1985

Charley Partanna and Irene Walker are both hit men. When they fall in love, it's only a matter of time before they realize they were hired to kill each other.

Directed by John Huston
Produced by John Foreman

Jack Nicholson as Charley Partanna
Kathleen Turner as Irene Walker

Irene Walker: *I can't get over it. What kinda creep wouldn't catch a baby?*

I did *The Jewel of the Nile* after *Prizzi's Honor* and at the end of *Jewel* went directly into *Peggy Sue Got Married*. We couldn't delay the start of filming *Peggy Sue* because it was August and we had to get in and out and finish filming the scenes that take place at the high school while it was empty, before school started in September.

It was a tight and stressful schedule, but *Peggy Sue* was so worth the effort. The whole premise of *Peggy Sue Got Married* is that a woman jumps back in time, taking her knowledge of the future with her. Well, how the hell were we going to do that? Francis Ford Coppola's direction set up the mysticism of the film right away. He pulls the camera through the mirror that Peggy Sue is looking into. You're going to see my face and the back of my double's head at the same time, doing the same things, putting on lipstick, fluffing the hair. And the mind accepts the impossibility that you're seeing the front and the back of this woman at the same time.

You don't even realize it when you start to watch the movie. But then you've already gone to a place where you're subconsciously saying, 'Yes, I will accept what the designer, Dean Tavoularis, wants us to think.' When Peggy Sue goes back in time, all the colors are altered. The street is sprayed with a purple wash and the sidewalks with a yellow, and the lawns are sprayed with green and the tree trunks are sprayed a reddish brown. All of which is not sharp enough for the eye to notice, but it creates a magical picture, a slightly unreal sensibility that makes you accept the premise of the story. And then of course you must believe that this has happened to Peggy Sue, and I must portray it in such a way that you can mix the ideas that she has gone back to the past and she also knows the future. We did it without using makeup tricks, too – no added wrinkles for the older Peggy Sue. It was all done with acting and body language – the perkiness of a teenager, the slower thought process of a woman in her forties.

It's a brilliant script. I love these characters. The idea that you would have the chance to go back and change or reexamine your choices, take another look at where you got with the steps you took, is universally understood and attractive. We've probably all wished for it at one time or another, haven't we?

We were filming in northern California, at a high school in Petaluma outside Santa Rosa. My grandmother and grandfather, both in their mid-eighties (although, Grandmother's age was always a point of dispute because my grandmother claims that the courthouse burned down with all her records and she really was younger than my grandfather's recollection), were visiting me on the set. We were shooting a poignant scene with the grandparents in the movie. Leon Ames, who was playing the grandfather, was a dear, sweet man. But he was having a lot of trouble remembering his lines. And that wonderful actress Maureen O'Hara – brilliant, wonderful, sweet – Mia Farrow's mother, was totally professional, totally clear, sharp, gentle, as the grandmother.

In this scene, after Peggy Sue's gone back in time, she starts to talk about when she lost her grandparents, and then she says, 'No, I'm sorry, I don't want to go there.' The grandmother says, 'It's all right, dear. I know exactly when I'm going to die.' And Leon as the grandfather says, 'Oh, when is it going to be, Katie? Tuesday or Thursday?' But he kept forgetting her name, saying, 'When's it going to be, Mary? No, not Mary – well when is it going to be, Sus— no, not Susie. When's it going to be, Kay? Kay? Friday or Monday?' This happened time after time after time.

My real-life grandmother and grandfather were sitting behind the camera and Grandmother's patience ran out. Leon blew the line again and she blurted out, 'Oh, for God's sake, it's Katie!' I said, 'You're going to get kicked off the set.' And she said, 'Well I'm eighty-five. If I can retain it, why the hell can't he?' Grandmother claims I got all my talent from her. And, it seems, my penchant for taking action.

Nicolas Cage, the male lead, has apologized to me for years for his behavior during the filming of *Peggy Sue*. But I must say that I have not pursued working with him again because of that experience.

Look, he's Coppola's nephew. Coppola truly believed he could do it. The problem was that once Nicolas got the role, he wanted to prove that he wasn't there as the result of nepotism. And so everything Francis wanted him to do, he went against – just to show he wasn't under Francis's wing. Which was ridiculous, because Francis's instincts and direction were excellent. But Nicolas had to do the opposite to everything: that stupid voice and the fake teeth – oh, honestly. I cringe to think of it.

Peggy Sue Got Married, 1986

Peggy Sue faints at her high school reunion and surveys her past with her older sensibilities. She has a chance to go back and change her future that holds an unhappy marriage and young motherhood.

Directed by Francis Ford Coppola
Produced by Paul R. Gurian and Barrie M. Osborne

Nicolas Cage as Charlie Bodell
Kathleen Turner as Peggy Sue

Peggy Sue: *What am I doing here?*

He came into my trailer the last night when we were in the midst of shooting literally for twenty-two and a half hours in a row so that we could finish in the time required. He'd finished all his filming and he'd been drinking heavily. He fell on his knees and he asked me if I could ever forgive him. And I said, 'Not right now. I have a scene to shoot. Excuse me.' I just walked out of the trailer. He didn't manage to kill the film but he didn't add a lot to it, either. For years, whenever I saw Nic he would apologize again. I'd say, 'Look, I'm way over it. It's okay now.' But he obviously had a sense that he could have done better. And since then, he has shown that he can.

Family planning

After *Peggy Sue*, I finally took a break. I was exhausted, and quite thankful to be done with a grueling film schedule. I'd been so wrapped up in the work and so wired that when Jay came to visit me when we were filming in Santa Rosa, he says I awakened one night after he turned over in bed, turned him back over, and chided him loudly, 'It won't match.' He says he was afraid to go back to sleep for fear of what I might do next. So yeah, it was nice to have a little time off after that to recuperate.

I'd always imagined that if I got married, I would want to be a mother. Before I met Jay, my biggest doubt had been that I would ever marry. I was afraid I would never have that stable a relationship, partly because I didn't think any man would be secure enough to be married to as successful an actress as I hoped to be. The fame, the success, and the exposure frighten men off as much as they attract them. But once I decided to marry, the idea of having children fell into place fairly naturally. We talked about having two or three.

For a year or two, we'd been planning to have a baby and we

had been trying. I was thirty-two; it was time. I'd missed a period and thought I might be pregnant. We were very excited. We went to Sandi and Michael Kaufman's wedding one weekend. The next day I had to fly to Italy to shoot a film, *Giulia e Giulia*.

On the flight, I started to bleed, which made me simply frantic. I had the flight attendant call ahead to the airport to have a doctor waiting. The minute I landed in Milan, they took me to the hospital. By then the bleeding was quite heavy. The doctor was brusque, unsympathetic to my situation. He said he wasn't even sure if I was pregnant. But I was sure. It was six weeks, seven weeks maybe, but then that was before pregnancy tests could diagnose you five minutes after you become pregnant as they can today.

One out of every three pregnancies is miscarried in the first three months. Not that anybody ever told me that, of course. And in hindsight I think there was probably something wrong with the fetus and thank God that it was self— what would you say? Self-cleansing? You just don't know in these situations, can't know. But that was really sad, really tough for me. Jay couldn't get over to Italy to be with me. Maybe I didn't make it clear that I needed him to be there. Trying to be invulnerable again, perhaps. But it was very hard to be alone going through that feeling of loss while the hormones whipsawed back and forth. I bled heavily for weeks, which was also a reason I thought that I had indeed been pregnant.

When I got back from filming *Giulia e Giulia*, Jay picked me up at the airport and informed me that we had bought a house in Amagansett, out on the ocean. We got caught up in our life again and started remodeling the house. Babies remained on my mind as I looked toward the time when we could try again. And I began to get involved in the community.

The Long Island fishing industry had collapsed. There was no bluefish fishing allowed anymore. The waters were overfished and the fishermen had to go so far out to make a decent haul that the local families were in terrible financial trouble. Sometimes, the result of poverty and men feeling like they can't provide for their families is that they take their feelings of powerlessness out on women and children.

So there was an abuse problem. A few brave women offered their homes as safe houses. It was a secret network. A woman who had been abused would be told to call someone in Bridgehampton. And somebody in Sag Harbor would say, 'I'll come pick you up.' These volunteers would hide the women who had been abused. They couldn't keep them in their houses indefinitely. But the women knew that the result of going to the police was often that the abuse intensified to the point of being life-threatening.

Some of these volunteers came to me and said they needed to establish an organization to rent safe houses and to have an emergency number. I helped them raise money for that. We rented some houses at first, and later we raised enough money to build a shelter at a secret location, well protected by the police, where the women and children can get counseling and can stay for weeks at a time if they need to.

They now offer the men counseling as well. I know because my gardener came to me one day and said, 'My wife has left me. I know she's at this shelter, and I can't live without her. What do I do?' 'Well,' I said, 'you go in for counseling. You start there. Then you start the dialogue again with your wife. But you don't go near her until you learn a few things.' It felt good to be able to help him directly – to see the result of having helped to start this organization, especially because I now had a stake in the community. As I said before, there are so many ways to serve, if we just banish the *yet* and get involved.

About a year after I had the miscarriage, Jay and I decided to try again. But I said, 'I'm not going to just hope or wait and see if it happens this time.' Turner takes action on everything else – why not this? I was keeping track of my cycle. I think it was when we were shooting *Peggy Sue*, and I had promised my mother that I would stop in Missouri on my way back to New York.

That was going to be my most fertile day, wouldn't you know. So I called Jay and I said, 'You have to meet me in Missouri.' He said, 'Do I have to – in your mother's house?' I said, 'Yes. Yes, you do.'

It caught. Oh, yeah. I was pregnant for sure this time. Which proves that it does help to plan.

Hold on to the power to say no

By this time, David Guc wasn't my agent anymore. It was becoming too uncomfortable for me because it wasn't comfortable for Jay. Sometimes the two of them saw things differently in respect to whether I should take a particular role, and both of them have a bit of a temper. But I'm grateful that David had put some New York edge on my Missouri niceness so I didn't just accept what was offered to me. He taught me this important lesson: 'You will be known as much for what you don't do as for what you do.' A great lesson, which I pass on to all the young actresses I work with or teach.

Ultimately, the only power an actor has is the ability to say no. You've got to hold on to that and not make choices based on money or they will own you.

I think my most unhappy film experience was *Switching Channels* – the only one I ever chose to do for money, which is probably why it was so unhappy. I'd had two rehearsals in New York with Michael Caine, who had signed to be the male lead. This was supposed to be like *His Girl Friday*, that wonderful old film with Rosalind Russell. For many films you have to cram a lot of exposition into the beginning so that as you go on people understand the relationships. Michael and I worked out this great idea on how to handle that in *Switching Channels*. In the film, we had been married for seven years but had worked together for fifteen. So we thought it would be funny if I would start a sentence and he would finish it. And he would start one and I would finish it for him. We'd immediately assume that we could finish each other's sentences, that I knew what he was thinking and he knew what I was thinking. All this tells the audience much about their relationship.

Michael was finishing *Jaws* . . . God knows what – *IV*, *V*, *VI*, whatever, and the shark machinery kept breaking down. He didn't have a stop date for when he'd be free. Well, I had already shot for several weeks while we'd been waiting for Michael. I'd shot as much as I could without the male character.

And I had a stop date, for a very important reason.

It was early in my pregnancy. We designed a wraparound skirt and a double-breasted jacket, so I could grow a little without it being that noticeable. But obviously I was going to get a lot bigger real soon and had to finish before I would become too apparently pregnant to explain away.

Since Michael Caine couldn't do the film in time, the producer hired Burt Reynolds. Burt came into a group that was already working together and knew each other, so he might have felt a little bit like an outsider. For whatever reason, he immediately said to me, 'I've never taken second billing to a woman.' I excused myself, ran to my room – we were rehearsing in a hotel – and called Jay, breaking into tears, saying, 'I don't think I can do this.' Burt was just nasty. I don't do well with nasty people. I actually turn into a puddle if somebody yells at me. Plus there were those pregnancy hormones at work.

Switching Channels, 1988

In a modern *His Girl Friday*, cable news producer John Sullivan tries to woo back his ex-wife and best reporter, Christy.

Directed by Ted Kotcheff
Produced by Don Carmody and Martin Ransohoff

Burt Reynolds as John L. Sullivan IV
Kathleen Turner as Christy Colleran

Christy Colleran: *When have I EVER used foul language, you rotten son-of-a-BITCH?*

Jay said, 'Dry your eyes, be cool, go back, just do the film.' Okay, okay.

I'd go back. Oh, every day there were these nasty little digs. They'd given me a golf cart so I didn't have to walk around too much since they all realized I was pregnant. And Burt even made fun of that.

We were shooting that first scene that Michael Caine and I had rehearsed, where we answer each other's questions and finish each other's sentences. It's got to be fast; it's got to be sharp. These are two really smart people who have known each other for a long time. Burt just couldn't do it. The director finally said, 'Look, why don't we just shoot line by line.' And, idiot that I am, I shot back, 'Because it's called a *scene*, that's why.'

Well, from that day on Burt and I were sworn enemies.

Burt later said publicly that the sound of my name made him want to vomit or something very nice like that.[12] Although I must say I never bad-mouthed him. Ever. Even though he said I tried to get him fired every day. But boy, it was not a happy set. It was not happy shooting at all. I was absolutely miserable. If the crew hadn't been so kind, and Chris Reeve, who was so very nice, hadn't been there in the cast, it might have been impossible.

For the first and only time, I had taken a role because of the money. I was going to have the baby and would be unable to work for many months. I thought, *All right, I need to make enough money to last the year*. I had said yes in part because of Michael Caine but mostly because they'd offered very good money. It came back at me. I learned that's what you get when you don't exercise the power to say no, and I never put myself in that position again.

And I learned that if I do realize I've made a bad choice, I should own it, fix it, and move on. The worst mistake can be waiting too long to say no.

I had to banish the *yet* when it came to saying a necessary no, too.

Chapter Eight

Separate the real from the reel

Rachel Ann Weiss came into the world ahead of schedule, on October 14, 1987. She was very little: five pounds, seven ounces.

If there had ever been a question for me about where the actress stopped and the real woman began, then pregnancy and parenthood answered it once and for all.

It was rather amazing, bizarre, actually, to watch the changes in my body take place. I've always thought that if a man's waist ever went from twenty-eight to forty-two inches, he'd jump off the penthouse. But I didn't have as tough a time during my pregnancy as I know some women do. I didn't have morning sickness or any of that, so I was quite fortunate. I felt good and I wanted to work if I could.

I was offered the perfect job for a pregnant woman: the voice-over role of Jessica Rabbit (she of the heaving breasts that had to be drawn after I recorded her lines so that the undulating motions would match the cadence of the sultry voice) in *Who Framed Roger Rabbit*.

Who Framed Roger Rabbit, 1988

Roger, the cartoon rabbit, is worried his sexy wife, Jessica, is cheating on him. He hires Detective Eddie Valiant to find out. The plot thickens when Roger is accused of murder and relies on Valiant to find the truth.

Directed by Robert Zemeckis
Produced by Robert Watts

Bob Hoskins as Eddie Valiant
Charles Fleischer as Roger Rabbit
Kathleen Turner as Jessica Rabbit

Jessica Rabbit: *You don't know how hard it is being a woman looking the way I do.*

Jessica has been dubbed the sexiest animated female ever. If only they could have seen what Kathleen, the thirty-three-year-old real woman, looked like hugely pregnant. The last day I was to record was the day I gave birth. Early that morning, my water broke. I yelled to Jay, 'There's a lot of water coming out and I'm not peeing!' Shortly thereafter I was in the hospital prep room, yelling, 'Get the studio. Tell them I'm not coming in today.'

Rachel's birth was kind of scary. The last thing to fully

develop is the lungs, and the doctors were concerned about that because she was early. So they did a C-section. She came out yelling. The doctor and nurses all thought that was funny. They put her in an incubator one floor above me right after she was born during the afternoon, and they didn't bring her back to me that night.

Once the epidural wore off, I wanted her. I just *wanted* her. It was late at night by this time, I'd just had abdominal surgery, and my legs were still a little numb. I got out of the bed and literally crawled down the hall to the stairway. I'd gotten about three steps up the stairs when I heard a loud 'What do you think you're doing?' behind me. Shit. I looked around and saw a very large nurse looking down at me. She asked me again, 'What are you doing?' I said, 'I want to see my baby. I'm going upstairs.' And she said, 'You are not going anywhere. You will stay right where you are till I get a wheelchair. And I will bring the baby to you.' I was rather petulant: 'Why didn't you bring her before?'

I was a new mom. I just wanted my baby with me.

We stayed in the hospital for a few days, and fortunately Rachel was fine. For the most part, we were treated like any other new parents and their newborn by the hospital staff, and we appreciated that. But the real and the reel collided once. It was one of those awful things that people do when they can't respect the privacy of someone in the public eye. I was breast-feeding. There was a curtain around the area where the babies were kept and that's where I was sitting feeding Rachel. I looked up, still breast-feeding, and there was a camera pointed at me through a crack in the curtains, taking pictures of Rachel and me. Somebody heard we were there, crept into the hospital, and was taking pictures – I suppose to sell to a tabloid. It sent shivers through me. First I was frightened for Rachel, and then I was furious. I'm happy to say the hospital was angry too; they took care of him quickly, for which we were very grateful.

Jay got up every morning at five o'clock to be at the hospital when Rachel and I had our first feeding. And when we took her home, he took the six a.m. feeding. I had the nine p.m., the midnight, the three a.m. I would lie in bed to feed her. We always gave her a bottle also, partly because I was afraid that I didn't know how much milk she was getting from my breasts. I mean, you can't measure it. And also because we wanted to share the experience of feeding her.

Jay would take her downstairs for her six a.m. feeding. The idea was for me to get some sleep, but I would creep to the top of the stairs so I could look at them. The only programs on TV at that hour were the business news shows – before Tivo, you know. I'd see Jay sitting there giving Rachel her bottle. And the TV would be blaring, 'The yen is up again.' It was so sweet. He was just wonderful with her. Jay is a very good father. He really has always been terrific with Rachel.

Having a child was a new kind of love experience, unlike any other. It opened my heart in a new way. I imagine all mothers find that motherhood teaches the deepest lessons about what's real and really important in life, and what's not.

Our house in Amagansett was finished by Christmas, and in my happy memories of spending the holidays there, I can still see Rachel all dressed up in her little red suit with the footies.

Nobody suffers from too much love

I'm happy with what we've produced . . . Oh, I think Rachel is fantastic. During her young years before she started school, she usually traveled with me, and often after that for shorter periods of time when it wouldn't interfere with her school schedule. And even after she was in school, in all the times when I've been away on location, we never went more than two weeks without being together. Either I would put into my contract tickets for Jay and Rachel to fly to me or I would negotiate a number of long weekends when I could fly home to them, depending on their schedules, how intense the schoolwork was, or where he was in his business. So not until Rachel was about seventeen did we ever spend three weeks apart without seeing each other.

Young actresses have asked me, 'How can you possibly have a career like yours and a long marriage and a child who's happy and stable and confident – a child who's secure? How can you do it?' I tell them quite frankly that one of you, either your partner or yourself, has to earn enough to be able to hire a wife. Because you cannot do everything all the time. You cannot make sure that you don't run out of milk or diapers or that the dry-cleaning came back and that the house is clean. You just can't do it. You need somebody else there to handle the details. And without that help, I could never have done it. I never looked on it as anyone taking my place or any kind of interference. I always thought of it as another person to care for Rachel. And to love her. I don't think anybody suffers from getting more love rather than less.

Get a wife

We had a wonderful nanny for Rachel's first two and a half years. She did what I could never do. She'd sit there with this infant for hours, talking to her, singing to her. I would have gone out of my entire mind. Just couldn't do it all day, every single day. But Jay and I never had any help in our home on the weekends. That was our time together with Rachel.

When Rachel was about two, a lovely young woman from Ohio, Tara Feldkamp, who has become like a sister to me, became her nanny. I've always asked of the young women who've worked for me that they continue their education. These are smart, interesting young women and I want them to develop their talents. Tara is now a head librarian in upstate New York. Another young woman who was our nanny went back to school and got her nursing degree. On the whole, my nannies have turned out pretty well in their own lives.

I think I was something of an example and a bit of a pusher, saying to these young women, 'Why don't you take some courses?' Especially when Rachel was in school full-time, what did they have to do all day? And I would help arrange Rachel's schedule and mine and help them financially.

Not that I could ever imagine anyone else doing all the things for Rachel that I would do. Jay once pointed out to me when I had been away on location, 'Rachel's still alive when you come back.' But I swear to God, every day I was thinking about whether she had eaten, what did she eat, how much sleep did she get, did she finish her homework? Had she been brushing her teeth? Every single day, and I would think the same sort of stuff about him, you know. *Is he feeling good, has he strained his back again, is he eating well?* Honestly, I would think about them before I would even think about my day's work.

Oh, I do know how much I missed in the daily living. I've always felt that it's not time that creates distance, it's the things that you don't get to be part of with them – the experiences they have without you or you have without them. These are the choices men have always made without criticism, of course, but they are difficult choices nonetheless.

Not that everything went smoothly all the time. I was appearing in *Indiscretions* on Broadway when there was a frightening incident one night. I had been at a meeting. I remember I was all dressed up in a beautiful blue Cerutti suit. I'd come home to kiss Rachel and change and go to the theater. And there was a hysterical phone message from the nanny that Rachel had fallen from her bike in the park and cut open her chin. And that Jay, who was out at the beach house in Amagansett, had sent her over to a plastic surgeon that was a friend of a friend.

I raced to the doctor's office. Rachel was in full, terrible hysteria. Blood was pouring down her chest so you couldn't see how bad the cut was. She wouldn't stay still so the doctor could see what to do. I finally had to take her between my legs and my arms and the nanny held her head so the doctor could give her an injection to numb the wound and then clean it and stitch it. She got about six stitches. I noticed there was some blood coming out of her ear, so I had him check her ear and he said it was just a cut from gravel or something. Nothing to be worried about.

We took Rachel home. By now it was seven-thirty. I put her in my bed and stayed until she fell asleep. Since Jay was out at the beach house, I called my friend Sandi Kaufman to be on alert and I asked my mother-in-law, Irene, to come over and stay with Rachel because I felt that I had to go to the theater. 'I think Rachel will sleep until I get home,' I told them. 'I will call at every intermission and make sure everything's all right, and if it's not I'll come home.'

I called during the first intermission. Everything was fine; Rachel was asleep. I called at the end of the second intermission and there was no answer. I didn't know what to do. This was before everyone carried cell phones with them at all times. I called Sandi's house and her husband, Michael, answered. He said Irene had called and told Sandi that she saw blood on the pillow and was taking Rachel to the hospital. So Sandi went with her to the hospital. But nobody had bothered to call the theater to tell me, and neither had they said which hospital.

Well, I was fucking hysterical. My dresser stood offstage left, calling my house every five minutes. Every time I would look offstage, she would shake her head 'no answer.' *Indiscretions* is Jean Cocteau's *Les Parents Terribles*. It seemed an ironic title at the moment. I played the bedridden invalid, Yvonne, who dies at the end of the play. That was some death scene I played that night. I was literally sobbing. I was out of control as an actress. The second the curtain came down I was off the deathbed and running – screw the curtain call, I had to get home. I raced offstage, where the dresser said, 'They just called, I just talked to them. They're home, Rachel is asleep, everything is fine.' I was shaking like a leaf. I took the curtain call and ran home.

Rachel was fast asleep and fine. Irene and Sandi had taken her to a different doctor, who said the same thing as the plastic surgeon had said before: it was a minor cut in the ear, probably from gravel when she fell, no damage done. Well, I went into the other room. I closed the doors and I grabbed my mother-in-law by the front of her shirt. I said, 'If you ever, ever, ever withhold information from me about my child again, I will kill you. I will absolutely kill you. Do you understand?'

She said, 'Oh, I didn't want to worry you.' 'This is my child!' I yelled. 'What the hell do you think my priorities are? Are you insane?' I don't remember ever being so enraged in my life. I scared the hell out of her. I can be pretty scary, anyway.

Fortunately, we never had a crisis like that again. Despite the adage 'The show must go on,' there were three people for whom I would not go onstage or I would leave the stage if something happened to one of them. The list was Rachel, Jay, and my mother. If one of them had a problem, then I was gone. And of course Rachel was top of the list. So the only thing that had kept me onstage that night was the fact that I had no idea where she was and so I couldn't go to her. And knowing Sandi was with Irene, to help make sure Rachel was all right. That had kept me from going completely insane. I gave Sandi a big talking-to afterward also.

That was the only time I thought, *It's not worth it, it's just not worth it. What if I'm really not able to get to them when something happens?* I was terribly discouraged because I thought that I could fulfill the responsibilities of motherhood and everything would be all right. As long as I was on a stage in New York and a few blocks away from home, I could get to them if they needed me. But what if I went on location again? I just simply wouldn't take a job that took me away for any length of time for a good while after that.

But Rachel got older. And on balance, the advantages my work gave Rachel far outpaced the liabilities. She had opportunities and experiences that not many kids have.

In New York City and at the schools Rachel attended, there

are a great many people with a lot of money, pull, and position. So in terms of her peer group, she wasn't that unusual. But in terms of traveling the world, staying in wonderful places, meeting people that one would seldom meet, she has had great advantages, and I think she appreciates it.

This kid has spent half her life backstage. I mean backstage in every sense of the word. I don't think she has any illusions about how hard it is to do this job. It has encouraged her desire to perform, though as a musician, not as an actor. She makes herself the absolute darling of any company I'm working with, be it theater or film. They all adore her. She gets away with outrageous behavior and has a ball.

When I took her to the *Friends* television show set, she was in the audience in the wedding scene. And they all hugged her and kissed her – she was the belle of the ball. Rachel thinks it's pretty cool that I want to live in Italy part of the time now. She can drive home from college to New York. New York will always be there for her, and I'll be there too for a long time. Or she can fly over to Europe. She's amazingly confident. She gets herself around quite well. I wonder where she got that! I love it.

I had some qualms when she first was visiting in London with her girlfriends and they said to me, 'You go to the theater – we're going out to clubs.' 'Oh no,' I said at first – and then I thought, when I was seventeen, I was in London and I never thought twice about going all over on my own, and I didn't have a cell phone, either. I must have driven my parents nuts. But we had pretty strict guidelines. Be home or call by such and such an hour. We didn't abuse the freedom. And she doesn't, either. She hasn't always come home when she was supposed to, but she always calls to say that she's not home yet. And I say, 'Yes, I know that. Yeah. No kidding.'

We have a joke about how things will change now that she is getting old enough to be on her own. For New Year's Eve in 2005, I took her and one of her best friends to Paris. Which is a custom we have, to take a nice trip over the New Year's holiday. The previous year was London, and next year we're planning on Italy. In Paris, we were walking through the Place de la Concorde and the Hotel de Crillon is there, where I often stayed when someone else was paying for it. I once had a lovely suite right on the top floor called the Leonard Bernstein Suite, with a balcony and a little sunroom. 'Rache,' I said, 'do you remember the room up there on the top floor where we stayed?' And she said, 'Oh yeah, yeah, I do.' I said, 'Well, wave goodbye, because you're not staying there now. This is up to you now, kid. We'll find you a nice hostel you can afford.'

The world of Rachel

My friend Margo MacNabb, who has known Rachel since she was born, made a funny comment at dinner the other night. She said, 'There's the world of Rachel and the world of us.'

Physically, Rachel is a good mixture of both families. She's got my legs, I'm happy to say, but not my bust, honey. That's got to be from Jay's family. She has a beautiful face. Again, a real mixture of her father's eyes and my nose, his mouth, my chin. Really nice – she came together rather well. She doesn't think of herself as beautiful because she's not a typical American blond beauty at all. But she will be very beautiful. And in a lovely, personal, individual way.

She's always demonstrated her own flair in terms of style with her clothing. I still don't think I have a style, one that lets me say with assurance, 'Oh that would be good for me.' Maybe it's too many years of costuming and being dressed in somebody else's idea of how I should look. But Rachel's always had a very strong sense. When she was very young, I'd buy her clothes and she'd say, 'That doesn't go.' Excuse me? In those days she wanted to match everything, of course. Now you have to mismatch everything. She's very smart about things she cares about. She's easily uninterested, too, if her attention isn't piqued.

She does have passion, for which I am very grateful. She's passionate about her guitar playing and the guitar jazz music that she's involved with. Passion is a better quality than anything else. I see many young people who go to the right schools, are from stable backgrounds, join the right company, maybe ascend the ladder in their careers – and still are waiting for something to give them meaning. As though the thing outside will give meaning to them rather than their bringing meaning to what they do. I'm thankful she escaped that. Because I don't know how you instill passion in someone.

Honestly, I think most people are pretty much born the way they are. And we as parents can only do a little more or a little less to help children's natural personalities unfold. Rachel is bright, she's funny. She has a good sense of humor. She's quite ironic and irreverent. I took her with me to the big 2004 March for Women's Lives in Washington and she's participated with me in many other causes and service activities. So I think she has the commitment to service instilled in her just as I had it instilled in me by my parents.

Rachel has a great sense of other people. She will see that someone is timid or needy or not feeling well and she will immediately respond to that.

When I was doing the film *House of Cards*, I played the mother of a child who's diagnosed as autistic. We filmed in a North Carolina school with autistic children and Down's syndrome children. Many of these kids were truly locked away in themselves. Rachel came for a visit; she must have been six or seven years old. In between setups, we would gather the children and their parents in a large classroom where there were books and toys and puzzles, whatever they would interact with. Rachel was running around there one day when we were on a break, trying to get the other children to play with her. But these kids wouldn't talk to her, mostly because they simply didn't talk at all. They would completely retreat in what seemed like terror.

But instead of walking away and saying, 'Mother, what's wrong with these children?' she looked around, and you could just see her mind going, *Huh. I see. Well then, this is what I will do*. She went to the cooler and got juice boxes. Then she went around to each of the children, saying, 'Will you have a box of juice? Have a box of juice. You want apple? You want cran— no, you want apple, I can see you want apple. I've put the straw in it for you. I'll just set it there on your desk.' And she went about communicating with these kids in this way. I was amazed. It was fabulous. She's always been empathetic like that. Nobody told her to do this. I was just teary to see her compassion and her acceptance.

And she has her own quirky way of operating in the world, of creating chaos and crises. The world of Rachel can drive a parent crazy.

We managed to get her graduated from high school, but she made sure it was right down to the wire. Three days before graduation, her history teacher, Mr. Howard, called. He said he's not yet received her term papers. I thought, *What the fuck?* Rachel had told me that she e-mailed them on Friday. I had a call from her dean on Saturday; I told him Rachel had said she'd e-mailed them in, because of course I took her at her word. Now it's Sunday and Mr. Howard says he never received them. I said, 'Let me call you right back.' I went into Rachel's room and there she was with her computer, desperately typing, trying to finish the twenty pages she had left. I said, 'So what I'm hearing here is that you haven't actually finished and that you lied to me about having sent them in.' And it was the second time something like that happened, by the way.

'I didn't want to be a hassle,' she said. 'I didn't want to worry you.'

Isn't that nice, you don't want me to worry. That's so sweet.

I was not amused. But I encouraged her and made damn sure she finished those fucking history papers. Okay, now it should be smooth sailing.

Then I discovered she had neglected to fulfill one physical education credit that she needed to graduate. Rachel is a field hockey player. She was on the field hockey team; that had always been her PE, but there was no field hockey season in the spring semester. And she had simply ignored the fact that she had to get that credit some other way. So now she might not graduate from high school because she lacked one goddamn PE credit. Honestly! I dissolved in tears. Jay exploded and blamed me when we told him.

I was already feeling totally fucking inadequate as a mother.

I knew when I was twenty that I wanted to play Martha when I was fifty. This New York opening night photo of me as Martha and Bill Irwin as George in Edward Albee's *Who's Afraid of Virginia Woolf?* reminds me what can happen when you take your dreams seriously. (© *Carol Rosegg*)

This sexy photo was taken around the time of *Cat on a Hot Tin Roof*, when *Vanity Fair* said, accurately, 'Turner has never run as an ingénue'. (© *Terry O'Neill/Hulton Archive/Getty Images*)

I spent first grade in Clearwater Beach, Florida, after Mom and we kids were evacuated from Cuba in the wake of Castro's takeover. Dad stayed in Cuba to close down the embassy after the United States broke off diplomatic ties.
(Author's collection)

Grandmother Gladys and Grandfather Russell 'Daddy Russ' Magee. I loved Daddy Russ so much for teaching me that there are times in life when 'You just have to, don't you?'
(Author's collection)

MARY KATHERINE TURNER "KATHY"
Springfield, Missouri
President-7; Editor of Newspaper;
Art; Drama; Madrigals;
Varsity —Volleyball, Softball;
Americanism Speech; Outspoken...
Extremely Intelligent
Forecast —Lady Ambassador To The Moon.

My eighth-grade classmates in Caracas, Venezuela, thought I'd become lady ambassador to the moon. I'd rather be ambassador to Great Britain while simultaneously playing the West End in the evenings.
(Author's collection)

This family photo was taken in London not long before my father's sudden death changed everything. *Left to right:* me; Mom (Pat Magee Turner) and Dad (Richard Turner); my older sister, Susan; older brother, Andy; and younger brother, David.
(Author's collection)

My very first head shot! I think I was about twenty.
(Author's collection)

My mom was always there for us kids. This is one of her favorite photos of her four children, taken when we were all home for Christmas. *Left to right:* me, Andy, David and Susan.
(Author's collection)

With Bill Hurt in my first film, *Body Heat*. The steamy sex on-screen belied the weather so cold we had to suck on ice cubes before we spoke to keep steam from coming out of our mouths. *(Body Heat © The Ladd Company. Licensed by Warner Bros Entertainment Inc. All rights reserved)*

Yes, you can read *Playboy* for the articles. Their profile of me in 1986, with this photo, is one of my favorites. And I'm nothing if not consistent – I'd answer the questions the same way today. *(Reproduced by special permission of* Playboy *magazine, © 1986 by* Playboy; *photo by Benno Friedman)*

Michael Douglas, Danny DeVito and I were like the Three Musketeers. We had so much fun and so many adventures working together on *Romancing the Stone*, *The Jewel of the Nile* and *The War of the Roses*. *(© Corbis)*

Four generations of women in my family, taken when Rachel and I were back in Springfield, Missouri, visiting with my mom and grandmother. I'm the fifth generation of college-educated women. *(Author's collection)*

Being a mother teaches you how to separate the real from the reel in life. *(Author's collection)*

Jay, Rachel and I on vacation in Florence. *(Author's collection)*

Sandi and Michael Kaufman are like family to Jay and me, and I'm godmother to their sons Daniel and Ben. Here, with Ben, now a teenager, when he was about five. *(Courtesy of Sandi Kaufman)*

With Sandi Kaufman, my best friend. I appreciate all my women friends more each day. *(Courtesy of Sandi Kaufman)*

Coauthor Gloria Feldt and me hamming it up at a book signing when her first book, *Behind Every Choice Is a Story*, came out. *(Courtesy of Planned Parenthood Federation of America)*

It's important for me to stand up for what I believe. Fortunately, that often puts me in good company. Here at a fundraiser for the Planned Parenthood Action Fund are (*left to right*) actor Stanley Tucci; our host, political activist Sarah Kovner; me; actor Julianne Moore; Gloria Feldt, who was then president of Planned Parenthood; the late former Texas governor Ann Richards; and *Glamour* magazine editor-in-chief Cindi Lieve. *(Courtesy of Planned Parenthood Federation of America)*

I call my Citymeals-on-Wheels phone buddy, Muriel Fleit, every week. *(© 2006 Citymeals-on-Wheels)*

My television roles tend to be a little *outré*. I couldn't resist the chance to be a woman playing a man playing a woman. Here I am as Chandler's father in the TV sitcom *Friends*.

The show must go on – soon after knee-replacement surgery, I'm arriving at the Children at Heart gala benefit for the Children of Chernobyl. *(Brad Barket/Getty Images)*

The Graduate gave me my body back after years of struggle with rheumatoid arthritis. This full-page ad was my fuck-you when the show didn't get a single Tony nomination despite playing to packed houses every night. *(Reproduced by permission of Sacha Brooks and John Reed; photo by Alastair Muir)*

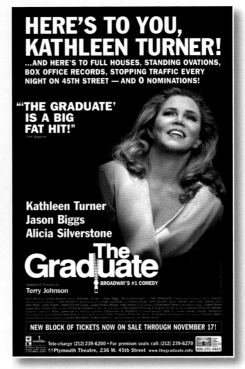

I canceled my appointments, sobbing and telling everyone, 'I just can't see anybody today. I had another problem with Rachel and with Jay and I cannot see anybody today.'

What sent me over the edge into such an emotional state wasn't just what Rachel had done. It was my own self-recriminations: *What if I had been here with her this semester rather than in London doing* Virginia Woolf? *Is this my fault? On the other hand, Jay was the parent in residence; he was supposed to have been taking care of all this. He was supposed to have been paying attention. And he obviously didn't. But how can I say that Jay was a bad parent or that he was a neglectful parent when I was the one in London? What can I do?* More tears, more self-recriminations.

I was sure Rachel wanted to go to college, but I could not for the life of me understand why she was not doing the things she needed to do to get herself there.

In my way of looking at the world, I instinctively see the steps that are to be taken to get where I want to go and I take them. So it's a big mystery to me why in the 'world of Rachel' she doesn't seem to take those steps. And I simply do not know what to do about it. That night I had a terrible coughing spell and then a full-blown asthma attack that took several days to recover from. I was just a mess.

Somehow, everything turned out fine. I finally came to the view that Rachel had taken the steps as she saw them – she got my attention. She finished her history papers and the school let her work off her PE credit deficit by cleaning out all the nasty lockers in the gym to get them ready for the next school year.

By the end of the week Rachel had graduated. It was a lovely graduation. And we spent the next day, a lazy rainy day, snuggling and watching DVDs and everything was all cozy-cozy.

Which again is the kind of thing every parent experiences. But it's tough going through it. Takes a few years off your life, now, doesn't it? One day I'm throwing up my hands and crying because I cannot seem to get through to my child about something incredibly important to her own life. And the next day after the crisis is resolved, we are back into our usual joyous relationship. She does know how to get a reaction, though, that kid, knows how to pull her parents' strings.

Waiting in the car

Being judgmental about things like what Rachel did – seeming to sabotage her own high school graduation – gets me nowhere. But children usually think we're judgmental whether we are or are not. That's because they're kids and they expect us to judge them.

Rachel, for example, came to the gym in our building not long ago when I was working out to say that she and her girlfriend wanted to go skydiving. I was startled: 'I'm sorry – you want to do what?' And I thought, *You did this rather well, didn't you, young thing?* Here I am in the gym and there are other people around. And her girlfriend.

I said, 'Hold on. Let me finish working out and I'll come right back upstairs and you'll show me all the information you have on it.' I came upstairs and they showed me how they'd done their research on the Web. You dive with an instructor and if you fail to pull your chute the instructor will pull another – but if the instructor fails also, there's a computer backup that triggers the chute, so there are three fail-safes. And I'm thinking, *Okay, all right, that makes sense. They did their homework.*

Then we got to the price. She wasn't planning to pay for it – she expected me to. And of course we came to the realization that we could not tell Jay about this because he would freak, so she couldn't ask him to pay for it. And I would not be telling him if I went, either – which I did a couple of weeks later and had an absolutely wonderful time.

Oh, what we learn from our kids!

The reel Kathleen can use her powers of observation very effectively as a tool for learning. In acting, I am very sure what's good and what's not. I'm positive. I'll read a line or play a scene and I'll say, 'That's exactly right. Thank you. Keep that, that's it.'

Yet as sure as I am in acting is as unsure as I can be in real life. I can know so clearly and quickly why I make the choices I make in my work. And at the same time, I can be so insecure and uncertain about the choices I make offstage with the people, with relationships closest to me. And I feel especially challenged in mothering Rachel. So you see, I cannot be too judgmental, because my insecurity kicks in. I can just observe and try to figure it out.

Where the insecurity comes from is a good question. Not to blame my father and mother, because I don't feel they ever deliberately did this, but somehow I felt I was never able to please them totally. I know some of it was their parental philosophy. They thought if they overpraised, then we would stop trying. I would do these remarkable things and my parents would say, 'Oh yes, that's just what we expect of you.' Which has, of course, driven me to treat Rachel in the opposite way. Every time Rachel did the smallest thing, I would say, 'How wonderful, how amazing! You just astonish me – I'm so proud of you.'

Maybe I overcompensated with Rachel because I felt I never got the praise from my parents I rightly deserved. I always felt I should be doing more, I have to do more. Even though there might not have been any more to do. That stayed with me much too long. But there's a point at which you've got to stop thinking about what your parents did or said and just move on. I have been working on that over the years. And I hope Rachel will do the same for me.

Now that she is over eighteen and technically an adult, my greatest angst about being a mom is how to give her the right measure of support and input without being too intrusive – being available to her without being overbearing. We're at a very touchy time in terms of her growth. But I know she feels, as I did about my father, that I would move heaven and earth to help her in any way that was necessary.

It's like my dad waiting in his car while I was acting in my high school play. Even if I don't approve of Rachel's choices – can't bring myself to go to the performance, as it were – I'll be waiting in the car. I'll be there for her no matter what.

Chapter Nine

Speak in your own voice

One day when Rachel was in elementary school and I was very much at the height of my film success, I wanted to go grocery shopping. I've never given up going to the supermarket to buy food and to plan meals. It makes me feel good. I took Rachel with me. I thought I would try out a disguise in the hopes of doing my grocery shopping without being noticed. So I bought an auburn-haired pageboy wig. I put the wig on, and I put on dark glasses, trying to do the Garbo-wants-to-be-alone thing. I was shopping when Rachel took off, just started running wildly around the store, and I lost sight of her. Without thinking, I yelled out, 'Rachel – come back, please.'

This guy came over, tapped me on the shoulder, and said, 'It would work a lot better if you kept your mouth shut.'

Thank you, yes, right. I never tried that again.

People don't necessarily recognize me by my face because I have played so many different kinds of roles (convincingly, it would seem) that I have never been stereotyped by my appearance. In fact, once I was to meet the *New York Times* columnist Maureen Dowd for an interview at one of my favorite Mexican restaurants. Inevitably, I got to the restaurant before she did. I'm always on time for appointments. I cannot stand to be late. In fact, I'm usually early. When she came in, I walked toward her to greet her. She thought I was the hostess.

But when I open my mouth, that's a whole different thing.

My voice has been called smoky, husky, sexy, sensuous, tobacco-cured, scotch-laden, iconic, and evil, to name just a few. I rather enjoy all these adjectives. It's a real pleasure to me to have a distinctive voice, and I've worked on making it more so over the years. There are advantages. When I call up a restaurant and say, 'This is Kathleen Turner – I need a reservation,' they say, 'Yes, yes it is.' I always get a table. And I find that when I put crying children against my chest, the vibration soothes them and the lower tones of my voice seem to comfort them.

I take the idea of voice quite literally because I truly believe the sound of my voice is terribly important to my overall presentation and how I will be received by others. It started with my being an actor, but it is much more basic than that, really. A resonant voice is first of all a practical communication tool for anyone at any time.

But voice to me also means empowerment, especially for women, children, and other groups that have not always been heard equally in our society. And voice represents service: the responsibility I believe we all have and the courage to use the power of our voices to advocate for our principles and causes.

In all three of these aspects of voice, authenticity is the key to effectiveness. You must speak in your own voice or no one will hear you. And your unique voice is a special gift that no one else can give to the world.

Voice is a practical tool

I saw an article recently about female executives training their voices to be lower in order to garner greater respect from their male colleagues.[13] The article mentioned that these professional women were trying to sound more like Kathleen Turner, which I took as a compliment. But a voice, like a fingerprint, is unique. Everyone has a unique voice quality, but the effectiveness of one's voice can be improved upon. And should be.

Training it is tremendously important. And that's not inaccessible to anyone. But for some reason we tend to ignore voice as part of how we present ourselves. It seems to me that, particularly for women, having a good vocal presence completes you. I mean, what does it matter what you look like if people cringe when you open your mouth?

That nasal whine some New Yorkers have – ouch. Then there are the Valley girl inflections, with all sentences ending on an up note as though they're questions and including the word *like* half a dozen times. I have told Rachel she must never talk like this. Oh, there are so many annoying examples. When I first went to college in Missouri, I was required to live in a girls' dorm. There were nights when I thought I was going to have to kill myself. All those squealing, high-pitched talkers. 'Honey – Polly, I thought I was gonna die! The other day, he looked at me, he looked at me.' I thought, *If I have to stay in here, I'm going to go absolutely insane*. So I finagled a way out.

Because of that experience, I used to think I couldn't stand the sound of women's voices in general, but that really wasn't true. I certainly can't come near the higher tones that many women have and that are quite pleasing. It depends very much on the sound, the resonance. You can have a higher voice and have resonance, or clarity, or just a purity that I can't match. So women's voices don't have to be low to be appealing. It's more about the quality of the tone, the timbre, that makes a voice more or less pleasant to hear.

We in the United States haven't attended to using voice as part of our personality. Everybody talks and we think it's the words that matter. But it isn't *just* the words that matter. Voice as a practical communication tool is a skill, like how you move and how you sit. Women take a great deal of care in how they present themselves visually. For some reason we've never extended that to our aural world. Yet close your eyes and you can flesh out the whole world in the sounds around you. Hearing is one of our strongest and most used senses. So why shouldn't we polish that part of ourselves as well? Why not consider it an aural world where you exist as sound?

It always amuses me when I see American actresses who go to great lengths to gain weight or shave their head or change their teeth or other kinds of radical changes to play a role – and then they open their mouth and you know they're the same person as in the last role they played. Every character sounds the same. I meet women who look very glamorous – they've got about five thou on the hoof, right? The hair, the clothes, the jewelry. And then they open their mouth and their voice is so annoying and off-putting. Why don't they take the amount they spent on one outfit and go get voice lessons?

Partly because of my voice, I've always played older than I am, although I'm now caught up with Martha, who is fifty-two. My voice worked against me when I first came to New York, because I was clearly young but my voice sounded mature. I made the rounds, trying to get commercials to pay the bills. A national commercial can pay you residuals for years. I once tried out for a commercial for a product to mop the floor. The line was something like, 'Oh, how shiny it is!' They just couldn't buy it coming from me. I lost that one to an ingenue who could do a high-pitched 'Oh, how shiny it is!'

Another time, I went to a commercial call for a car company that had some large cat on top of a sign, and it snarls at the end of the commercial. I was in the room with these beautiful women, all of them models, I am sure, with their suitcases and hair curling irons and makeup. I was thinking, *What the hell am I doing here?* Then I looked over the ad copy and thought, *Okay, I can snarl. I can't look like these women, but I can snarl*. The woman casting the commercial came out and said to all of us, 'Snarl, please.' Within seconds the room was full of beautiful young things all snarling away. It was the funniest damn thing I'd ever seen. I was laughing so hard. I snarled very convincingly, I thought. But I still didn't get the commercial.

But my voice was working for me by the time I auditioned for *Body Heat*. Can you imagine Matty with a high, squeaky voice?

Though a higher-pitched voice can produce beautiful tones, a lower, heavier voice, which comes across as more masculine, is an asset to being taken seriously. Many women are tuned out, not heard, because their voice is light and lacks authority. You do not dismiss my voice.

Often in other countries I'm addressed as 'sir.' When I pick up the phone in a hotel to order dinner, I'll get, 'Yes, sir,' in response. Always in London this happened, even though I lived at the same place for months during the run of *Virginia Woolf*. I gave up trying to correct them. I just wanted my dinner.

And a low voice certainly does not diminish sex appeal or femininity. Just the opposite. I've been considered a sexual icon in substantial part *because* of my voice. In *Nip/Tuck*, which is obviously not real life but has something to say about sexuality and sex roles in our culture, my character, Cindy Plumb, is obviously my age – fifty-two – and she's one of the most successful phone sex artists. So clearly, whatever fantasies these men she is talking to are having bear no relationship to her actual appearance. They're visualizing some twenty-year-old babe who happens to have this very effective voice. And as soon as her voice gets too low to give them that fantasy, they want her to get the twenty-year-old voice back. So she goes for a vocal cord lift.

I don't know if my voice shaped me or if I shaped the voice. When I was in junior high school in Caracas they put me with the boys in the choir. I could sing alto but I was more valuable with the boys in the tenor section. It didn't seem odd to me at all. So I wonder if there is an element of always having had a low voice that determined some of my character. It's entirely possible.

In any case, both my natural voice and vocal training paid off in the end. I've been kidded for practicing with erasers between my teeth. Here's how that came about: There's an excellent teacher named Arthur Lessac who wrote a book on voice and voice production. He recommends taking the erasers off the ends of pencils and putting them in the back of your mouth, in between your teeth. It teaches you how to stretch the muscles in the back of your mouth, between your upper and lower teeth, and you become more aware of them. Some say that Demosthenes, the Greek orator, overcame his speech impediment using pebbles this way. It gives you a fuller, rounder tone. The tighter your neck, the tighter your shoulders, the more pinched your vocal cords are. Keep the vocal cords relaxed and they have the most vibration. When they get tight, the sounds get sharp. It's really not a mystery. You just have to work at it. As long as people can hear themselves or know what they want to sound like, they can make those improvements.

Maybe I should start a voice class.

Voice is power

Arthur Lessac, who wrote that definitive book on vocal production, was the father of Michael Lessac, who directed me in the film *House of Cards*. The story was not well understood at the time because it dealt with autism, which was even less understood then than it is now. And voice played a prominent role in the story.

I thought it was a very beautiful idea, a beautiful script, and I helped Michael, who's a good man and a great director, raise the money to do the film, which took seven years because of the challenging subject matter. My character, Ruth Matthews, is an architect and her husband is an archaeologist. One night her husband finds a pyramid in Central America and falls to his death. They have a daughter named Sally. Sally seems to become autistic: she stops talking, stops responding. At first they think it is temporary from the shock of the father's death and having to move back to the United States and redesign their lives. But it becomes apparent that the child is not going to communicate. The mother frantically starts looking for treatment. And she's told by everyone that the child is autistic, there's nothing to be done about it, and Sally should be placed in special care. Ruth refuses until one night the child climbs out of an attic window and is found balancing along the top of the roof. This frightens her so much that she agrees to put the child in a special-care facility.

House of Cards, 1993

Ruth Matthews's husband falls to his death at an archaeological dig and her daughter stops speaking. Risking her own sanity, Ruth tries to enter her daughter's mind in order to reach her.

Directed by Michael Lessac
Produced by Vittorio Cecchi Gori, Wolfgang Glattes, Lianne Halfon, Edward Khmara, Gianni Nunnari, Dale Pollock, and Jonathan Sanger

Tommy Lee Jones as Jake Beerlander
Kathleen Turner as Ruth Matthews

Ruth Matthews: *We all go a little crazy sometimes, Doctor.*

One day, Sally builds this incredibly complex beautiful tower of playing cards, all perfectly balanced one on the other. So Ruth tries to understand this structure and to create a computer model of the same structure Sally has built with cards, thinking this is the only way to reach this child. Another reason the film wasn't understood at the time it came out is that we were using a virtual reality model before that idea had become well known. Ruth creates a virtual pattern through the computer and walks the path of the construction of the house of cards using virtual fields.

Ruth is terrified of heights since her husband was killed by a fall. As this construction gets higher, it becomes more and more difficult for her, but she's determined that this is a way she can communicate with her daughter. And finally when she reaches a certain height in creating the structure, it starts to wobble. The daughter sees this and she has a vision of her mother falling to her death. She screams, 'NO!' and starts running up the 'steps' of the house of cards that her mother built, to grab her and save her.

Sally speaks, she talks. It's miraculous. This trigger released the child and she regained her voice, which was her power to communicate, to connect with and be understood by the people around her. Regaining her voice was the first necessary step toward having the power to do everything else in life.

Voice, in the metaphoric sense of being heard, being understood, being received and acknowledged by society, is such an essential part of empowerment. And it is one that has special resonance for women (pun intended). First you have to be able to get their attention.

Women sometimes complain that men simply do not hear

them. Part of this is no doubt cultural, but many men physically cannot hear women's higher tones. I think a good voice is an arresting voice. I mean by that, it gets attention in a positive way. My daughter is always complaining that I'm too loud. Even when I try to speak really, really softly, she says my voice still carries to such an extent that people around us hear me. I think that's a great asset, actually, and not just because I need it when doing stage work. (Though maybe Rachel has a point. When I do film or TV, they often ask me, 'Could you bring it down, be a little softer?' Because I'm too loud for the mike.) But I think to have an arresting voice in normal daily life, not a commanding so much as an arresting tone, helps people to hear you. You somehow seem more serious or more capable, and that alone is empowering.

Only recently I learned something about my own grandmother's life that really shocked and touched me. And it bears upon the notion of voice as empowerment to do what you want or need to do in life. My mother told me the story when I was visiting her in Missouri and we were going through old family photos.

My grandfather, Daddy Russ, was an engineer. But in the 1930s after the banks crashed and the Depression started, he worked as an automobile mechanic and salesperson. Everybody liked him and he was a great salesman. He could work wonders on an old beat-up truck, but if it was too far gone he'd have to sell them a new one, and nobody had any money. So it really got quite desperate.

Grandmother was educated to be a teacher. In those days if you were married, schools wouldn't hire you because they assumed a married woman was supported by her husband. Only unmarried teachers were hired. It was perfectly legal at the time. The family was in a dire financial situation. So Grandmother took my mom and uncle and moved back in with her parents. She divorced my grandfather purely so she would be eligible to be hired to teach school, which she then did. They remarried later on in life because they still felt the same way about each other. But Grandmother thought she had no choice but to divorce him so she could get one of the few jobs available to women during that time, and so her children would be fed.

Grandmother became very successful. When the county superintendent of schools died, the governor appointed her interim superintendent. Everybody said she couldn't do it, because, according to my mother, 'they were mean, stingy, crusty school boards, each one independent, by God, nobody was going to change the way they did things.' At the end of two years she had to run for reelection and she won in every school district in the county – the first woman to be elected to the post. Then she talked the school boards into spending money that they had said they would never spend. I guess she could have gone on running and winning as long as she wanted. But during World War II, Daddy Russ and Grandmother remarried and she left that county to be with him again. Come to think of it, maybe my grandmother was right when she said I take after her.

This is such a compelling story about a woman having to resort to great lengths to make her voice heard in the sense of taking action so she could earn a living. Grandmother did what she had to do to take care of her family despite the unfairness of the situation.

Voice is service

A great voice, a voice like James Earl Jones's, a voice like Roscoe Brown's, a voice like Maggie Smith's, or, heavens, like Barbara Jordan's, which sounded to me like the voice of Moses, makes people take notice. I revere those voices. I assume that any person who speaks with such a voice must be extraordinary, that I should listen to him or her. A great voice automatically brings with it the opportunity for influence.

It was a great honor to me when I was asked to narrate a documentary, *Answering the Call*, about the first sixteen horrendous days right after the 9/11 attack on the World Trade Center. There was so little I could do, but I had to do something. And there was absolutely nothing I could do alone. Yet because of the outpouring of thousands of people, the enormous task of sifting through the pile of rubble that had once been the Twin Towers was tackled. We were together taking a stand against terrorism. We were saying the forces of evil would not win the day: we would rescue who and what we could, we would rebuild, and we would prevail.

Using my voice to document the stories of those heroic people, from the firefighters and police officers to the emergency medical technicians and the volunteers, was the very least I could do. I was and am humbled by each and every one of them.

Any voice can become great if used to take a stand and do service – greater still when joined with others. And sometimes it is the unheralded action of a single individual that speaks most compellingly about righting a wrong of society. I was so touched by my grandmother's life because it made me think about how in my lifetime women have gained opportunities to achieve so much, whereas she had to take such drastic steps, to divorce the husband she loved simply to be able to get a job so she could put food on the table for her children during the Depression.

In my mother's day, women could be working wives in traditionally female jobs, though their income and accomplishments were usually regarded as merely supplements to their husband's. But I have always been a working woman, knowing that if I worked hard and took the necessary steps to advance myself, I could aspire to whatever I wanted to do in life and that I could control my own financial situation. I owe this to the many courageous women who used their voices to change the law and society to make all this possible for me. My daughter has grown up with even more of a sense of her 'voice' in the world.

Speaking with a united and arresting voice could make women more powerful in the world of business, media, and politics. We assumed that once women's capability became apparent and legal rights were set, they would stay that way. But like birth control options, like women's reproductive choice, who thought that would be at risk again? And it's truly all at risk now. It's as though people feel now that the need to have a just and equal place for women in society is no longer an important issue. Feminism, the empowerment of women, doesn't mean you have to take anything away from men, or that you want to. But that seems to be what has been implied to many younger people. I don't care if that guy has that position as long as he's good enough. But why not also a woman if she is good enough? So we still have work to do.

To use my voice on behalf of an issue, I first have to have a strong belief in that cause, a passion for it. And then I must have the knowledge to speak authoritatively about it. Sometimes I have to do as much preparation to use my voice in a service role as I do for learning an acting role. This happened when I was invited to speak at the National Press Club in Washington, which I'm told is quite an honor, on behalf of the organization called Childhelp USA, with which I worked for years. Childhelp has centers for foster children who are truly at the end of the line. They've been moved from home to home, they cannot seem to adjust, they cannot seem to fit into society, and they're understandably angry and destructive. These centers not only are places for these hard cases to live and learn how to socialize, but also they teach potential foster parents how to deal with the displacement issues the children have. My God, can you imagine a child who's been abandoned and then moved from one environment to another without ever feeling safe or loved? I admire this group very much. They have a network, 1-800-4-A-CHILD – you see it on grocery carts. Anyone can call that number anywhere in the United States and the Virgin Islands and they will tell you the nearest shelter, the nearest police station, the nearest medical center, whatever that child needs. This is great stuff.

So I was invited to the Press Club to speak about child abuse, foster care, how the government handles it, what the non-governmental organizations like Childhelp do. It's a big topic. I spent a month and a half working with Childhelp on the speech: getting the materials, reading the reference books they gave me, making sure that I knew every fact. I would be speaking for twenty minutes and then the audience would have forty minutes to grill me. I know when people go up there as actors and celebrities, the audience is going to try to find out if they know their stuff or are just fakes. Or whether they're just there to make themselves look good and don't have much actual connection with the topic.

When a reporter in the audience asked me, 'Where are your sources?' I said, 'Let me get them.' And I started to read out my sources, the publishing houses and the date of publication. I read five or six of them, then I looked at the reporter and I said, 'Would you like more?' The whole press corps burst out laughing because clearly this man had not expected me to have the resource material or the understanding that I had.

I later learned that the month before, they had asked Elizabeth Taylor to speak on AIDS. When it came to the question period, she couldn't cite the background or the sources of the claims she had made in her speech. She said they would have someone else get that information for them. So the press was expecting the same from me.

I was tremendously anxious and nervous about this speech and the responsibility I felt to Childhelp USA to do well. A journalist said to me at the end of the session, 'Miss Turner, the greatest compliment we have to give you is that we haven't asked you about any of your movies.' And I agreed, thank you.

Speak in your own authentic voice

It seems the better an actor I am, the worse liar I am.

It's like a price I pay. Here I am, a woman who can be incredibly subtle onstage or in film, and yet I completely give myself away in my own life. I'm afraid I tend toward bluntness; I always have. I can play a role onstage or in a film with absolute discipline. But being able to hide my own feelings and my own thoughts is impossible. It simply doesn't work. Anybody can read me like a book.

I suppose if I actually thought about hiding my feelings from someone, I could do it. But to me, one of the laws about acting is that the character cannot be lying. She must be authentic. Bad acting is pretending. Good acting is believing. It is the absolute truth as you know it, as the character knows it. When I tried to be the ingenue in one of my first stage performances, I was awful. When I tried to get the floor-washing solution commercial, it just didn't work. And when I went to the Food Emporium in disguise, I was quickly found out. My own true voice outed me.

Carrying that over into my daily life with my family and friends, I could try to pretend. I could say, 'No, everything's all right, I'm not angry, I'm just fine,' when I'm not. But that would violate one of my own laws about honesty and integrity. So I've never really tried to shield myself that way. Which can sometimes be wrong, because then I also don't shield others from me. Despite this downside, on balance, the old adage that honesty is the best policy is still true.

Usually when I'm sought out for a role because they want my authentic voice, the character is a little outré – not your average run-of-the-mill straight suburban housewife. I've even played a woman who becomes a house, in *Monster House*, in which I mostly just groan and make all kinds of strange and scary noises. I get to play these rather shocking parts, which are very, very appealing to me.

People know me professionally as sexy characters such as Matty in *Body Heat* and tragic-comic bombastic ones such as Martha in *Who's Afraid of Virginia Woolf?* but the truth is that I love to play anything that's a little weird and out of the mainstream. Especially in television, where many of the characters are caricatures anyway and the character's voice is almost always an important part of how you identify with her. There was Chandler's drag queen father, Mr. Bing, on *Friends*, for which I had the delicious irony of being a woman playing a man playing a woman. I've played roles on other sitcoms such as *The King of Queens* and *Family Guy*, and there's my *Nip/Tuck* character, Cindy Plumb, the phone sex operator who has a name that even sounds so – well, plummy. I loved playing the TV cartoon character named Stacy Lavelle on *The Simpsons*. Stacy is a doll maker who created a Barbie-esque doll. And the girl in the Simpson family, Lisa, goes all righteous and upset about this. She arranges a meeting with Stacy at which she talks Stacy into producing a strong, independent, intelligent young woman doll. And she can't sell one doll! This was such perfect satire on consumerism and feminism.

So people form opinions of me before they have met me. I think by and large, they take me as a package, because my voice is so identifiable in all the definitions I've used. Even if I weren't on camera, even if I were just on the phone, they're going to say, 'Oh, that's Kathleen Turner. Well, Kathleen Turner stands for things.' The overall impression may be that I'm a strong woman, an independent woman, a woman who is whatever *feminist* means to them. But certainly not a traditional woman – let's say that, yeah? My voice immediately says something about the character, the cause, or the show.

I imagine this commentary all makes me come across as this incredibly strong woman, and I think I am that. But there have been times when I lost my voice, as Sally did in *House of Cards*, and I feared I might never find it again.

Chapter Ten

The irony strikes when you're hot

Playing Maggie in *Cat on a Hot Tin Roof* was to be my big return to Broadway. We performed *Cat* out of town for a good three months before opening in New York; tried it out in Delaware, Boston, Philadelphia. We even went to Pittsburgh, God help me. I was in a high state of elation about being back onstage. At the same time, I was anxious about the New York opening. I was now known more as a movie actress than a stage actress. I knew full well that the critics and some theater insiders would be looking to shoot me down because of that.

Quite the opposite happened, I'm happy to say. We opened on Broadway in March 1990 to fabulous, fabulous reviews. It was truly exhilarating, night after night, to be performing live again, and for such enthusiastic audiences.

Cat on a hot tin roof, 1990

Big Daddy's sixty-fifth birthday brings his son Brick and Brick's wife, Maggie, into town. Brick has taken to drinking and turned cold toward Maggie. When it is revealed that Big Daddy is sick, Brick's brother, Gooper, and Gooper's wife try to push to take over Big Daddy's estate.

Directed by Howard Davies
Produced by Barry and Fran Weissler

Kathleen Turner as Maggie
Charles Durning as Big Daddy
Daniel Hugh Kelly as Brick
Polly Holliday as Big Mama

Maggie: *I'm not living with you! We occupy the same cage, that's all.*

Maybe a week after we opened the show in New York, I finished the performance and walked off the stage. Floated into the dressing room might be more like it. At that instant, the phone started to ring. I knew Jay would be calling, so I ran to grab it, eager to share my euphoria. He didn't ask how the night had gone as he usually did. He just said, 'Sit down.' I was still all keyed up from the show, and I bubbled, 'I can't sit down; it was a great show. I got a standing ovation.'

Jay said, 'No, no, sit down.' Something in his voice told me I'd better sit down right away.

'I have to tell you that eighty-seven people died in one of my buildings today.'

'Eight or seven people?' I repeated. 'No,' Jay said, 'I said eighty-seven people. And it happened because of a fire in an illegal club that I did not know was operating in the building.' He wasn't managing the building but he was one of the financial partners. The enormity of what Jay was saying slowly sank in. I dashed home, as stunned as he was and with no thought to anything but the tragedy that had befallen these people and their families.

The illegal club that was the scene of this horrible, horrible tragedy was called Happy Land. How outrageous.

This ushered in one of the most bizarre periods of my life. Jay, with his sense of responsibility and the horror of such a thing happening, became suicidal. One night he called at ten minutes to eight saying, 'I'm calling to say I love you and goodbye. I won't be alive when you get home.' I screamed, 'Understudy!' and ran out of the theater, jumped in a cab, and arrived home terrified. Jay hadn't done anything to himself, but he was so devastated and depressed that he had cried out, thank goodness. We got professional help to ease the emotional pain. But he couldn't get past it for a long time; it was so horrific to him, such a horrible, horrible event. Perhaps in some way he felt responsible even though in the direct sense he was not. He could not stop thinking about it. Maybe he should have done more, maybe he should have checked on the building more often, maybe, who knows? Maybe, maybe, maybe.

Jay became very depressed, and he usually slept in the evening as a result. He felt his life was wrecked. I not only had to stay strong for Jay, but I also had to keep things as normal as possible for Rachel. I continued to perform every evening partly for that reason. But, even more, I kept my normal performance schedule because I wanted to prove that he wasn't guilty, that we weren't going to walk away from the world. Not at all. I would proudly stand up there onstage every night as his wife, because I believed in him and I knew he was a good man and this was not his doing.

I'll never, ever forget my first performance after the fire. The fire happened on a Sunday. Monday was our day off. On Tuesday, Charles Durning, who was playing Big Daddy, came into my dressing room while I was putting on my makeup and he said, 'I'm going to be right behind you offstage. When you open that door, if you get any shit from those people out there, if they boo you, if they do anything, I'm walking out right behind you and telling them what's what.' I said, 'Charles, you're not on till the second act.' He repeated, 'I'm right behind you. Right behind you.'

Now I was really terrified. It hadn't occurred to me to fear an overt negative or threatening audience response.

The curtain went up. I threw the doors open with my heart pounding. I started my first line: 'One of those no-neck monsters hit me with a hot buttered biscuit so I have to change!'[14] I could see the audience begin to stand. I heard them start to applaud, softly at first and then more vigorously. The whole audience stood for me. Because I was *there*. And because I was there for Jay too.

Well, it was just breathtaking. It was all I could do to keep my composure. But one beat and I went on with my lines as usual.

The people were wonderful.

But oh my God, the press was a different story. I couldn't

possibly get into the theater through all of them and their cameras swarming around the stage doors. I had to be taken into another theater and go through the air-conditioning ducts to get into my theater. Photographers and reporters would come to my house. Rachel was very young then, so I would go out on the steps of our brownstone, and beg, 'Guys, please, do me a favor. I'll walk over there; I'll give you as many pictures as you want. Don't shoot the number on the house, don't shoot my front door, please don't do that. I have a young child.' Well, they took a picture anyway. We decided we had to move. And then, wouldn't you know, the *Post* published an article that screamed, 'The happy couple – who were happier before the Happy Land Social Club fire claimed 87 lives (a company Weiss controlled held the lease) – are moving to an even more elegant townhouse they have renovated uptown.'[15]

The *Post* will have my undying enmity till the end of my days. It's such a piece of shit anyway.

All of this was going on while I was performing eight shows a week and trying in some way to help Jay, in some way to protect Rachel. Everything was a blur as I juggled it all, including a temporary move to a hotel. Before the fire, we had started renovating a house in the West Sixties. Remodeling was something we enjoyed doing and did well together. Jay would handle the construction and I would plan the layout of the rooms and the lighting. Well, suddenly we had to move into that house even though it wasn't finished. I would sneak away and move things in without the press finding out where we were. They still thought we were living down on 10th Street for a long time. Which was good.

I stayed in the play. Jay had some good help, some good

support. And he had a couple of lawyers who are still dear to us, very good men. But it cost everything. It cost Jay his business. And imagine what that does to a man.

The whole story was slowly coming out: the fire was started by a man who was angry with his ex-girlfriend who worked at this illegal club.[16] A gasoline station sold him an illegal can of gas. None of this had anything to do with Jay's actions or with us, and he was completely exonerated in the end. But that didn't matter to the press or public chatterers, because I was Kathleen Turner.

Toward the end of the scheduled run of the play, I was asked to extend for three weeks. The audiences were so good. We in the cast felt we were doing a good job and we were enjoying ourselves. None of us felt that we'd used it all up yet. So I said yeah, we'll do another three weeks. And a wonderful thing happened that uplifted the whole cast. Ray Gill, who'd started with us playing Brother Man, had dropped out in Pittsburgh because a serious flare-up of AIDS put him in the hospital. They didn't know if he would survive. But he did and now was well enough to come back and finish the last three weeks of the run with us. Maybe the joy of Ray's return against all odds felt especially sweet to me because of what Jay and I had just been through.

After the three-week extension, the play was still selling out, so the producers considered having the run continue. I had to leave because I'd committed to doing the film *V.I. Warshawski*. I'm rather proud to say they were never able to get anyone who could replace me as Maggie. Not that they didn't try.

Charles Durning came into my dressing room one afternoon between shows and he said, 'You gotta come. You gotta see this,

Kathleen.' He took me around the outside to the back of the house. 'Shhh – be very, very quiet.'

We crept into the back doorway to where we could see the back of the stage. One of the producers was auditioning Raquel Welch to take over as Maggie. We heard her say, 'Well, I just don't think that Kathleen has ever been feline enough.' Raquel was going around the stage with her hands like claws, hissing and making cat gestures. Charles was cracking up. I had to shush him. He's so funny. The producers decided not to recast.

As things will do in time, things got better for Jay. When the play finished, we stayed out at our beach house for a while. We needed to chill out, to be together without the stress of being constantly in the limelight.

But Rachel was starting school. I had to go on location in Chicago. Soon we were back into life as usual. Jay started slowly to build his business back up, and to get a perspective on what had happened so that the depression began to lift. Mostly, it got better because we just stayed with it. We just stayed. You just have to . . .

Turner takes it on the nose

I had to keep working as much as I could because now we needed the money to pay the legal bills and make up for Jay's lost income. That meant getting back into film. V.I. Warshawski is a smart, ballsy character, and I love Sara Paretsky, who writes the V.I. Warshawski books. We filmed some wonderful material – much better than what made it into the final version. I was not pleased with the final cutting. Actors never get to determine the editing of a film. But I did have script approval, thank goodness, which after the *Jewel of the Nile* fiasco I always made sure I had in my contract.

V.I. Warshawski, 1991

Private detective Victoria Warshawski babysits for her new boyfriend, who ends up dead. V.I. teams up with his daughter, Kat, to find the killer.

Directed by Jeff Kanew
Produced by Doug Claybourne, Penney Finkelman Cox, Jeffrey Lurie, John Bard Manulis, John P. Marsh, and Lauren Weissman

Jay O. Sanders as Murray Ryerson
Charles Durning as Det. Lt. Bobby Mallory
Kathleen Turner as Victoria 'V.I.' Warshawski

V.I. Warshawski: *Never underestimate a man's ability to underestimate a woman.*

Jeffrey Katzenberg, the studio head, was pressuring me hard to change the end to resemble *Fatal Attraction* because it was a big hit film at the time with Michael Douglas and Glenn Close. Michael's character is having an affair and he tries to kill her at the end. He thinks she's dead. Just when you think it's all over, suddenly you hear this back-of-the-throat sound and she bolts up out of the bathtub brandishing a knife and the story starts over again. Well, V.I. skewers her villain at the end with a boat hook and throws him into the lake in order to save Kat, the victim's daughter. Katzenberg wanted the man to suddenly come alive again. I said, 'No, this story is about Kat and how she goes on.'

Night after night I got phone calls from Jeffrey. 'Oh, come on, I'll do this for you, I'll do that.' I finally said, 'Okay, you send me a written version of what you want and give me approval over whether or not we shoot.' He said, 'No actor's ever had that. That would be a precedent that would ruin the industry.' I said, 'Those are my terms. It's my choice whether or not we shoot the ending that way.' So that was finally the end of that discussion. Whew! Close call.

I missed another call, though, and broke my nose during a night scene where V.I. runs desperately to rescue Kat. In case anyone has been wondering why my nose looks different now from how it looked in, say, *Body Heat* or *Peggy Sue*, this is the story. I was running hell bent for leather to dive off the pier because Kat is out in the lake unconscious, in a boat that's sinking. The cameras were rolling. There was an uncovered cable on the dock. I caught my foot on it, went flying, and hit the edge of the camera trolley right between my eyes. The blood was pouring and everybody was screaming and running around and yelling for the nurse. This poor nurse came up and said, 'Oh my God, Katherine, Katherine.' I corrected her, 'My name is Kathleen.' Not a very gracious way to receive help, was it? They iced me and took me to a plastic surgeon and got my face stitched up. But then of course I had two black eyes, so I couldn't shoot for a week.

Since Jeffrey wanted me to change the ending to have the villain come back to life, I thought it would be funny, in my Turner way, to get a football helmet, pads, and jersey and to go on camera with my black eyes and say, 'I'll be back.' He didn't seem to think that was funny at all. 'Waste of film,' he grumbled. 'Waste of film.'

Unfortunately, Sara sold the character to Disney. I think that was a bad idea. I would love for us to take that character back because Sara keeps writing the books as the woman ages. So I'm still age appropriate for V.I. But I will not work with Disney again. I don't like their product or how they treat people, and that's that.

Losing that which I most took for granted

I was in Baltimore in 1992, filming *Serial Mom*, when I started to have inexplicable pains and fevers.

Serial Mom, 1994

A suburban housewife starts to take slights against her family a little too seriously. Taking matters into her own hands, Beverly Sutphin takes revenge. As the body count climbs, the police start closing in on the Sutphin family.

Directed by John Waters
Produced by Joseph M. Caracciolo Jr., John Fiedler, Pat Moran, and Mark Tarlov

Sam Waterston as Eugene Sutphin, D.D.S.
Kathleen Turner as Beverly R. Sutphin

Misty Sutphin: *He killed people, Mom.*
Beverly Sutphin: *We all have our bad days.*

One day I had to do a famous scene where I'm running in high heels with the knife after a kid who has said something bad about my child. I was playing Beverly Sutphin, the middle-class suburban mom who goes to great lengths, including murder, to defend her children against slights real or perceived. *Serial Mom* has become a cult classic that is revived and sometimes reenacted every year in some places. Fans have memorized the lines and can repeat them on cue, just like people do with *The Rocky Horror Show*. It always freaks me out when people stop me on the street and do this.

As usual, I was doing my own stunt work. I went to put on my high-heeled shoes that day and I couldn't get my feet into them. This was strange. Nothing else had changed. But my feet seemed to have grown two sizes. Well, of course, being me, I stuffed my feet into the shoes anyway. I spent the day chasing up and down the street in shoes that had become incredibly painful.

I finished *Serial Mom*. When I got home, I felt quite sick, but I thought, *All right, it's just the intensity of doing a film and then when it ends, I fall apart*.

But it wasn't just that at all. I started to wear Jay's sneakers without laces because I couldn't get into any of my shoes. My family doctor recommended a specialist who was the head of podiatry at a big hospital. He took X-rays and said, 'I don't see anything wrong. Are you sure you're just not being a little vain? Maybe you should buy bigger shoes.' *Thank you, sir. That was certainly helpful*.

I kept waddling around in Jay's sneakers. Then I realized I couldn't move my left arm. I went to pick something up and I couldn't straighten it. It felt like I was growing a second elbow;

it looked as though my elbow had moved over to the inside of my arm.

So I went to a sports medicine specialist who takes care of the Mets and Yankees pitchers. He took an MRI and said, 'I don't see anything wrong with the bones, but we could do exploratory surgery.' I said, 'You don't know what you're looking for and you want to do surgery? No, I don't think so.'

Soon I couldn't turn my head. I would have to turn my shoulders to look around. And I thought this was really odd and getting odder. I had an X-ray of the area all around my neck. They said, 'Oh, you've lost the curvature of your upper vertebrae.' But nobody could tell me what was going on. And nobody had a treatment that could make it better.

By now I was almost a year into the symptoms without a diagnosis that made sense. I had gone to the top doctor of every fucking department of medicine in one of the biggest cities in the goddamn world and they couldn't help me.

I decided, *All right, I'm dying. I'm dying. There's some terrible disease – I don't think it's cancer, probably we'd know that, but I'm clearly dying.*

So I went back to my GP. I said, 'You know, Bert, I'm dying and I'm really scared. Jay just got through all this terrible stuff and I can't afford to die right now.' Bert said, 'Well, we'll just find out what this is.' So he took blood and had a full workup done once again. This time he called me up and said, 'Kathleen, most people have a rheumatoid factor of maybe sixty. Yours is sixteen hundred.'

Stunned, I said, 'Oh. And that means?' He said, 'That means you have a serious case of rheumatoid arthritis. It's a chronic, incurable disease that destroys the lining of the joints.'

'And what do I do now?' He didn't have an answer for that.

That same day, right after Bert called to give me this mind-blowing news, I was scheduled to go to a parent-teacher conference with the kindergarten teacher at Rachel's school. Being me, I went despite my state of shock.

There were all of three stairs up to the door of the school, and yet I struggled to pull myself up step by step. The kindergarten, thank God, was on the ground floor. But the room had cute little furniture with chairs about twelve inches off the floor. I looked at those fucking little chairs and burst into tears because I knew that even if I got myself down onto a chair I would never be able to get up again. The teacher saw me and asked, 'Oh my God, what is it?' I said, 'I just found out I have rheumatoid arthritis.' 'Oh, poor thing' was all she could say. She felt very bad for me and gave me her chair.

'Oh, poor thing' was about all anyone could say at the time. Now, this was less than twenty years ago. Nobody knew much about RA, or about autoimmune diseases in general. They often thought RA sufferers were just complaining. Oh, you worked out too hard. You must have had too much to drink. You probably ate something bad. Or maybe you're getting a bit of the flu. They'd assume anything or everything. But it's a *disease*, you know.

It was a relief to know the diagnosis. At least that gave me something specific to deal with. But as we started to learn more about the disease, it got increasingly scary. Rheumatoid arthritis is an illness where the body's immune system reacts inappropriately and actually creates the problem in seeking to cure it. The ultimate ironic illness, you might say.

I went to meet with an RA support group. All the people I'd met up to that point with rheumatoid arthritis were disabled and disfigured for life. Their hands were crippled or their hips were frozen in place. The knee replacement hadn't been perfected then. Their feet were gone. It was terrifying to see this as my future. I would not be able to take care of my family. I would not be able to act, to pursue my passion and my profession.

It was a complete and total nightmare. I'd never realized how dependent I was on my physical ability. It was the basis of my confidence. I'd always been an athlete. I'd always felt I could do almost anything that required physical strength and skill. I took pride in doing my own stunts. I loved throwing myself around physically.

I was accustomed to my body moving about with ease in response to whatever I told it to do. I took for granted that this would always be so. And suddenly all of it was stripped away. My body could respond only with excruciating pain whenever I tried to move it at all. The joints in my hands were so swollen, I couldn't hold a pen. Some days I couldn't hold a glass to get a drink of water. I couldn't pick up my child.

I simply could not, would not, accept this fate. But I was in deep despair over what to do.

One day I was coming out of the shower – I couldn't get in and out of the bathtub but I could stand in the shower – and I had a big plastic bottle of body lotion that I was trying to squeeze so I could moisturize my body. I could not make my hands squeeze that bottle. I started sobbing. Rachel happened to go by my bathroom. She asked, 'What's wrong, Mommy?' I tried to stop crying because I didn't want to upset her or to be helpless in front of her, but I couldn't help sniffling, 'I can't get the lotion out of the bottle. I can't, I can't.' Rachel planted her feet and said, 'Oh, don't be silly. I can.' She took the bottle and squirted the lotion all over me. And I said, 'Well, thank you. That is the sensible thing to do.'

I hated so much for her to see my weakness. A mother is supposed to be strong for her child. It completely changes the balance of the relationship when you are no longer the all-powerful parent. I felt a constant sense of letting her down, of not being able to be a full participant with her. It was hardest when she would be playing outside and she'd say, 'Come on, Mom, let's run.' Or she'd yell for me to catch her as she jumped off the swing and I'd have to say, 'I can't.' But Rachel was great, even when she was still elementary school age. As a child, she had the ability to accept what was happening in a matter-of-fact way even when she didn't understand it. When I couldn't hold a spoon to feed myself, she fed me without being asked. Or, oh, God, there were days when the pain was so terrible, and she sat on my bed and read her Dr. Seuss books to me. She just went about finding solutions and she did not judge me nearly as harshly as I judged myself.

But oh, Lord, that was so, so hard. We were living in the beautiful brownstone that Jay had completely renovated. We had put in an elevator, fortunately. Because the only way I could get up and down the stairs otherwise was by sitting on my bottom and pushing myself with my hands from step to step. Oh, dear God.

Jay was very, very supportive. He was as staunchly there for me as I had been for him when he was at his lowest emotionally after the fire in his building. He must have gotten terribly fed up with it, though.

The greatest shock to me was how I lost belief in my own attractiveness, my own desirability, everything. With my loss of confidence went a loss of sexuality. That is a strain on the marriage, a strain that then is multilayered. RA made sex difficult because physically everything hurt so badly that it was so hard to feel sexy, hard for me to be a good partner, hard to be intimate. There was no position that didn't hurt like hell.

Refusing to accept despair

I felt quite worthless. It didn't really matter what I said. I felt I had no voice. I had lost my power to set the course of my life. I felt unworthy of being heard because I could contribute so little to anyone. I couldn't move, I couldn't do the normal things in life, and I couldn't work. Even with my husband and my daughter, I became tentative, questioning and insecure. I felt I couldn't ask for anything from them because I couldn't give it back. And if they asked something of me, I couldn't necessarily do it, which would make me feel even lower. I felt silent, silenced by my inability to act. And I mean act in the most basic sense of taking any kind of action, even the most mundane.

Jay helped me get by in public situations where I didn't want people to know how ill I was. We were at a fancy restaurant once with the head of a studio. I'd worked with this man in the past and we liked him, but also I needed to keep in professional contact with him. I managed to get down into my chair, but I couldn't get up. So Jay behaved as a perfect gentleman. I'd say, 'I need to use the ladies' room.' He'd come around behind me and, under the cover of pulling the chair out for me, he would slip his hands under my armpits from the back and lift me so that I could stand. Once I was standing, I could move. I just couldn't go from sitting to standing.

At that time, doctors were still treating RA with medicines

that had been used for the past century and didn't work very well at all. Immunosuppressants (steroids) and anti-inflammatory drugs were tried on me first. With the steroids, I blew up like a balloon. They not only warp your appearance; after these drugs are taken for some years, they also eat bone and muscle tissue, and that damage cannot be undone. They can also harm the vital organs: the liver, kidneys, and even the eyes. But since I literally could not move without them, I didn't feel there was a choice but to take them and keep monitoring the cure that was as bad as the disease.

Later, they tried a form of chemotherapy that had seemed to help some people. These drugs made me feel horribly angry and depressed. I'd wake up in the morning in a rage and not know why. I'd have nothing to be angry about. I mean, other than life in general – and my life at the time was enough to make any sane person angry.

It was only then that I got a doctors' reference book and found out that the side effects of all these drugs include depression, anger, and rage. Boy, did that ring true. Yet not a single doctor had discussed any of that with me. And I had been so concerned about RA's physical effects that I had not thought to ask about psychological effects of the disease or the drugs.

It was a period in my life when I was not terribly kind to people. Now I can see that, and I only hope they understand and can forgive me for any hurt that I caused. I had no idea until I did research that at least some of my behavioral changes were related to the drugs I was taking. I do know that simply living through every day was a miracle. RA isn't just physically debilitating; it's also like having a constant low-level flu. You're always feeling a little off, a little like you're about to get sick.

And I was so demanding of myself that I turned that judgment onto other people. I mean, if I could goddamn well get through this day, then they goddamn well could, too. I didn't want anyone to know how difficult it was for me. I didn't want people to praise me for my long suffering or incredible stamina. I didn't want to let them in on my personal health situation, but at the same time I felt very hard used that I had to keep going under these grueling circumstances. And here these wimps were, complaining or slacking off on the job, and they didn't have nearly the difficulties that I was having. How selfish of them. I was projecting my struggle onto other people and finding that they came up short. Which I had no business doing. But it was part of the anger and the depression that was heightened by the drugs.

I tried to tell myself over and over that I was not angry with Jay or Rachel or anyone else. I had to remind myself over and over that it was the drugs talking, not me. It must have been very difficult for Jay to put up with all this.

I agonized as I saw before me the possibility that I would never get better and this might be the rest of my life. And I said, 'I cannot live like this. I know some people can accept that this is the way they are going to be for the rest of their lives, but I can't. It's just too awful.' In my almost total despair I thought, *If I can't carry on as an actress, then I don't know what I can do with my life. I might as well let myself die or kill myself, because I'm not much help to anyone.*

I was asking so much from everyone, from Rachel, from Jay, from my co-stars. I couldn't bear owing so much.

At that moment when I could feel nothing except sheer desolation and despair, I reached a point of decision. I either had to give up entirely or say definitively, 'No, I will not give up. Now what can I do to change this?'

I am much more the second sort of person. I decided I would not accept it. I mean, there's just something in me. I will not accept certain things. No. Sorry. Not in my life. Just no. I got to that place of utter despair and I could not accept it. I would not have the rest of my life be permeated by this feeling of helplessness. And once I believed that I could not live with this desperation, then I had to believe there was another way to go, something I could do to improve it.

The physical part was just physical; I could have dealt with that. The emotional part was much worse. Why get out of bed, why care, why struggle down to the kitchen to make a meal for Rachel, why do anything – that kind of thinking is just not possible to me. There had to be a reason always to get up and *do* something.

And there was Rachel and there was Jay and they were worth living for. As bad as I felt about Jay having to do so much for me, still, I loved him and I knew he loved me. And then there was this child, this amazing person that I wanted to be around for and to be involved with for the rest of my life. In the very worst times, the thought of leaving Rachel was the strongest pull.

I kept searching, searching, searching for solutions, and finding none.

Then one day I went to Rachel's school again and as I was hauling myself up those three little steps and trying not to cry, the mother of one of Rachel's classmates was coming down the steps at the same time. Sale Johnson took one look at me and asked, 'What the hell is going on with you?' I said, 'I have rheumatoid arthritis.' And she said, 'Don't move. Just stay right there – I'll be right back.'

She went in, got a pen and paper, and wrote down the name of a Dr. David Trentham and the hospital he was at in Boston. She told me that her middle daughter had juvenile RA. Sale was married to Woody Johnson of Johnson & Johnson pharmaceuticals. And they were funding Dr. Trentham's research. Because of course, as bad as it is for adults with RA, a child's joints aren't even formed yet. And unless they can get the RA under control, they never will develop. So, understandably, the Johnsons were pouring money into this research and, fortunately, getting some results. Sale said, 'You're going to Dr. Trentham tomorrow. I'm calling him as soon as I get home.'

I was so grateful. I went to Boston as soon as Dr. Trentham could see me. The medicines he was testing hadn't all been approved by the FDA, but there were special allowances for compassionate needs, and once he examined me, he said I'd qualify. The medicine was just part of it. Unlike other doctors, Dr. Trentham said that the last thing I should do is go to bed. If the pain is terrible, that's when I should get into a pool. He said, 'No matter how much it hurts, keep moving. Go backwards if you can't go forward. Crawl back and forth in the water if you have to, get some resistance going, get some movement in your joints and get the blood flow going. Do it as long as you can possibly bear it. And it *is* unbearable, but you also know that you have to do it.' Dear Daddy Russ, thank you for showing me once more, 'Well, you just have to, don't you?' And once more, I did.

I started swimming at the Equitable Building. They had a nice pool in the basement. All I could do at first was rest my hands on a kickboard and slowly kick back and forth, back and forth, across the pool. Then I started to be able to do a little breaststroke, which was pretty exciting. And one day I actually swung my arm around in freestyle. It was such a momentous step forward for me that I stood there in the pool afterward, laughing and crying with happiness. The lifeguard saw me and thought I was drowning. He jumped in and rushed over to drag me to the side of the pool. I blubbered, 'No, no, you don't understand, I just did this. I just swung my arm all the way around.' Poor man had no idea what to do with me.

From that point, Dr. Trentham let me work with light weights to build my muscles so they would protect the joints more. If you can strengthen the smaller muscles around a joint, you can take pressure off the joint itself. And then he said I could try a bicycle and get my knees moving. It was a very gradual and extremely painful process.

This was the beginning of the turnaround for me. Dr. Trentham and the other investigators created a whole new generation of drugs that have completely changed the future for me and other RA sufferers. I was one of the first to be able to try them. It took several more years to get me off the chemotherapy that was so appalling, and the steroids, but gradually we began to determine a course of treatment that worked for me and would eventually put me into remission. (And if anyone with RA or who cares about someone with RA is reading this and wants more information, it's all available on www.RAaccess.com.)

One day will be forever etched on my heart. I was being met by Rachel and Jay at the airport when I got back to New York after one of my trips to Boston to see Dr. Trentham. As soon as I saw them, I started to run toward them. Then I heard Rachel saying, 'Mummy, you ran.' She was so aware and so happy for me. We all embraced. It was such a wonderful moment.

Regaining my voice a baby step at a time

The first real job I took after the crisis was beginning to abate but before I was in remission was a TV movie called *Friends at Last*. I thought I could handle it because it wasn't a very demanding script, about a middle-aged woman whose husband leaves her for a younger woman. She is confused and hurt and reacts badly, violently in some cases, and they battle over the child. She discovers a lump in her breast; it turns out to be malignant, requiring a double mastectomy. The husband comes back to help care for her. It's called *Friends at Last* because although they don't get back together as a married couple, they find the friendship and love that was always there. It was a sweet story. There was no adventure stuff, no stunts. And I had a driver, John Cox, who'd been my driver before in Toronto, where we were filming. I knew he would take good care of me.

One night we were shooting a scene after a long, long day. It was a very emotional scene in which the husband tells his wife he's had enough, he wants out. I was hurting so terribly; I was leaning up against the wall and I knew I couldn't make it back to my trailer. And Colm Feore, the wonderful actor, took one look at me, scooped me up in his arms, and carried me to my trailer. He helped me get out of my costume, which luckily was just a robe and nightdress because it was a late-night scene. He got my clothes on me. John picked me up from the trailer and put me in the car, took me back to the hotel, and literally carried me up to my room.

You have to imagine how the pain was so terrible that I couldn't sleep. Even though it was Canada in the late fall, I couldn't bear to have anything touch my feet. Not even a sheet, because anything touching me hurt so badly. I would get so cold because I couldn't have any covers on.

Faith Prince was playing my girlfriend. Everybody was very kind. They were patient when I had to take my lunch hour to go to the hospital and have cups full of icky yellow fluid drained from my joints. In one scene where I was in a group therapy session with women who had been abandoned by their husbands, we were to sit around on the floor in this gymnasium. I said, 'I'll go down but I won't be able to get up, so you'll have to cut and lift me up.' I was supposed to get up and leave during the scene. Somebody had to haul me up onto my feet so I could sort of stagger out. Fortunately I could make the staggering look like it was emotional.

It seemed as though it would never, ever end. But gradually I did get more mobility from the exercise as the months went on. And the medication was keeping the inflammation down so I didn't have the constant fever and flu symptoms. Slowly, slowly, I was getting better every day, until at long last I felt I could begin to get back to a semblance of normal life.

There would be many setbacks. Recovery from RA does not move in a straight line between two points. It could be as simple as Jay asking if I could pick up Rachel at school that day. I would say, 'I don't know. I don't know if I can get there.' Never being able to assure someone that I could be relied on was terribly difficult for me, because I've always prided myself on being reliable. If I say I will be there or I will take care of it, I do. But sometimes I simply could not. That was hard to accept.

I missed just a couple of shows when my feet would blow up so badly that I couldn't get them into any kind of shoes, let alone walk on them. By 'blow up,' I mean that the skin is stretched so tight because of the fluid in my feet, it starts to crack. When that happens, my toes look like little sausages and my feet don't look very much like feet anymore; they're just these huge things at the end of my legs. I can't see an instep, can barely stand up. Sometimes they literally burst, exposing bone and muscle, if I don't stay off them and take care of them right away.

But through force of will, I missed very few shows. Knowing I could do eight shows a week, that's the biggest test. Filming for a couple of hours a day, so what? But doing eight shows a week, week after week after week, was the test that proved that if I can do this, I can do almost anything. Just my ability to stay with it and fulfill my obligations brought back much of my confidence. And as my confidence grew, I began to regain my voice in the world.

Sometimes just to endure is enough

The RA brought many changes into my life. Though it's not fatal, the chronic pain and deterioration of the joints kill parts of your life. The disease certainly changes your lifestyle enormously. You can't do or be everything when you've got RA, baby.

I need more rest now. And forget vanity – I have to keep exercising just to be able to move on a daily basis. And to keep the muscles strong so they compensate for what the joints cannot do.

People have varying thresholds for pain. Mine has always been quite high – I can stand a great deal of pain. I think women generally have more tolerance for pain than men. It's sort of wired into our bodies because of childbirth, and I think we accept it more. It's not the exception to us that it is to men.

But conscious acceptance of the pain has actually helped me

deal with it. I've learned over the years simply not to let pain take charge of my life. I mean, yes, it hurts. Okay, fine. Just accept it. On the nights when my feet blow up on me, which still happens, or when there is a flare-up in some other part of my body, I ignore it. I put it out of my head. And the fact is that once I step onstage, I don't feel anything. I don't feel pain, I don't feel tired, I don't feel anything. I don't take pain medication because I don't like what it does to my mind, and to my ability to remember my lines. I get massages, eat healthy food, and use a warm paraffin bath on my feet and hands.

You learn a lot through pain. Too bad you don't learn as much from being happy. First of all, having RA changed my notions of beauty. Before, my looks were just a given. It's a good thing beauty was never central to my sense of self. My mother had always told me, 'Don't pat yourself on the back for something you didn't earn.'

My sexuality, both sexual attractiveness and desire, felt threatened at times. I became a little timid. As I said before, I lost my voice, yes. But fortunately my core self-image was strong enough that it didn't feel as though I was losing my*self* so much as losing a part of myself. I learned to replace that part with other strengths that I have gained from the struggle.

Perhaps I was arrogant before RA, to take my health, my sexual attractiveness, and my beauty for granted, or maybe I was just young and naive. The great thing now is that I demonstrate over and over how I can still project sexuality and attractiveness with the toss of my head or the confidence in my eyes. And, of course, with my voice. I love that! Once, being seen as a sex icon weighed like a millstone on me. Now it's the icing on the cake, to be savored down to the last lick.

Second, my ideas about being in control, especially of relationships, are different from those I had before I was diagnosed with RA. I have come to especially treasure the change in my relationship with Rachel, from my being the all-powerful parent to being the more vulnerable human I actually am. I think that we are closer as a result.

The most significant thing that having RA taught me was to prioritize. I'd always been superwoman. I thought I could do anything. I still think that in a lot of ways. But once I knew the RA would be part of me forever, I sensed that I'd lost control of my life and I had to sort out the competing priorities if I wanted to regain control.

I had to say definitively: 'This I must do myself. I must get on the phone, I must write this, I must show up there, I must do what only I can do.' The next category is things I can delegate to my assistant or the agency or to friends, things they could do in my name. And then the third category is 'I don't give a shit. This doesn't need to be done at all. Let it go.' It turned out there is a lot more in that third category than I ever realized.

Prioritizing helped me to know what is important to me. My family is important. My relationship with the people I work with is important. What the gossip columnists say is not important.

What's important is to endure. And sometimes, simply to endure is the greatest victory of all.

Chapter Eleven

Wait till the choice is inevitable

These words I read in a novel by John Berger settled over me like a comfortable shirt: 'Everywhere there is pain. And more insistent and sharper than pain, everywhere there is a waiting with expectancy.'[17] It is almost hopeful, this thought that yes, something better is possible.

Waiting with expectancy must have sustained me during that time when RA dealt an almost fatal blow to my health and sense of self-worth. When I had to face the shocking and terrifying loss of my physical capacity and I felt powerless and voiceless. When I simply could not do many of the things I was so used to doing.

But then I would tell myself to buck up: *Well, okay, I can't make my body do whatever I want it to do anymore. But there are still things it can do. What are they and what else can I train it to do so that it can compensate for what I have lost?* From learning to prioritize, I had gained a healing clarity about who I am and what is really important in my life: I could wait with expectancy in a way that would not have been possible before I struggled with RA. This isn't a passive waiting but a waiting that allows me to focus my intellect and energy.

Once I decided against giving in to despair, there came a more profound ability to wait until I know intuitively what a choice will mean or what meaning I will give to it, and to trust that 'more insistent than the pain' will be the inevitability of the choices I make. Yes, the impatient Kathleen who at age five tried to make an airplane fly faster has learned it is possible to let things come to her.

Life is all about risk and choice to me. I don't need to know exactly what I'm going to be doing next. So in that way, I was in familiar territory. I was just exploring yet another new role.

I fucking well needed that attitude to pick up the pieces of my life that had been shattered in no small part through my own obstinate reluctance to tell the truth about my RA.

No longer a leading lady?

I stubbornly refused to parade my illness all over the tabloids. During the time I was so ill and even after I was beginning to get the RA under control, the wags and the press were merciless. Because I was working less and on smaller projects, they'd say that obviously nobody wanted me anymore. They'd say I was no longer a leading lady. They snipped that I had become fat and unrecognizable because I was an angry, washed-up diva, an out-of-control has-been, when in truth the changes in my physical appearance were caused by drugs and chemotherapy and were not within my control.

Still, I did not reveal what was happening to me. But oh, the paparazzi loved to reveal me in the most unflattering photos they could possibly take. You take fifty milligrams of steroids a day and everything on your body puffs up to look a lot like the consequences of prolonged heavy drinking. They speculated all kinds of things, and I couldn't challenge them because I wasn't willing to talk about it honestly. Inevitably, when you don't give people accurate information, they make up their own stories to explain what they see.

You name it; they said it. Turner can't get the big jobs anymore, except perhaps in the sequel to *Body Heat* called 'Body Fat,' and all that shit.[18]

Perhaps the press and the critics would have treated me more sympathetically if I had disclosed my illness and revealed my disabilities openly, but I simply could not – not even when their barbs hurt as much as my swollen joints.

Was it false pride, or stubbornness, or was it the family trait of not asking for help, that persistent inability to be vulnerable? Yes, all of that. I was trying so hard to work at all, and I was terrified that I'd never work again if people knew the true nature of my situation. These were tough, tough, tough times. All I could think about was continuing to make incremental improvements in my health, to keep putting one foot in front of the other, fulfill my family obligations, and do the work when I got it.

For years I worked when the RA was in full-blown active mode even while I refused to speak candidly about it. I still had financial pressures. Jay was rebuilding his business, so I needed to earn some money. And like Virginia Woolf, I appreciate the importance of having my own income because it frees me to be me. But most of all, I wanted to keep working because acting is my passion and continuing to act was a central part of what made my life worth living.

I was constantly trying to weigh how much I could do with the illness, feeling I would be irresponsible to take a job that I couldn't physically do.

When I did *Indiscretions* on Broadway in 1995, my RA was still acute. Oh, God, did that hurt. The first and third acts take place in my bedroom. It's set in the 1940s, and my character, Yvonne, was a diabetic. In those days they had insulin, but they had no way to measure with precision how much to use. So the chance of taking too much insulin or not having enough was a constant dice roll. The play starts with Yvonne collapsed almost in a diabetic coma, and her sister, who is played by Eileen Atkins, rushes in and forces Yvonne to drink a glass of orange juice so she can get up and into bed.

Since two of the acts took place in Yvonne's bedroom, I thought, *Well, I'll be lying in bed most of the time, so that's good*. But this would just not be Turner, you know. I still couldn't resist the temptation to try to be a semblance of my former athletic self.

Yvonne had an inappropriate and incestuous attachment to her son. But he falls in love with a young woman and is about to leave his mother. This is completely impossible for Yvonne to bear, absolutely the end of her world. So she climbs up on the bed, stands at the very edge, and falls backwards as though she is dying. I insisted on playing this to the hilt. I'd miss the headboard by about two inches when I fell. I never did hit it. But I scared the hell out of everybody else night after night. That was my paltry substitute for the gymnastics I used to be able to do, and I rather enjoyed it.

The big problem came in the second act, which took place in the fiancée's apartment. It was the first time Yvonne had been out of her house in years. I was dressed to the nines in a stunning forties tight suit with those big shoulders, a hat, and very high heels in which I had to climb up a three-story metal staircase. I had said, 'Oh, I can do this,' because of course I would not admit that I shouldn't even think about doing it.

During every performance, I would climb up to the top of the stairs. By the time I got up the three flights, tears would be rolling down my face. I'd sit in the catwalk, waiting for my cue to come back down. I kept tissues, lipstick, powder, and a mirror at the top of the staircase. I'd let myself cry until I heard a certain line just before my cue. Then I'd clean up my face, put on powder and lipstick, and walk in excruciating pain back down.

Once after I did the matinee, my feet swelled up hugely, just completely blew up, and I had them up in ice packs. Not that that really helps, but it makes me feel like I'm doing something for them. I said, 'I can't walk. I can't go on tonight.' The producer came backstage and cajoled me, 'Oh, come on, you went on this afternoon. You did the matinee – why can't you do the evening?' I took the ice packs off my feet and showed him, 'Take a look. Just look.' He took one look at my feet and said, 'Never mind, we'll get a car to take you home.' I said, 'Thank you, yes.'

At that time, my right wrist was intensely painful. I couldn't bear to have it touched. There's a climactic scene in the end where Yvonne overdoses on purpose in a bid to make her son leave the woman he loves and stay with her, but she miscalculates and takes a suicidal dose. So there's a ten-minute deathbed scene with everybody trying to bring her back to life. They're sitting her up and trying to make her swallow – so they're handling me physically. Oh, Jesus God, I'm supposed to be dead and it's all I can do not to scream. It was fucking terrible.

And the drugs I was taking at the time weren't helping. Aside from the rages I could fly into – I was doing *Indiscretions* when Rachel had the bicycle accident and I flew off the handle at my mother-in-law – I was having trouble remembering lines. I think Eileen Atkins, and maybe some of the others, felt I was just a lazy American actress who didn't do the work, didn't study enough to learn her lines properly. That hurt my feelings so much, because I had that script every night in my hands before I went onstage and every night afterward, studying my lines as hard as I could. But I kept paraphrasing the lines; my colleagues let their disapproval about that be known.

Apparently I was not too congenial myself, because Eileen called me an 'amazing nightmare.' And I suppose I was.[19]

Better drunk than sick

I went on letting others believe anything they wanted to about my behavior and physical changes. Many people bought the assumption that I'd turned into a heavy drinker. I couldn't publicly refute them because I believed it was worse to have people know that I had this terrible illness. They'd hire me if they thought I was a drunk because they could understand drinking, but they wouldn't hire me if I had a mysterious, scary illness they didn't understand.

Indiscretions, 1995

Michael is the center of his mother Yvonne's world and has just fallen in love with Madeleine. Yvonne's husband, George, has suffered from Yvonne's focus on their son and has taken a mistress. It is soon revealed that George's mistress and Michael's love are one and the same.

Directed by Sean Mathias
Produced by Roger Berlind and Scott Rudin

Eileen Atkins as Leonie
Roger Rees as George
Jude Law as Michael
Cynthia Nixon as Madeleine
Kathleen Turner as Yvonne

Yvonne: *If that's the sunlight, I'd rather stay in the dark.*

We – Jay, my agent, myself – felt it imperative to keep my rheumatoid arthritis quiet. Until the last six or seven years, nobody had any grasp of RA or autoimmune diseases in general. After all, Michael J. Fox hid his Parkinson's disease for many years so that he could keep working. There has been a huge change in public awareness over the last two decades, thank goodness. But in Hollywood back when I was taking the heaviest medication, if you said, 'Look, I'm a drunk and there are some days I won't be able to function,' they'd say, 'Yeah, we can deal with that.' They tolerated it just as we all had tolerated

Ken Russell's drinking when on the set of *Crimes of Passion*.

But if you said, 'I have this disease called rheumatoid arthritis and I don't always know when I will have a good enough day to do a full day's work,' you could just forget it. Forget it! It was like being a witch or something. You'd never get a job. It was all because of fear of something they didn't understand.

Right or wrong, I concluded it was better for people to think that I was a drinker than to think that I was ill.

I soon proved them at least half right. As the pain got worse, I found that vodka killed it quite wonderfully. I mean, alcohol just fucking kills pain. It's been used as an anesthetic through the ages. Medicines don't necessarily work, but alcohol can be counted on to do the job. I didn't want to take pain pills anymore because I didn't like how they mucked up my mind, so I used alcohol instead. My rationale was 'My body's in enough trouble; I need to keep my brain clear,' but I stupidly didn't consider that alcohol does the same thing to your brain.

My drinking fed a self-destructive spiral. The drugs I was taking for RA were already depressive and alcohol is a depressant. When I took them in combination, their depressive effects multiplied each other. I started once again to question whether life was really worth living.

Alcohol is also a disinhibitor, as are steroids. An intense and immense anger would come out of me when I was disinhibited. And with the steroids exacerbated by the alcohol, what a terrible, terrible person I must have been to live with.

There was a progression. I drank consciously at first to kill the pain. But then I began to accept it just as drinking. I never drank to excess before a show; if anything, I would drink on an off night or when I was between jobs. Later, after I got the new medicines and the pain began to subside, I kept drinking too much. I became dependent on vodka. It didn't damage my work, but it did damage me personally.

I lost the ability to know when I'd had enough, more than enough, alcohol to dull the pain. Until then I would say, 'Whoa, all right – I'm starting to lose control here, that's enough.' Somewhere this line dissolved. I'd think I was absolutely fine, so I'd say, 'All right, I can have another drink.' I would be able to continue talking and functioning and people would say I was delightful at a dinner party. But then I'd realize the next day that I didn't remember anything about what had transpired.

Adding to the problem, I was starting perimenopause and my body chemistry was changing. I turned from a charming drinker into a really nasty drunk. I could keep the facade of the nice person, the good girl, the charming celebrity, most of the time when I was working. But I would drop that facade when I got home. I just couldn't keep it up indefinitely, and home is, after all, where we always think there will be unqualified acceptance. That's usually a positive thing, but its ugly underbelly was that it was easier for me to shed the veneer of niceness at home, to stop making the effort to smile in the face of the intense pain and decreasing physical ability. So inevitably, that's where I received the most criticism, because those who knew me best were the most aware of my excesses. And they bore the brunt of it.

I now know I injured Jay and our relationship very, very much. The toxic combination of drinking and the RA drugs was certainly a precursor to other problems we were beginning to have.

You would have thought that the Happy Land fire tragedy and

rheumatoid arthritis would have been enough for any human being to deal with, but, no, Kathleen Turner the verb always pushes the limits. I now had the drinking demon to slay. I wasn't quite ready to deal with that one, though. It would have to lurk in the background awhile longer.

The impatient one learns to wait

In the midst of the worst of it all, what increasingly helped me live through the sharpness of the pain was learning to wait until my choices seemed inevitable. I had somehow developed an even sharper expectancy that life *must* get better and opportunities to work *would* come along so that I'd have choices I'd want to take.

And things were getting gradually better. I was off some of the worst medications. The side effects of the newer drugs weren't yet known, but to me it was worth the risk to try them. I was experiencing a slow progression toward remission even though the damage already done to my joints could not be repaired. Family life was entering a more stable phase. Rachel was older, more self-sufficient. Jay was all right. And I was getting much stronger physically. My do-it-yourself physical therapy could even be replaced by more rigorous workouts. I became a regular at the Reebok gym in my neighborhood and began to work out with a trainer as often as I could.

Before that, when I lived in such fear that I would have a flare-up at any moment, I felt too terribly vulnerable. It was part of my armor that I didn't show fear, didn't tell people. To have chinks in my armor, to let someone else see those chinks, let alone share them with the public, is just nuts to me. Who wants to air their fears in public? The very idea of talking publicly about my disease, my vulnerability, was way too frightening. Only when I knew it was under control and felt secure enough about my ability to function in life and work could I start to talk about my RA publicly.

By this time, it was also known that the sooner RA is diagnosed, the better the symptoms can be controlled. People who are diagnosed today need never to suffer what I went through. They don't have to lose joints or go through all those surgeries if they simply have the information to get it diagnosed and treated early. Knowing that, it became terribly important to me to spread the word as a public service. It got so I felt that I had to tell other people. I had to do this.

Once I started talking about my RA, I wasn't nearly as afraid of it. At first people still responded as though I had some exotic, weird thing. I felt some of them pull away, but others responded with compassion. And because I have always come across as strong and what some interpret as arrogant, there was something of a 'So there, Superwoman!' attitude. No matter. Talking about my RA liberated me from the debilitating grips of silence.

I now know what I was most afraid of was the RA itself. I have not fully conquered the fear to this day. It stays with me. When I wake up achy or feel some swelling, I get an atavistic response, a primal terror. I immediately think, *Oh God, it's coming back, Oh God, please don't let it be coming back.*

I honestly don't think I could fight that fight again knowing how bad it would be.

In 1998, I got an offer to go shoot a very wry, very sardonic version of *Cinderella* in England with a director, Beebar Kidron, a woman whom I admired. I'd always wanted to support women directors. It wasn't a long shoot, just a couple of months. Jay and Rachel both felt it was okay for me to go. And I had set up a better security system with my mother-in-law in case Rachel needed anything. This presented me with a little practice run back to my normal work life. I went off to shoot in England.

While I was in England, the producer Terry Johnson came to see me on the set to talk about doing the stage version of *The Graduate*. At first the whole thing seemed preposterous. I was forty-six. When Anne Bancroft played Mrs. Robinson she was thirty-six, and I didn't imagine the culture had changed so much that sexuality in older women would be appreciated even – at this point – two decades later. Far from dissuading me, the challenge immediately attracted me. And I liked Terry. But still, I said I wasn't sure about doing *The Graduate* as it had been constructed for the stage.

The original ending Terry showed me didn't work, in my opinion, because of its treatment of Benjamin, the young man Mrs. Robinson seduces. And whatever conclusion Terry wanted to leave the audience with at the end, the script didn't seem to me to hit the mark. So he promised to take another look at the ending.

I have made my biggest mistakes when I jumped at choices before I had to. But I was honing the ability to refrain from making a choice before I could feel viscerally as well as know intellectually that it was right for me. There is almost always a point at which that happens if I will be still and wait for it. If I don't jump, if I don't choose something too soon, before the choice absolutely has to be made, it usually becomes very clear what the choice should be.

Soon after I finished *Cinderella*, Terry got the script back to me in New York. He had taken my ideas and made them work well. The play was funnier and gentler, more powerful, and more loving all around.

One thing Terry did, which the movie hadn't done because, after all, it was an accurate reflection of the 1960s, was to create a more prominent character for Mrs. Robinson's daughter, Elaine. Everybody who saw the film remembers that Katherine Ross was beautiful as Elaine, but they don't remember her opening her mouth – because she didn't. In the play, Elaine had a substantial role, which helped to flesh out the complexity of the mother–daughter relationship. It made her a full person. I liked that change a lot. There's a particularly great scene between her and Mrs. Robinson in the play.

Now it felt right, and I said, 'Yeah, okay, I'll do it.'

Now I was talking about spending six months in England, because we were to rehearse there and go right on to performing in the West End. That was tough to imagine. By then my new medication was allowing me to move pretty well. I had lost the puffiness caused by the medications that had given the gossip columnists so much fodder, and I felt physically fit to do the Mrs. Robinson role for the length of time that would be required. I was able to work out harder and become a little shapelier. That would be rather important for Mrs Robinson, who bares it all on the stage, where one's imperfections are ever so visible. I was even able to wear high heels – very painfully, but I could do it.

Rachel and Jay, God bless them, flew back and forth between New York and London. Rachel liked it because she was getting out of school, and jet lag didn't seem to bother her as much as it would an adult. I was happy to have them there with me as often as possible.

The Graduate was highly successful in London. But I didn't think that would translate to the United States. Because of our attitude toward sex, because of our attitude toward women, I just couldn't see it having the positive reception we got in London. In Europe, older women are still considered powerful sexual entities. I mean, nobody would say that Catherine Deneuve is past it. No one would dare speak ill of Sophia Loren or even Jeanne Moreau. They don't say these women have no attractiveness, no power left. But here, they would and they do. Frankly, I just didn't think I needed to take that shit. So I declined even to discuss the possibility.

I felt sure my career was on the upswing after years of smaller roles and lesser fame. I couldn't declare victory yet, but I came back from my six months in England feeling so happy that I had been able to take on a major stage role again and knowing that I could wait till my next role presented itself to me as the one I should inevitably choose.

Childbearing choices become inevitable

While my career was on hold, I could always imagine making a film or stage comeback. But I hadn't taken into account that my biological clock kept ticking too. For that there is no going back, even if like Peggy Sue I'd had all the cinematographic magic Francis Ford Coppola could bring to bear.

Jay and I had always hoped to have more children. But once RA hit, the drugs I had to take were so destructive to a fetus that it was impossible to consider having a child even if my body could have handled a pregnancy, which was doubtful. It would probably have been a choice between carrying a child and walking again. And the thought of being a mother who couldn't walk raised an entirely new set of issues to consider.

We waited until new, less invasive medications came along. But by then, I was in my midforties. I had reached that jolting moment when after decades of controlling fertility and assuming it would be there when I wanted it, I didn't get pregnant. We went to see infertility specialists to inquire about in vitro fertilization. They said that my eggs were probably not able to make a sustainable pregnancy. In addition, there are theories that RA so often hits women in their late thirties because of a link to perimenopausal hormonal changes. They thought I might be too far into the menopausal process.

We considered the option of using a younger woman's eggs and Jay's sperm. And I thought, *Well, a baby conceived this way would be Rachel's sibling, so that would be a positive*. I would love any baby that was put into my arms regardless of whose egg it was. But I felt so left out of it, particularly because we also probably would have had to use a surrogate since I'd still have all the hormonal changes that worked against my being able to carry a pregnancy in my body. We talked at length about the limited options left to us. This time the obstacles seemed too insurmountable to overcome.

When we came to the end of that line, the choice not to try for a pregnancy was, for me, inevitable. I felt sure it was the right thing to do. But certainty didn't make it any less devastating.

I felt as if I weren't a woman anymore. I think it's a lot like the feeling many women get when they realize they're in full menopause. Only I wasn't through menopause yet. And yet I felt as if all my childbearing choices had been suddenly, precipitously stripped away. Just at the moment when I was beginning to feel as though I was overcoming my illness and could return to a more normal life after all those years of pain and struggle, once again I had to face the harsh reality that my body couldn't do everything it was designed to do. I felt crippled once again, in a new and sharply painful way. I was so sad.

But after the tears, when it was clear that I couldn't conceive and carry a pregnancy, I said, 'In that case, why don't we adopt a child who needs a home?' In some ways, I wanted to adopt to help a child, especially a child who might not have had other opportunities to be adopted. Because I spoke Spanish and loved South America, I suggested that we consider adopting a child from there, because I would be able to help him or her retain the culture. So we looked into adoption, talking with several agencies. I think in the end it was more my ambivalence than Jay's that kept us from taking the step. Once I got over the emotional hurdle of dealing with my biological inability to become pregnant and give birth, I began to realize that in some ways my desire for another child was not rational and perhaps even a little selfish. I'd just gotten the RA into remission, was getting my work back on track. Rachel was well along in elementary school. And I was frankly afraid of all the responsibility and the rededication it would have taken to bring up another child at my age, with the constant fear of RA encroaching further on my physical abilities.

My experience with infertility reinforced for me how very personal all decisions about pregnancy and childbearing are, how everyone's circumstance is unique. We needed to think these tough questions through without pressure from anyone. We had to go through the whole complex process to get to what became a painful but inevitable choice.

I want other women to have their choices too, to be able to realize their options about having or not having children. Maybe mine were over insofar as childbearing was concerned, but other women should have choices. In the moral sense, making a choice is a precious ability. So to waste it or to misuse it, to not be educated about it or be unable to get the necessary health care to exercise your choice, just seems like a crime.

I know that Jay wanted more children. Maybe he will have more. He's a wonderful father. But I am done.

Choice and inevitability: a paradox but not an oxymoron

Over the years the definition of *choice* has changed for me. If I can hold off from leaping at a choice, if I wait for a while to accept or reject what has been presented, what I need to do becomes inevitable. The right purchase, the right job, the right action, the right word, becomes clear. It was impossible when I was younger to conceive of waiting for a choice to become clear. But now, when you say the word *choice*, to me it means what is clearly the best option, and I can wholeheartedly embrace the responsibility for taking it.

Maybe it sounds paradoxical to talk about any choice as being inevitable. I mean, isn't the essence of choosing having the free will to eliminate inevitability? And if something is inevitable, how can you be in control of weighing the possibilities and making a conscious choice?

In actual practice, having the patience to wait, not to jump too soon, not to be pressured by any external force, allows me to make the best choices. I can listen to my heart and my gut as well as my head. So perhaps it is a paradox, but waiting until the choice is inevitable is definitely not an oxymoron!

I laugh now looking back to long before *Body Heat*, when I clearly *didn't* wait until I could judge whether a role was right for me. I just wanted to be onstage. Tommy Hulce and I were doing *The Seagull* at the Manitoba Theater Center in Winnipeg in 1980. I didn't know myself well enough yet to realize that the role wasn't authentically me.

So here I was, trying to do Nina, who is an ingenue – duh, that should have tipped me off right there. Every day I was struggling. Now, I don't find Chekhov easy to understand in the first place. To make matters worse, we had a first-time director who was not very confident, and he knew it. In fact, on opening night, he came into the dressing room, fell to his knees, and begged my forgiveness. I thought, *Not today, honey – I'm in too much trouble*. The fourth act did not work at all. Finally, Tommy and I went in with the lighting guy and reblocked almost the entire fourth act ourselves. The director didn't even notice.

Part of the deal with this theater was that we had to give special performances for schoolchildren. On those days there'd be an additional ten a.m. curtain. Coming in at eight o'clock in the morning to put on makeup, I thought, *What am I fucking doing?*

One morning we were in that fourth act that we'd never been able to get to work. Nina falls onto the desk crying, 'I am a seagull, I am a seagull.' And this kid's voice says, 'Wait a minute – she thinks she's a bird?' I lost it. I just lost it. Tommy turned upstage. His shoulders were heaving in silent laughter. I was on the desk. I looked like I was sobbing but I was actually laughing my goddamn head off. I thought, *Of course, that's it. It's a comedy. Chekhov said* The Seagull *is a comedy.* Oh, God, it was terrible. Absolutely terrible. We were lousy. I'd jumped too fast to take the job and it wasn't right for me. The audience always knows – even if they are elementary school kids.

Many people say to me that choosing is the hardest thing. Well, it seems to me that *waiting* is the hardest thing. There's almost always a point at which the choice is inevitable if you don't jump, if you don't choose too soon. If you wait until the choice has to be made, it becomes much clearer what that choice should be.

Now, if I'm in doubt, say, about taking a film and I don't have to decide yes or no yet but the time is coming up when I'll have to either accept it or reject it, almost always I'll get another piece of material that clarifies whether or not I need to do the first. If I wait, I'll get a script that clearly says to me, 'This you must do; this you mustn't.' So when I can wait, which is so hard for me, things do have a way of clarifying themselves.

Knowing when the choice is inevitable

If only I could be as sure about my choices in my personal life as I am in my professional life. It's been even harder to learn to wait until those choices seem right and inevitable. That's almost always because personal choices are about beliefs and values, and are fraught with emotion.

When Jay's business crashed there was never any question in my mind that we would get through it together. He later said to me that I could have, should have, left him because he felt like a failure in his eyes. But that was Jay feeling so terribly, terribly responsible for the whole thing. It never occurred to me to leave him. I don't think it ever occurred to him to leave me when I got so sick. These are inevitabilities in a sense. I didn't feel there was any choice to be made. And I think he would agree that he felt that way too, when it was his turn to take care of me. That was our personal value system. Not that it would have been an inevitable choice for everybody. Look at Newt Gingrich, who left his wife to die of cancer. But look at Newt Gingrich, period.

I have made other important personal life choices such as staying in New York rather than moving out to California. I imagine if I'd lived in California and made an effort to be part of the lifestyle there, I might have had a more constant film career, with the financial rewards that brings. But there was no way that Jay would have moved to Los Angeles. And once I had Rachel, there was no way I was going to bring up a girl in Los Angeles. It is anti-women out there, altogether. Women are, without a doubt, second-class citizens. There's almost a palpable contempt. And there is such pressure to conform to extreme ideas of beauty or wealth. Plus, I wanted Rachel to have good schools, and I have no doubt the schools are better in New York. I wanted her to have the exposure to the city and the culture.

Also, I was always planning to continue performing in the theater as well as film. So for me it became an inevitable choice to live in New York. I thought that if the film work was really good, they could fly me out or they could come see me to talk about it. That's exactly what happened on occasion, so I was beginning to understand the concept even before RA.

Like in 1987, when Danny DeVito flew into town with the script for *The War of the Roses*. I told him I had already agreed to do *Cat on a Hot Tin Roof* and that I wanted very much to get back on Broadway and to play the exceptional role of Maggie. Danny was insistent. He came to my house and said he was going to read me for it. I humored him: 'What? All right, fine, I'll read for you.' We read the script, and it was so clear this script was going to bring out the best of each of us. I started thinking of the triumvirate that we are – Danny and Michael Douglas and me. Oh, I could really see myself in this one right away. I couldn't wait for that last gesture when Michael would reach out, dying, to put his hand on my shoulder and I'd make this moaning exhale sound and push him away. I just loved it. I couldn't wait, couldn't wait, couldn't wait for that moment! And because we all had script approval and Danny was directing, I knew no one could screw it up.

Then I was in a quandary. Sometimes it isn't doubt but too much of a good thing that presents the conflict for which you have to make a choice.

Once I give my word, I do not ever go back on it. Not professionally and not personally. I'd already met with Howard Davies, who was going to direct *Cat on a Hot Tin Roof*, and said I'd do it. But it hadn't been fully cast yet, and Charles Durning, the actor who we most wanted to play Big Daddy, wasn't available at the time.

I told the producers I wanted to do *The War of the Roses* first. We were able to show that they had not laid out any money for the stage production except for the director's transatlantic flight. So I said that if I refunded that amount, they wouldn't be out any money. And then we could postpone starting *Cat on a Hot Tin Roof* until after I finished *The War of the Roses*.

The War of the Roses, 1989

Barbara and Oliver Rose are happily married until
Barbara starts to wonder what it would be like without
Oliver around. They decide to end the marriage, but they
both want to keep the house and they're willing to do
nearly anything to get the other person to leave.

Directed by Danny DeVito
Produced by Doug Claybourne, Arnon Milchan,
Polly Platt, James L. Brooks, Michael Leeson, and
J. Marina Muhlfriedel

Michael Douglas as Oliver Rose
Danny DeVito as Gavin D'Amato
Kathleen Turner as Barbara Rose

Barbara Rose: *Was it as good for you as it was for me?*

Making that choice was tough, and it was high-roller risky for
me. I could have lost them both. But as it happened, things
worked out very, very well. Charles became available about the
time I finished *The War of the Roses*, and he turned out to be the
fucking pillar of the play. Everything just sort of went into its
proper place. Both the film and the play were great successes.
Well, that's an understatement. They were also both great
productions.

We shot *The War of the Roses* in L.A. Danny and Michael both
had homes and families there. Jay could fly out fairly often and

Rachel was staying with me because she had not yet started school. So Danny, Michael, and I didn't hang out together off set as we had in our previous films, but we still had a lot of fun.

There are some incredible scenes, like the amazing one where Michael and I are swinging on the chandelier. Oh, God, was that painful, and I didn't even have RA yet. We were filming the scene for a couple of weeks at least. It's a long scene, and they had to shoot up, shoot down, shoot sideways, all angles. Every morning they would lower the chandelier down to the ground so we could get into it. We could always tell if we were in the right position because where every branch of the chandelier was, we had bruises on our bodies from lying around on it for so long. The continuity woman appreciated this. We would just line up our bruises and then we'd know we were positioned exactly where we had left off the day before. Sometimes you've really gotta figure we actors are out of our minds. But by God, we matched.

Danny later told me his wife, Rhea, had instructed him that if I said no when he came to New York to offer me the part, just not to come home. Which struck me as very funny. But maybe Danny has the same idea as I have about inevitable choices.

If I have the patience to wait and watch for them, the doors keep opening. If I put it out there and say, 'This is what I want to happen,' I don't necessarily know when or under what circumstances, but it usually turns out that I'll get to do what I had wanted to do or some better version of it than I ever imagined.

Allowing a choice to happen because it is intrinsically the best choice for me requires not being pushed by influences outside myself. There is one thing I have never delegated to anyone else.

No one has ever chosen the work that I do. No agent, no manager, no producer, no family member, has ever been able to say to me, 'Don't do this' or 'Do this.' Because that is simply not possible – it's unthinkable to me. I'll take their opinions if they want to give them, but that's it.

The choices I make are who I am. Even if they're wrong choices, to delegate or to cede the right to make them – to anyone – would be to give up myself. So the right and inevitable choice is worth the wait.

Chapter Twelve

Don't repeat your successes

True, some choices came easier in my pre-RA days. When I managed to get the best of both the theatrical and the movie world by rolling the dice and watching them land on a way of doing both *The War of the Roses* and *Cat on a Hot Tin Roof*, I didn't have to think twice about whether I could swing from the chandelier or sustain the energy for eight high-emotion performances a week. I just had to maneuver the shooting and opening schedules so I could stake my claim to both of them.

But even after I had RA and now while I am living with it in remission, I have always been willing to take chances, to risk. I don't know beforehand whether something I do is going to work out; I don't know whether I am going to get hurt or not. None of us can ever know before we plunge in and do something precisely what the consequences will be. I'm not afraid of emotional commitment, either. I have been committed for many years to people in my life. And sometimes, yes, I have been very hurt by them or I have caused hurt. But that hasn't made me afraid. I'm willing to have an abundance of emotion again and again, and I'm hoping that will always be true.

In the same way, I don't know whether a film or play I do is going to be loved or not until it's out there naked before the world. I like not knowing everything in advance, not planning for everything. A full and meaningful life must involve some risks or there can be no growth. Risk to me means going to the point at which you may not be able to do what you have set out to do, or at which you might seriously fall short of what your vision is. Risk is the willingness to fail.

That's why the point of making choices in my work is not to go for what is easy or most lucrative but to go for the challenge. I especially relish roles that push me to try something I've never done before. I'm willing to try to do almost anything in a role so long as it's new and my character is necessary. I take risks not just for the thrill – though I do enjoy the thrill – but for the learning. I do work that I think is interesting and important. I don't like to be bored and I definitely don't like to be typecast.

I do not repeat my successes.

Serial risk taker

If I had taken those pseudo-*Body Heat* roles or the awful five-million-dollar *King Solomon's Mines* that was offered to me as a continuation of the *Romancing the Stone* and *The Jewel of the Nile* genre, I would have been pegged for all time. I think the payoff from not repeating successes is longevity and timelessness. I'm always surprising people by doing something new. No one can ever say I've worn out my character's appeal, or become too old for her, because she keeps changing along with me.

That's why after playing the sultry, scheming Matty in *Body Heat* I played the comic Dolores in *The Man with Two Brains*. And after *The Man with Two Brains*, I played the mousy and shy Joan Wilder in *Romancing the Stone* just before I played the sexually boundary-less hooker China Blue in *Crimes of Passion*. Next the coldly purposeful Mafia hit woman Irene Walker in *Prizzi's Honor* and from there to sweet *Peggy Sue*, and so on down my checkered career path till I arrived at the larger-than-life Martha in *Who's Afraid of Virginia Woolf?* Martha, who at the time I got her was the pinnacle but now that I've played her is the beginning of the next phase of my life.

I love the fact that because of my range of roles, while my generation thinks of me as Matty or Joan or V.I., the twenty- and thirty-something generation thinks of me as Beverly Sutphin or Chandler's father. Gloria's young grandson recognized me as Stacy Lavelle on *The Simpsons*.

What's consistent is that I choose my characters precisely because they *are* strong and I find it intriguing that so often 'strong' also turns out to be written into the script as 'evil' when the adjective applies to a woman. Our culture is still afraid of strong women and tends to demonize them. Some of my characters have been nice, but most of them have been morally challenged in some way. For a role to interest me, my character must be strong. She must believe she can effect change in her life. She might fail in what she sets out to do, but she must try. It seems to me looking back that most of the women I am attracted to are basically intensely selfish, which is also seen as an evil attribute for a woman. Now, in the first place, selfishness defines the lead in drama – the lead must be someone whom the story and other characters revolve around. In the second place, let's face it: someone who is focused – even if only on herself – is a powerful draw.

The risk is that I have to figure out how to make the audience love or at least admire the character in spite of her failings. Sometimes stories are straightforward. In *Serial Mom*, as bizarre as that was, as soon as Beverly kills the fly in the first shot, you think, *Uh-oh, we've got trouble here.* My job is to stay true to the ultimate story but to misdirect the audience a little so that when the reveal comes they are with me, they believe my character is capable of what she does at the end. My leap of faith is that I will take the audience with me on this journey. I will convince them. And I am happy to say I can and I do.

I don't always know how I do what I do, so I think, *What if I were to fail? What if the magic didn't happen?* God, it's so scary. But I am a lucky woman whose talent and passion are suited to my job. And in the course of taking risks and succeeding, I have become ever stronger in my willingness to risk the next time. Because usually, not only does nothing bad happen when I summon my courage and take a risk, but most of the time, something very good happens. Isn't that a wonderful surprise to learn as we get older and better?

My friend Sandi Kaufman has said that when I took *Serial Mom*, a smaller film after I'd done such megahits, she thought, *Are you nuts? You don't need to do that. Why are you doing something that's really twisted?* But it turned out to be a funny, very cool film that has become iconic in a diametrically different way from *Body Heat*.

Beverly Sutphin was so morally challenged that even my co-star, Sam Waterston, wasn't sure about doing this movie. He's a real New Englander, an upright, God-fearing man with a great sense of humor and an amazing talent and charm. I don't think he quite got the director, John Waters's, sense of humor, which is admittedly rather sick. The things that John finds funny you don't want to know about most of the time.

Sam felt that Beverly, the serial (killer) mom, was becoming a celebrity heroine: the community where we filmed was supporting her; they were selling 'serial mom' T-shirts and one of the kids in town even wrote a book about how his mom was a serial mom. Sam said to me one day, 'Aren't you worried that we're glamorizing serial killers?' I said, 'No, Sam, I don't think so. First of all, it's a movie. Second, it's satirizing celebrity-ness, not glorifying serial killers. It's saying that in our culture, it doesn't matter what you've done; once you reach a certain amount of exposure, you become an important person. Look at Charles Manson, for God's sake. He's a cult hero. Ugh. *Serial Mom* is making fun of that to make the point about how warped our values are.'

My daughter, Rachel, hates the part of this film that I think is the funniest. Beverly and her husband have one lovemaking scene in bed. Now, I thought it would be hilarious if it was done with a trampoline effect so that we would bounce impossibly high. Sam thought that was funny, too. So we had a big sheet over us, and I'm on top, throwing myself up and he's pushing me higher and higher till I was bouncing three and a half feet in the air. Well, Rachel thinks it is absolutely disgusting. I think it's a hoot. And so did the crowds at the 1991 Cannes Film Festival when *Serial Mom* was the closing film there the year after it came out.

The closing film at Cannes is not in the competition. It's a popular selection. John was so nervous. The year before, they had closed the festival with the American film – *Days of Thunder* – and the audience had booed it mercilessly. So John seriously had this on his mind. To make the situation even more nerve-racking, there is a very wide aisle about two-thirds of the way down the theater with thrones set up where the director and lead actor have to sit. There's no sneaking away.

The problem with showing a comedy at Cannes is that most of the audience is reading subtitles because they don't speak English as their first language. So the laughs come at different times. We weren't sure how the humor was being received.

When the film ended and the lights came up, the whole audience stood up and cheered. John was absolutely childlike. Well, he is a child in many ways, but he was giggling and trying not to clap for himself, just happy-happy. After the showing, we walked out to the Palais de Festival where the red carpet starts, and up onto a huge platform, where we could see the three thousand or more attendees chanting *'Je t'aime, je t'aime,* Kathleen, *je t'aime,* John.' It was heady as hell.

We went across the street to an end-of-festival party, but it was too crazy and we were too wiped out to stay long. We were starving. We asked one of the numerous French secret police-men stationed all around in plain sight, 'Can we get a pizza nearby?' He said in his heavily accented English, 'My brother has a pizza parlor. I'll call him and while you are on the way to your hotel, he will open up and make you a pizza.'

John, Jay, and I were staying at the Hotel du Cap. The policeman called his brother and we picked up our pizza on the way back to the hotel. We walked into the Hotel du Cap with our takeout pizza. There we are at one of the swankiest hotels in the world with the most extraordinary food and service, and all we wanted was a pizza. It was a terrific evening. Terrific pizza, too.

Virgin role

The Virgin Suicides, which was released in 1999, was something completely different for me once again. Sofia Coppola sent me the script; it was her first film as a director. Somebody else owned the rights, but she felt so strongly about doing it that she had developed the script without the usual permissions. I first read the Jeffrey Eugenides book on which it was based because I wanted to understand it as completely as I could and to be sure that I felt Sofia was on the right path. She was dead-on. I loved the script.

Whoever owned the rights finally released them. Sofia was there to grab them with a script ready to be turned into the movie. I went out to meet her in Los Angeles. She noticed I was looking at her a little oddly over lunch. She had played my little sister in *Peggy Sue* and that was the image I still had of her. I started laughing, thinking about this. She said, 'Why are you laughing? Because I'm not wearing green?' I said, 'You got it, exactly.' I guess I expected to see this thin little girl in a green Girl Scout outfit.

I agreed to do the film with Sofia. Right away, I got a call from her father, Francis. He asked me, 'So do you mean that you really will play in this film?' I said, 'Absolutely. I saw what a great script this is.' And he said, 'Well, it's hard for me to see – it's my daughter, after all, and I can't help but express my doubts.' I said, 'This movie has to be made.'

The Virgin Suicides, 1999

The five beautiful teenage Lisbon sisters, children of a domineering mother and math teacher father in an affluent suburb, commit suicide. The community struggles to understand what prompted them to kill themselves.

Directed by Sofia Coppola
Produced by Francis Ford Coppola, Julie Costanzo, Dan Halsted, and Chris Hanley

James Woods as Mr. Lisbon
Kathleen Turner as Mrs. Lisbon

Lux Lisbon: *I can't breathe in here.*
Mrs Lisbon: *Lux, you are safe in here.*

I helped to raise money and get people to work on it also, which was satisfying. Francis said he wasn't going to interfere but would help in producing it. Well, he couldn't stop himself. He showed up on the set every day for a couple of weeks. He swore he'd just sit there and watch. But Francis can never sit and watch. He kept talking to Sofia and was taking her attention. His wife, Ellie, who's a terrific woman, was doing a documentary on the making of the film. Ellie and Sofia ganged up on Francis and said, 'Go home.'

Mrs. Lisbon is one of the saddest characters I ever had to play. It was very challenging for me, actually, to be so sad, so lifeless and depressed. Sofia's direction for me often would be, 'Kathleen, you're coming to life! Pull back.'

Shit, did it again, I'd think. So I made up this image of a plug in my heel, and when I was ready to be in character, I would pull the plug and let all the life drain out of me. Then I would be ready to play Mrs. Lisbon. Still, every once in a while Sofia would have to remind me, 'You're coming alive again.'

'Shit – okay, pull the plug, pull the plug.' Keeping in my head this vision of all my blood draining out of my body to do this poor woman was not a happy experience. And it was tough to think about her daughters committing suicide and not to worry incessantly about Rachel, just approaching her teen years. It was desperately difficult to play Mrs. Lisbon because she was so unhappy. The thought that there are women like that breaks my heart. But it was very happy for the film and for me that I was able now to portray the character full tilt.

When *The Virgin Suicides* came out in London I was there doing *The Graduate*. Two blocks away from each other on Shaftesbury Avenue, I was the lifeless Mrs. Lisbon in one place and the randy Mrs. Robinson in the other. And I thought, *Now, that's range. Now we're talking range, guys. Anybody wonder about my range as an actress? Take a look on Shaftesbury Avenue.*

Living larger

In the world of economics, playing such diverse roles would be the equivalent of spreading the risks. But that's a rather defensive posture to take about one's life and life work. I look at not repeating my successes as expanding my future rather than circling wagons around the past to protect it. I want my life to get larger, not smaller. And now that I have fewer responsibilities at home, I'd like to go out and explore more experiences rather than sit in the background waiting for somebody to need me.

Our children will always need us, and that's nice. But I'm glad Rachel is away at college now. At long distance, dealing with the ups and downs in the World of Rachel seems a lot easier: 'Mom, I've hurt my knee.' 'Well that's too bad, hon – did you go to the clinic?'

Okay, I'll admit that I had to declare an official Depression Day after I first returned from moving her into her dorm. And I'll admit that a few weeks later, when I wasn't receiving sufficient e-mails and calls from her to satisfy my maternal quota, I finagled an invitation to go and spend the night with her there. But then I was perfectly happy to drive myself back home, stopping on the way to pick up my new kitty, Tiger Lily, at the pet store and settle us both, purring, into our comfy perch overlooking the Hudson River.

It's a very exciting idea that we have all these choices in life, when the independence that we once had in our early years is coming back to us at the stage at which many of us women find ourselves moving into our fuck-you fifties and beyond. We know ourselves and our bodies better and we have become more comfortable with who we are. There's just less pretense. The children are pretty much paid for. We might still have their college expenses, but pretty soon they're going to be earning a living, almost all of them.

We may or may not be married. Did you know that most Americans will spend more single years during their life span than in a continuous marriage, especially women, because we live longer?[20] But hopefully if we are married, our husbands are able to support themselves. So that once again, as we were in our younger days, so long as we can support ourselves, we're free to say no or yes to whatever we choose.

First we need financial independence, or at least the ability to earn our own way. It is so important that every woman gets an education and marketable skills. With a basic level of education and some skills and good health, anyone should be able to earn enough to pay for food and rent and, hopefully, health insurance. Those are the basics that give us our independence. Once we can manage to get them, then there's no reason in the world we shouldn't be able to say no to anything that makes us doubt our own worth. And to be at a place where we can say a resounding 'Yes!' to whatever we choose to.

Goals have to be realistic – for example, I couldn't be a mathematical genius no matter how hard I tried. But beyond that, the most critical factor is to be willing to risk failure. And not take no for an answer. If anyone tells me that something can't be done, I change the question to 'How *could* we do it?'

I feel now as I did when I was a teenager in London before my father died: that I have the whole world open to me. I can go almost anywhere and be accepted, be welcomed. Isn't that amazing? I wanted it and somehow my steps along the way led me to it. People will help me, take care of me. And that's such an extraordinary thing that I want to take full advantage of it. I'm so excited, even though I do not know yet what my next role will be. I have all confidence it will be a good one, better than the last.

My timing was good. I'm right in the middle of the baby boomer generation of women. I think the greatest social change is happening now. This is the first generation of women that has earned and commanded their own financial resources throughout our adult lives. Now, that is a huge change from previous generations. And I think the scale is going to expand exponentially in the next ten years.

We're so different from previous generations, and it's a generation so big that it changes everything as it sweeps through each age range along the way. Already, boomers think that they won't consider themselves old until age seventy-nine, so for us midlife lasts until we are almost eighty![21]

And in large part, women intend to keep working. Look at this from About.com on the differences between men and women: 'Baby boomer women are dreaming of retiring to Mars while baby boomer men hope to retire to Venus. Baby boomer men are looking forward to working less, relaxing more, and spending more time with their spouse. Baby boomer women view the dual liberations of empty nesting and retirement as providing new opportunities for career development, community involvement and continued personal growth.'[22] Whew, that describes how I feel to a tee!

Kathleen Turner is my brand

When the idea sprang upon me forty years ago that I could earn my living by acting, that it was a profession and not some kind of fantasy world, it was like a bolt of lightning. It took me years to say, 'Yes, I am an artist,' because we Americans don't have or encourage that respect for the acting profession. Everybody thinks you were found in Schwab's drugstore and somebody said, 'Oh, baby, I'm going to make you a star.' No, the fact is that I am a businesswoman and I am my most important asset. My acting is an art, but not just an artistic pursuit. My choice of work, whom to work with, what material I perform, and how to do it, are my product that develops me as a brand. It creates my future, my ability to protect my loved ones or give them what they need financially. Yeah, I'm a business. Acting is my industry. That's the plant that I've built.

Jay's best friend, Michael Kaufman, used to say that if I hadn't been an actor, I would have been CEO of a Fortune 500 company. Of course, he also said I didn't do anything I didn't know I was good at. Ha! Perhaps I am a little controlling – no, not really controlling: I just don't like to promise what I can't deliver. I say it, I do it, remember?

I think the first response to my brand would be affection, likability. Even though I do these outrageous characters, people like them. People like them a lot. They even love poor Martha. Or Beverly the serial mom. Managing and protecting the Kathleen Turner brand can be tricky. It would have been easy to accept more jobs and make a lot more money. But I always believed ultimately it would be at the cost of the product, that is, quality versus quantity. So my goal basically was to stay ahead of having to take a job to pay my rent. I have lived within my means so that I would never have to give up my idea of quality.

You learn as you go along how to safeguard your product, how to present yourself better, how to control the way other people are presenting you. Right after I did *Body Heat*, I had a publicist who told *Playboy* I'd do an entire nude photo shoot for them, including a centerfold. When I found this out, I said, 'I'm not doing that.' She said, 'What does it matter? You were naked in the film." I said, 'That's a film. That's a character. It's acting. A centerfold would be *me*. I'm not posing nude for any magazine.'

She said, 'But I promised them.' I said, 'Well, that's too bad, isn't it?' Can you imagine? I was shocked to my core. I said to her, 'Okay, from now on you check the publicity with me before you make a promise.'

She was furious. 'I promised them, I told them you'd do it,' she threw back at me.

'Well, I didn't say I'd do it. And guess what? I'm the product,' I replied.

So I got out of that one. But it was a terrible moment. She saw a dollar sign. She'd gotten a *Playboy* spread for me, right? I guess she thought, *Who wouldn't want that?*

Kathleen Turner, that's who.

And it all turned out very well, because later, *Playboy* did a lovely, sexy photo shoot for *Babes on Broadway* in which I was clothed in pink organza. And one of the best interviews ever done of me was published in *Playboy* in 1986. Really, you *can* read *Playboy* for the articles.

Tallulah!

I had begun to work on a show based on the life of Tallulah Bankhead (to whom I have been compared) in the south of England at the 1997 Chichester Theater Festival. The producers were excited about it but they thought it needed a lot of work, and so it did. We set up a fourteen-city tour in the States and Canada. I went on the road with my one-woman show, *Tallulah!*, in early 2000.

Doing *Tallulah!* gave me another milestone in my recovering health. I showed myself and others that I could do a two-hour monologue onstage and not miss any performances. Do you have any idea how many words there are in two hours? As I've said, I love to throw myself around, and Tallulah is drunk all the time, lurching and falling all over the stage. I was able to do that day after day: two full hours of one woman going through her life. That's a tremendous arc, and she's such a character, so out-of-control much of the time.

For almost a year, I traveled from city to city. I loved doing this because I had felt out of touch with the country after being in London for so long. I learned so much about people and how things played in different parts of the country.

You can get really lonely doing a one-person show. So wherever I went, I would contact a university ahead of time and say, 'I'll be here three weeks. I would be happy to teach a masters class for your senior students who are serious about a profession in theater.' We'd set it up ahead of time. Planning the classes helped to fill my time and my days.

When we got back to New York, two of the producers took me to lunch and gave me the bad news: 'We aren't going to bring *Tallulah!* to Broadway.' I argued with them because of how well received the play had been outside of New York. I dissolved into tears, I wailed, I went home and I threw things against the wall, which is not my usual way of behaving – I think that came straight from Tallulah.

But the truth was that they were right in part. I was forcing some of the play through on my own personality. When something flows naturally and easily, you have a sense that the words and the thoughts are connected. The flow from one thought to the next and the drive of the play work. When you have to force your own thoughts and in effect explain the script, then the performance isn't being carried by the material. You really feel it when you are on the stage. The script needed work, but the writer didn't agree and wouldn't redo it.

Throughout the *Tallulah!* tour, Terry Johnson kept asking me to bring *The Graduate* to Broadway: 'Will you please—?' I kept saying 'No, no, no. I don't think it's worth doing in New York. I'm busy developing this piece, *Tallulah!*, that will be one of my legacies.'

When it was decided that we would not do *Tallulah!* on Broadway, that left a hole in my schedule. Terry came to New York again to try to persuade me to do Mrs. Robinson. He said the producers felt it had to be me in the role. They offered me a great deal: I would be the highest paid actress on Broadway. They challenged me. I do like a challenge. I went through the 'what if' stage, then I went through the 'to hell with them' stage. And at that point, everything I needed to make the choice was there and I decided to do it. I just thought, *Fuck 'em, you know? Fuck American puritanical hypocrisy, fuck it all. People love this show, and I'm going to go for it. I'll do* The Graduate.

The critics were tremendously harsh on Terry as the writer-director. But we had sold-out houses for almost eleven months. We had the largest advance booking ever on Broadway. How much of this popularity was due to the nude scene? That was the buzz, as you might expect. But people had so loved the film version of *The Graduate*. The nostalgia factor made them want to see the play too.

Getting myself back in full

I was forty-eight, two years older than when I'd opened in London, and I had to summon the guts to go onstage nude again. Terry said to me that if I could figure out a different way to carry the story forward and to effect the shock on Benjamin when Mrs. Robinson first tries to seduce him, I was free to try it. But various stages of undress, even underwear or just a slip with no bra, none of it matched the impact of standing there and dropping that towel.

The crew and everybody backstage were tremendously respectful and protective toward me. When we were out of town, a local crew member, not one of the staff that traveled with us throughout the tour on the way to Broadway, made a comment about 'what a piece of ass' or something crude like that. And the next thing I knew, our prop guy had him by the throat, pulling him up by his shirt and saying, 'That's Miss Turner – you knock it off.'

Fortunately, I have always been able to know the difference between acting Mrs. Robinson on the stage and being Kathleen Turner. Still, at first, it was terribly, terribly frightening when I allowed myself to think about being nude on the stage in my hometown, New York. The nude scene was what, twenty seconds? It wasn't that big a deal in England. But this is America. You would think after two hundred plus years we would have gotten rid of some of that puritanical crap, but it's still there.

But here's the miracle. It was in doing that nude scene night after night that I realized what a gift had been given to me. It gave me confidence as we went along. I hadn't thought to hope that doing the nudity or assuming the very sexual persona again would give me back some of what I'd lost in my personal life. But it did. This awakening came gradually. *The Graduate* literally and spiritually gave me my body back. And that meant *I* was truly back at last.

Then, when I started getting those letters from women telling me how my willingness to bare my forty-eight-year-old self had helped them feel better about their own middle-aged bodies, I became absolutely grateful for the opportunity to play Mrs. Robinson. I was no longer fearful of playing a role where nudity was an essential part of the story. I embraced it.

That left me with one last big fear I had yet to face before I could get my life fully on track again. It was time to face the music on my drinking.

Left to my own vices

One night when I was in rehearsal for *The Graduate* in New York, just before Christmas, I got out of rehearsal a little early. I hadn't had time to do any of my Christmas shopping. So I did my usual Turner sweep, trying to get everybody's presents in one afternoon. I'd promised to go to the theater that night with my director, Terry Johnson.

I got almost all the shopping done. We were to meet at Orso, a restaurant on 46th Street. I got there, put my packages in the cloakroom, and downed a vodka. Terry met me and we went to the theater. At intermission I said, 'Excuse me.' I told myself I was so tired that I would just sneak out, gather my presents from Orso, and go home. But when I got back to the restaurant, I had another vodka. Then I had another vodka. And another. How many, I don't remember.

I went downstairs and collapsed in the bathroom. Someone found me and told the manager, 'There's a woman in the bathroom, sitting on the floor.' Very discreetly, I must say, the manager got me up to the office and called Jay to come get me.

Evidently I fought Jay when he got there. I didn't want him to touch me. So he had to call a friend, who came to help him and whom I allowed to help me into the car.

This wasn't the first time I'd been drinking until I passed out. But it was the worst and most public. The next day, after I apologized to Jay, I went to rehearsal and I said to the cast, 'I'm having a drinking problem. I have these pills. If I drink they will make me desperately ill. I'm going to give these pills to the stage manager and he's going to give me one a day. So I want you all to know, I will be taking one of these pills every day. And I will not be a problem again.'

And that's what I did. It was one of the most painful things I ever had to do because I am so self-contained about my personal problems. I felt as though I had failed and, worse yet, failed others who were depending on me to carry the show for all of us. The stage manager gave me a pill every day. That's a statement to make to the cast and crew that they could trust me, that it would not happen again. Jay didn't want to be my jailer. He felt – and probably rightly – that would create resentment in me toward him. And he was probably wise in that way.

If revealing my personal problem within my family and to the entire cast and crew was excruciating, it was still only the beginning of what I had to face. Honey, you can imagine how the media had a field day. Check this from the *Austin Chronicle*:[23]

The occasionally appealing Kathleen Turner was found flat on her face with a split lip on the bathroom floor at the restaurant Orso's in NYC. 'Drunk as a skunk,' I believe the phrase is. Her husband was called, and he escorted her out, and according to a source, 'Kathleen was reeking of booze, slurring her words, and almost broke her neck leaving the restaurant . . . She was rambling incoherently and, on the way out, she stumbled on the stairs. If her escorts hadn't caught her, it would have been really bad.' Sounds like it's *already* bad . . .

I don't think anybody beats herself up more than the person who got drunk. I didn't need anybody telling me what a terrible person I was, because I felt that already. I was sure I was a terrible person and should be punished.

But I am so fortunate to have friends who didn't judge me; they just said, 'How can I help? Do you need me to come over? Do you want to come here?' They were like solid bases I could hold on to when I drank too much. And they helped me to know it was past time to do something about my problem. But first I had a commitment to keep.

True to form, I was able to control my drinking once we opened *The Graduate* on Broadway. You can't drink and do eight shows a week. Not the characters I choose, anyway. A member of the crew who had abused drugs in the past but had been sober for years at this point, helped me out. We'd have weekly poker games with the crew and the cast. Everybody else would be drinking and he and I would be having fruit drinks and laughing about it. Because, after a while, we usually won. The others got a little too sloppy playing their hands.

I'd promised myself and my friends that after *The Graduate* closed, I'd check in to the rehab clinic. I feared that when I stopped working and had time on my hands, I would start to drink to excess again as was my pattern. I wanted to really explore alcoholism, what it is, where I was in relation to it. So it seemed to me the best insurance would be to go right from the play and to check myself into the center for a while.

I recognized the damage I was doing, not just to Jay and my relationship to him, not just to Rachel, but also to myself. And to my whole belief in living, which had, thank God, rescued me from RA. But now I was destroying myself by myself. And I couldn't figure out why I was doing this now, just when I was making both a physical and a professional comeback.

At first, when I got into rehab, the center staff said to me, 'You're not drunk.' I said, 'No, I'm not drinking now.' As I stayed there, I realized that people would come in desperately addicted to drugs or alcohol and they had to detoxify before they could even be treated. These people had stories that were shocking and fascinating. We had group sessions, and I found the dynamics of them very interesting. There were women who had killed their children while driving drunk. Doctors who had performed operations while flying high as a kite. I mean, these stories were so horrific. People confessed the most heartrending things. I could see lives in shambles before my eyes. Some of them, especially those in the medical profession, were mandated to be there by the courts in order to retain their licenses or to have a shot at getting them back. Then there was a woman in her seventies from a very gracious upper-class background, with completely different stories.

I heard some scary stuff. I learned a great deal and became more aware of what behavior to watch for in myself, to be more aware of what the drinking does to me, both physically and emotionally. And what it does to those around me. It gave me a perspective that I couldn't reach on my own.

For about six months after that, I went to Alcoholics Anonymous. But for me it was not anonymous at all. I'd be waiting outside to go into a meeting and I would hear someone saying, 'Oh, I have Kathleen Turner in my group.' AA is supposed to offer a safe environment, and I felt no safety there. So I stopped going to Alcoholics Anonymous, but I continue to work on improving, first with another private group and now with private counseling.

I took Rachel with me to my counselor to talk about alcoholism. I also thought she should be aware that it can be genetically present. We talked about it a lot, and God knows I've told her how very, very sorry I am. Actually, apologizing drives it home.

And then some important things changed. First, I managed to become more aware of how much I was drinking, and second, my doctor changed the drugs I was taking for RA once again. The new regimen gave me so very much more relief. Part of the drinking had been caused by the pain or the fear of the pain and the constant fear that any day I could become acute again. Or I'd have a month in remission and I'd be thinking, *Okay, the worst is over*. Then suddenly it would flare up again and I'd be right back where I'd been.

That constant insecurity – not knowing when I would be immobilized again – had made me always on edge. I'd wake up every morning, and before I got out of bed to walk to the bathroom, I'd just hope I could make that walk. That fear is tough to live with, honey. And when I'd get out of bed and find I could walk to the bathroom that day, I'd go, 'Hallelujah, it's going to be a good day.' But I couldn't count on that with any certainty then. Now I'm in constant remission, but I was just on the cusp of getting to that point when I started doing *The Graduate* in New York.

The odd thing is going from drinking socially for thirty-five years to losing control of this pleasurable aspect of my life. It's very confusing. My mother told me that her grandfather was an alcoholic. I don't think my grandparents were, though they were quite some drinkers. Good old Daddy Russ always said a shot of bourbon a day was the secret of his longevity.

Truth telling: I was still drinking to excess on occasion right up till about halfway through the New York run of *Virginia Woolf*, which opened in the spring of 2005. Following the pattern, I was great during the week and then on Monday, my day off, I would drink too much.

Maybe by drinking I was looking for a release; maybe some of it was the boozy character I was playing. A lot of the reason I drank was my relationship with my husband. This is not to blame him at all, because there was nobody pouring that drink but myself. But when we did make the decision to separate, my need to drink compulsively slowed measurably.

I cannot say it was the marriage alone. There were lots of factors. Maybe I just finally grew up enough. Maybe I don't feel like I'm hiding so much anymore. Maybe I'm not as afraid. Maybe I'm just calmer or happier or reached a point where I have more self-awareness. But I don't feel that pressure to drink anymore, or to hide when I do take a drink. I think a lot of the drinking was shutting myself off from the world. Because it does put you completely out of contact. It's like going into a room and locking the door. You're not there. Nobody can reach you.

I justified it in many ways. I blamed the pain and the fear and the pressure – all kinds of things, any one of which could drive someone to drink. Nevertheless, I wasn't coping. I wasn't dealing with the fundamental problems at all. I know that now.

I probably knew that then, but now I can name it and face it.

So it's something I have to watch and I'll always have to watch. But at least now I can enjoy a drink without being afraid that I'm going to abuse it automatically. I don't *have* to have that drink.

And I have a good psychiatrist who says to me, 'All right, don't be so judgmental about yourself. Find out why you do this. And let's deal with that, not the aftereffects that you're so ashamed of.' And she tries to help me do something that I'm trying hard to do but is almost impossible for me: to stop judging myself and to stop blaming myself for everything that happens.

I'm learning forgiveness and I'm learning more self-awareness. Why do I want that drink? Is it because I'm having a wonderful meal with friends and a good glass of wine would be icing on the cake? Or is it because I don't want to deal with what's going on so I'm going to drink? The difference is immense.

Hey, listen. I've beaten the rheumatoid arthritis into remission and come back to accolades as an actor. I have a kid who is sane, funny, good, and smart. I have a wonderful life, wonderful friends, and so many things that I want to do in the next half of my life. I might be a risk taker, but why would I want to risk losing all of that?

Maybe this is even one successful role I *do* want to repeat.

Chapter Thirteen

Send yourself roses

So there's a big flood and a man climbs up on his roof to escape the waters. He's not afraid because, as a religious man, he puts his trust in God to provide for his rescue. A raft carrying a family floats by and offers to take him with them. 'Thanks,' he says, 'but God will provide for me.'

Pretty soon, a motorboat comes by and the driver offers the man a ride. 'Thanks, but God will provide,' the man replies. The water is almost up to the roof now, and a helicopter flies overhead and drops down a rope ladder. The man, still unafraid, waves the copter away, saying, 'God will provide.'

The floodwaters continue to rise. Soon the entire house is underwater and the man drowns. He enters the pearly gates. Standing before God's throne, shaken and wet, he says, 'I believed you would provide for me, God. Why did you let me drown?'

To which God replies, 'Look, I sent you a raft, I sent you a boat, I sent you a helicopter. Why didn't you take any one of them?'

That's one of my favorite jokes. I mean, what the fuck was this guy expecting? An angel swooping down from heaven? I love the message that we have to help ourselves and that the tools to help ourselves are right there in front of us. But we have to be willing to use them.

Before an opening performance, when I am feeling like I really need an affirmation, I'll send myself a big bouquet of roses. Why not? Why should I wait around and hope that someone else will send me roses? If someone does, that's delightful, and I will receive them with pleasure. But if no one does, I won't have to be blue. I will provide for my emotional needs just as I provide for my material needs. If I don't treat myself well, if I don't show my belief in myself, how can I expect anyone else to?

That's why I treated myself to the Lanesborough Spa after the close of *Virginia Woolf* in London and before I returned home to the demands of life in New York. I always try to do something nice for myself after I finish a play or film. I'd like to share some of the ways I have learned through experience to make my life as rich and full as possible.

Sometimes solitude is the greatest gift I can give myself. The quietness, the space and the time to be with my thoughts, or just to *be* have become quite precious. My days get eaten up with busy-ness if I let them. I have to consciously plan to give myself the gift of solitude. Time alone recharges my spirit and mind. Time away from the usual fray is even better. My decision to spend two weeks at the Cal-a-Vie Spa the summer after I returned from London was the first time I have done anything like that for that long just for myself. It was remarkable how much I enjoyed the conversations Gloria and I had about this book in that atmosphere and how much more easily the thoughts about my life flowed when I could relax into solitude and reach deeply into myself.

I like to do silly things alone, too, like walking around the city, watching people, just being part of it. I like to stop in at little restaurants I have never seen before. And I love to read at a meal. So I go off alone with a book and read and eat someplace I've never eaten before. It's a treat even if the food turns out to be unfortunate.

Even when I was young and poor and just starting out in New York, I'd find some way to give myself a gift once a week, like taking a cab instead of the bus, or buying a single rose even when I couldn't afford the whole bouquet.

It doesn't have to be a big expensive thing. Just something to make sure you remember that you're special, because you can get pretty downtrodden. You have to celebrate yourself. And giving yourself a little affirmation helps you shake off the many slings and arrows we all get from our critics every day.

Speak truth to critics

Oh, the critics. Critics go with my territory as an actress, so I'm accustomed to putting myself out there and exposing my heart to the world only to have some critic try to take me down a notch. There is such a cat-and-mouse game between critics and actors, because all actors want so much to be loved and we tend to take it pretty hard when the reviews aren't 100 percent positive, which they usually are not. Virginia Woolf, as always, made an observation that is so true. She said, 'Unfortunately . . . it is the nature of the artist to mind excessively what is said about him. Literature is strewn with the wreckage of men who have minded beyond reason the opinions of others.'[24] And the wreckage of women.

Some critics seem to be personally malicious, not reviewing a performance so much as attacking a person. I won't name names, though I could. Well, maybe I will name John Simon from *New York Magazine*, who eventually got fired, thank goodness.

Sometimes the critics just don't do the work to understand the context of a play. The very core of Albee's *Who's Afraid of Virginia Woolf?* is the culture that defined women's and men's roles in 1960. That's where the brilliance of it is. Those who saw the show only as alcohol-sodden marital conflict missed it. And if they miss it, they're reviewing a different play.

There *are* times when I get bad reviews, and as much as it hurts, I know they might not be altogether wrong. If they are right, I try to learn from them. If they are wrong, I say, 'Screw them.' Keep on with the performance that you believe in.

As everyone knows, the New York critics gave *The Graduate* very poor reviews. Not of me necessarily, but the play as a whole. Then Tony time came around. Now we were sold out every single night, and every night there was a standing ovation. But we didn't receive a single nomination for anything. Not lights, not sets, not anything. I was so angry, I made the producer take out a full-page ad in the *New York Times* with a big picture of me laughing. The ad said, 'Here's to you, Kathleen Turner! . . . and here's to full houses, standing ovations, box office records, stopping traffic every night on 45th Street – and zero nominations!'[25]

That was my fuck-you. I framed that ad and I gave it to my wonderful and always supportive agent, Sam Cohn. I love Sam because he truly loves the art of theater and he is totally committed to his people. He has it hanging on his office wall. It still makes me laugh when I see it.

As Michael Douglas would say, 'Revenge is the best revenge.'

The audience is the ultimate critic, and audiences do react differently according to their culture. A funny thing happened with Dustin Hoffman when he was playing *The Merchant of Venice* in London. He had been told that, unlike audiences in the United States, British audiences rarely give standing ovations, especially for plays. Sure enough, he wasn't getting standing ovations. They wouldn't stand no matter how great the performance had been, and it was just driving him nuts. Then one night it fell to Dustin to announce to the audience the death of Sir Laurence Olivier. He made the announcement right after the curtain. The audience slowly and silently rose to their feet. Dustin was shaking his head as he was going off the stage, saying, 'You have to fucking die to get a standing ovation here.'

Fortunately, nobody had to die for us to get the London audiences to stand for us in *Who's Afraid of Virginia Woolf?* As thrilled as we were about the critics' reaction, the four of us in the cast still tried to appreciate our own worth first and foremost and to give ourselves some rewards for our very hard work.

Give till you feel good

I like to give things to people. This makes me feel good and I hope it makes them feel good. Not huge gifts usually, although my traditional opening night gift was always pretty goddamn big. I had a wonderful jeweler, the late Helen Woodhull, whose work I love and hers is the only jewelry I've collected. I first asked her to design a pin for me for *Cat on a Hot Tin Roof*. Then she would break or change the mold so no one else had this pin except the original group. For *Virginia Woolf*, we designed a wonderful laughing wolf, baying at the moon. Helen said it was the best thing she'd ever done. She cast it in silver for the four actors, the director, the producers, and one for Edward Albee.

Sometimes, we came together as a cast to help support each other. We all pulled together to help my dresser, Dawn Thomas, who had an extremely painful displaced vertebra in her lower back. The NHS, the National Health Service in England, put her on a waiting list for an MRI but told her it would be six months. Then she'd be put on a list for a consultation with a surgeon three or four months after that. Dawn was in despair. I said, 'This is unacceptable.' So I took her to a private doctor, got her an MRI the next day. We took the MRI to a surgeon later in the week. He recommended immediate surgery.

Well, the surgery cost four thousand pounds, the equivalent of almost twice that in U.S. dollars. Dawn didn't have anything like that. So we four actors got together some money, and others joined in, and then we went to a charity that helps the theater ushers and backstage members of the unions. They found a way to get a better rate from the hospital, and on the postoperative care, which we hadn't thought of. She had the operation two weeks before we finished the show. She came back and worked the last night, already nearly pain-free. Knowing we had worked as a team to help one of our colleagues made us all feel happy.

We four actors had dinner with Anthony Page, our director, a couple nights before we closed in London. It's amazing how we were still involved with each other, how we talked and joked. Anthony was at his most charming, very British, very funny. We pretty much said goodbye to Anthony, though he threw a little after-show party too, for the cast and crew and a few people who were involved with the theater.

After the curtain calls, every single show, we each hugged everyone. I hugged David, then I hugged Mireille, and I hugged Bill. From the very beginning I said, 'Look, nobody's walking off this stage without coming back to the realization it's you and me – it's not Nick and Martha, it's not George and Martha, it's not Honey and Martha. It's Kathleen hugging David, Mireille, and Bill.' We needed to dissipate any feelings that might have arisen during the play, with all the conflict that occurs. You can't really perform these strong emotions without feeling them – you perform them through yourself so there is part of you that's activated by the anger, activated by the lust or by the fear. You try to shake those off and replace them with positive actions and affirmations.

So one way we would symbolically send ourselves roses is by simply hugging each other and saying, 'Okay, we did it.' The last night after the last curtain of *Virginia Woolf*, the actors gave each other a four-way hug. And we just looked at each other and said, 'Well done. We did a really great job. And we're done.'

Change the definition of 'sexy'

Maggie Smith, my dear friend, likes to say she's been 'Harry Puttering,' referring to the role of Professor McGonagall that she plays in the Harry Potter films. I took her to a farewell lunch at Green's just before I left London because she had enjoyed it so much when we had lunch there during the run of *The Graduate*.

One time my daughter and my niece wanted to meet Maggie when they came to visit. My niece was just goggle-eyed, looking at Professor McGonagall – and Rachel was trying to look cool. Maggie said in her self-mocking way, 'Oh yes, my brilliant performance, "Come along, now, children, get in line. You are dismissed. Now calm, please, calm." Sparkling dialogue, don't you think?' It was pouring rain, and my mom, who was also with us, had on a clear plastic raincoat and hat. Maggie said, 'You look just like a condom.' Rachel thought this was very funny. Oh, we laughed so much.

Maggie's had such a tremendously different career from mine. The British very often do. She was told when she was young that she would never be pretty enough to do film, so she went straight into the Royal Shakespeare Company, to tour the country and then to come into the West End of London. There was a solid cadre of British actors that could count on having work continually. No one thought you should stop working at a certain age. When you stopped playing Juliet you simply played the next older character. You don't stop working, for heaven's sake. So Maggie and her peers didn't have the same fear that their careers would end due to age as American actresses do. That got her through to the grande dame stature that means no one would question anything she chose to do. Like Miss Jean Brodie, she is always in her prime.

I feel extraordinarily lucky and I'm very, very grateful to have had a progression of amazing roles during my career so far. It's a progression I intend to continue. Every day, I learn more, build more on my experiences, which, I like to think, should make me of greater value.

That's the positive way to look at things. But facts are facts and the truth is that in Hollywood, as a woman ages she's not likely to be the romantic interest. She gets stereotyped, often as bitter and angry or just silly. Men, on the other hand, continue to get roles as the romantic lead in films well into their sixties. We often see a visibly older man with a younger leading lady – as though his wrinkles don't matter, or it's assumed we'll accept that they make him look more distinguished. He keeps reaffirming his youth and sexual power by showing he can attract what is considered attractive in this culture, young women. I often get summaries of the scripts the studios are developing. I got one that I sent back furious because it said, 'The main character is thirty-seven but still attractive.' I circled the 'but' in red ink and I sent it back and said, 'Try again!' Good, essential female character parts are much less likely in film than onstage, and that is why the theater tends to be better for women when they get older. The parts are more interesting and you have more authority to develop them intelligently.

There are better roles in both film and theater for older women in Europe than there are in the United States. Americans tend to dismiss the past, be it in architecture, art, music, or clothing. We don't look at older people – and in particular older women – as having inherent value that has accumulated because of their age. We're kind of like in the real estate business, where they flip properties without regard to the historical value. But there is an inherent value in accumulation of time, of the experience and what has taken place, whether you're speaking of a building or of the progression of art. You need to be able to see the older work to appreciate the new. And to see the growth of the innovative mind through each generation. That's why I'd like to work some of the time in Europe from now on. I'll just change my venue until Americans have greater reverence for the older actor's experience.

How our society views women will have to change, because today's women are changing how we feel about our own age and aging. We aren't going to be willing to accept any notion that we are no longer sexy or interested in love and sex the way previous generations might have been willing to do. Just today when I was getting my e-mail, I saw an ad flashing across my computer screen showing a picture of a gorgeous, healthy-looking gray-haired couple nuzzling each other suggestively. AARP is catching on to their market. As women get more economic power, we also become more respected for who we are, wrinkles and all. Sexuality and sexual attractiveness are part of the whole person from birth to death.

I'd like to think I have helped start that change as a toss of the rose for all women. I made waves early in my career as Matty, and possibly even bigger waves when I played Mrs. Robinson. And the message wasn't about the titillation of someone appearing nude onstage. It was about a middle-aged woman who was not only still interested in her own sexual pleasure but still sexually powerful and attractive even to men much younger than herself.

Come to think of it, I believe I would like to become the oldest goddamn sex symbol on the stage.

Women friends – a beautiful bouquet

I have amazingly admirable women in my life. More and more as I get older, I appreciate the closeness and the friendship of women. I find so many women my age now so interesting. I love their thoughts. I count on them. I can feel completely at ease with them. They are a varied lot.

There's Maggie Smith, of course. I love to be with her because we have very, very good laughs. I do enjoy good laughs. We got to be friends when she was playing the West End at the time I was doing *The Graduate*. She was doing *Lady in the Van* at the Queens; I was at the Gielgud, right next door. I went to see her performance before we opened. I sent a note over, asking if she wanted to have a glass of wine afterward. It became usual that every Thursday night we'd have dinner together at the Ivy; most times, we'd close the place up.

I have another extraordinary British friend, an artist named Rosalind Dexter. She's written a book on the philosophy of design and two books on feng shui. But she feels that feng shui isn't enough, that you have to take so much into consideration: how you live, what you use the space for, and how to apply it to industrial spaces, which is very interesting to me. She's a little like a super fairy. My image is of her flitting and fluttering and flying and swooping and soaring. Her exuberance, her 'Isn't it wonderful to be alive?' attitude is great – I love being around someone who loves life so much.

Another friend in London, Sabrina Guinness, helped to create and fund a TV studio for poor minority kids who've been kicked out of the system. I like her thoughts, and we share the commitment to service. So she's a great pleasure to be with.

These are women I've lived away from for years at a time, but we never seem to lose the connection. When they're in New York or I'm in London, there's an immediate bond – it's easy to come back together, easy to sit down and talk. Which is the way it should be with good friends.

Over heaps of steamed crabs thrown directly onto City Crab's paper-covered tabletop, several of my New York-based friends and I reminisced recently about when we met and how we became such good buddies. I always think that communal food you can eat with your hands is the best way to make people comfortable and stimulate conversation. Though this group didn't need any extra encouragement.

Sandi Kaufman, who became my best friend, and I met just after I got back from filming *Romancing the Stone*. I'd decided to have a little cocktail party in my new apartment on West 23rd Street that Jay had helped me find. Michael Kaufman – he and Jay have known each other since they were four years old – came with Sandi, who was then his new girlfriend. She's from Savannah and has lovely manners in that southern way, very courteous and warm.

Sandi is an accountant, and when we met she was just about to start her own practice. We talked about whether I should become her client because we didn't want to screw up the relationship – that's always a risk. But the friendship is still absolutely great, I am happy to say. At least once a month we'd have a women's poker game and she is one of the original members. We rotated from house to house with a wonderful group of women. One is a stand-up comedienne, one is a film editor, one a real estate broker, there's an art designer – they have a myriad of interesting jobs, which is more stimulating to me than just being with people who do the same thing as I do.

Sandi and Michael and Jay and I became like family. We always have our family occasions together, usually with whoever else from our circle of friends and family is around at the time. But we are the nucleus. We always have Thanksgiving together, even now that Jay and I are separated. I make the best stuffing, as everyone acknowledges – sweet cornbread and bread stuffing. We spend the Jewish holidays together. And for years, they and a number of other friends joined us at the beach house for Christmas dinner. We've watched our children grow up together. Jay and I are the proud godparents of their two sons, Daniel and Ben.

Sandi was there for me when Rachel had the bicycle accident, she was there for me when I thought my RA was too much to bear, and she was there for me when I needed to go into rehab for my drinking problem. She's been almost like a sister. We have not allowed my separation from Jay to make a difference in our relationship. I'd like to say I've been there for her in her crises, too, but somehow I haven't needed to. I don't know why she has so many fewer crises than I do, come to think about it.

My friend Margo MacNabb is a terrific travel companion. We went to London and Rome together. And I want to go to India next with her. We get such a kick out of each other. She has every outfit lined up with everything needed to accessorize it: the belt, the shoes, the sweater that goes with the jacket. This is unheard of to me. I marvel at it. I just take three pairs of slacks, four sweaters, a couple shirts. But if I could wear Margo's clothes, I'd take my underpants and that's it when I travel with her, because she always has everything.

We met when she worked with the singer Billy Joel's then-wife, the supermodel Christie Brinkley. Christie and Billy had a place near Jay and me in Amagansett. Christie kept reserving tickets to go see *Cat on a Hot Tin Roof*. And she kept canceling. Finally, she called at five o'clock in the afternoon of the closing night, saying that she hadn't left home yet. She never showed up.

Christie would just not show up for dinner parties, too – and you know how I feel about keeping my commitments. Well, she felt bad about canceling. So she had Margo buy Waterford tumblers and a beautiful bottle of bourbon, which they sent to me as an apology. I sent it all back because it was the fourth or fifth time Christie had canceled to see my show. And I said, 'No, I cannot accept this kind of gift to secure a friendship.'

Adventures and ventures with friends

When I was a judge at the Cannes Film Festival in 2004, my great pal Kathy Dougherty came with me. She's a film editor. We first met at a cocktail party in Paris, where she was cutting a film and Jay and I were on vacation after I finished *Giulia e Giulia*. We just loved each other right away. When we got back to New York, we realized we lived four blocks from each other. We've been fast friends ever since.

The Cannes jury included lots of really great people. The Chinese director Tsui Hark was wonderful, as was Quentin Tarantino, of course, and Emmanuelle Béart from France, Benoît Poelvoorde from Belgium. They were all terrific.

It was hard work and murderously hot while we were there.

But it was a fantastic experience. I felt privileged to be involved in the voting. The people on the jury were very generous and took the job seriously. There were mornings when we had to get up early to go see a heavy Chinese murder mystery at eight o'clock and then we'd see a completely different kind of film at eleven and then something else at two.

We were sequestered in a chateau up on the hill after all the screenings were finished, and we couldn't speak with anyone on the phone. We were there for twenty-four hours at least, still wearing our fancy outfits while we deliberated on the winners.

Michael Moore won the Palme d'Or that year for best picture for *Fahrenheit 9/11*. It was a big hoopla. I have to honestly say, I wanted Michael to get the Grand Prix, the second prize, because I didn't want people to think the choice was political. And I really thought the Korean film entry was more powerful as a film, though *Fahrenheit 9/11* is certainly a great film. But I was outvoted.

The jury held a press conference the next day, which was unheard of. We felt it was necessary to say publicly, 'Look, this was not a political decision; it was an artistic decision.' We voted because we thought this was the best film.

Kathy and I made good use of our downtime. We laughed a lot about people and their pretensions. There were fourteen nights of events, which meant I had to have fourteen different evening gowns. I don't dress like that normally. So I called up a number of designers and asked if I could borrow dresses, which they allowed me to do. Jewelers such as Harry Winston were providing jewelry for us to wear. They would show me something so outrageous that I'd joke, 'Don't you have something a little bit bigger? I want something just a little bit bigger.' I mean, it was crazy. They had bodyguards walking around behind all the people who were using this fine jewelry, to protect their assets.

Since I couldn't wear high heels, I had my dresses done very long so I could wear my clogs. One evening I lifted my dress a bit so I could walk up the stairs, and people could see my clogs. The photographers caught the picture and spread it all over the world. Apparently this was big news, Kathleen Turner in her designer evening dress, Harry Winston jewels, and clogs.

On our one really big day off, we went to the fabulous Hotel du Cap for lunch with my friend Yanou Collart. Yanou, who is Belgian and lives in France, is a well-known publicist whose clients have included actors like Michael Caine and Sean Connery. She got her start selling Bic pens in North Africa and then went on to represent nouvelle cuisine chefs in France when they were just beginning to develop that preparation, which she made internationally famous. I'd met her in the 1980s when I was in Paris publicizing *Romancing the Stone* and she had invited Donald Sutherland, Michael Douglas, and me over for dinner cooked by some of her chefs. Every one of these amazing chefs cooked one course, and as part of the fun Michael, Donald, and I served it. At one point, she started to laugh so much. I asked, 'What are you laughing about?' Yanou said, 'Imagine the hourly pay represented here!'

The scene over lunch at the Hotel du Cap was like that, only magnified. Kath and I were thinking we were pretty cool, all dressed up and looking like beautiful people, there with Yanou looking at other beautiful people on a gorgeous day. Then we spotted a huge helicopter landing on a yacht the size of an aircraft carrier nearby. It was a sheik dropping his school-age kids off for lunch. They hopped on a motorboat and came to the restaurant. Everybody was wide-eyed as they walked in, thinking, *Who are they?* I mean, we were already in a very rich environment and these are schoolkids being dropped off for lunch – I'm not kidding – in a full-size helicopter. All of us stopped eating. It was beyond ostentatious.

Then there was the amfAR fund-raiser that Sharon Stone threw. The amfAR group has done fantastic work to fight HIV/AIDS globally. Quentin took a number of us out for a lovely dinner beforehand in a little village away from Cannes in a very famous restaurant, Moulin de Mougin. We got to the event, which was quite over the top, late, and everybody there was drunk by that time. Liza Minnelli was singing 'New York, New York' as we walked in. But she knew what she was doing, even loaded. It's a wonderful thing. Sharon Stone was sitting on guys' laps, trying to get them to give more money.

Kathy was appalled. I'm sure she was thinking, *Oh my God, this is what these celebrities do?* There are sides to this business that just do not make sense. Maybe people assume that if you reach a certain level in your life, tacky events don't happen, unhappiness doesn't happen. But you know, the Academy Awards can be really horrible and the Tonys can suck. People can misbehave, and Liza Minnelli could have fallen on her face. The celebrity life is not what it's cracked up to be in the tabloids. We're all human. Celebrities have the same problems as anyone else. It's not any better, it's not any finer, it's not any richer – stuff still happens. It's just more public.

A couple of years ago, my very intense friend Charline Spektor and I got fed up with the media's lack of questioning about important political issues. We decided that if we were going to bitch about it, we'd better do something about it. So we started a radio show called *American Dialogue*. Our one-hour shows were taped and sent free of charge weekly to NPR stations. They were based on issues, not personalities. Some of our topics have been the failure of diplomacy, the changing media, the Patriot Act, women's health care, and the threat to reproductive choice.

To publicize our program, I went on Paula Zahn's CNN show. She asked me why we were doing the program, in a rather hostile tone. I said, 'Look, I'm not claiming to be an expert in your field. We are just trying to ask questions that we think many people want to ask. And we have an hour to talk to guests so we can have a more substantive conversation than a news show that deals with many issues.' This was in the early days of the Iraq war, when there was such censoring of information. While journalists were 'embedded' with our military in Iraq, their copy was being looked at by the government, which decided whether or not the information could be used.

Paula huffed that she asks a lot of questions too. I suppose she thought, *Who is this puffed-up little personality who's throwing doubt on my professionalism and commitment?* But I believe what I said is true, that the media was catering to a level of governmental oversight they would never have accepted in the past just to keep their access to the Bush administration. Many questions were not being asked. I'm sorry she took offense, but I hit a nerve that was sensitive for good reason.

Charline and her husband own bookstores called Bookhampton. She has written a wonderful play; I got Bill Irwin to perform a reading of it with me for some producers at my agent Sam Cohn's office, and I hope she'll be on Broadway with it someday. Perhaps I'll play the lead.

In the end, it is my friends who really count and make my life so rich and meaningful.

Tend to the spirit

I don't talk too much about religion and spirituality because I feel it is so personal. But spirituality is very strong within me and important to me. I believe in a supreme being. I cannot believe that humanity with all its imperfections is the highest point we can reach for. That would be just too disappointing, too horrific. The hurtful actions and the evil that we're capable of are so distressing; I must believe there is a greater good beyond ourselves. And I believe, almost Spinoza-like, that there is an element of God in everything and in everyone.

I do not believe in a God who sets down rules and says, 'If you don't believe this way I'll punish you.' Or, 'I'll throw down sickness on you or hurt someone you love.' Surely the Golden Rule, 'Do unto others as you would have them do unto you,' is common sense as well as simply the right thing to do. That's about the only rule I think you need. I don't like a religion, for example some Christian denominations, that would condemn my husband to hell because he's Jewish, or my daughter because she refuses to practice Christianity. I can't believe that's any aspect of a real God. I think it's man's personification of his own desires, of his own seeking after power.

Though my father was the child of Methodist missionaries and we always attended an English-speaking Protestant church wherever we lived when I was growing up, my parents were not dogmatic. I was in the bell choir, and we were pretty regular churchgoers. In London we belonged to a church. But my mother also wanted to see the great cathedrals of England. So on high religious days, like Easter or Christmas, we would attend some of the most extraordinary ones. We visited all the big cathedrals in England, France, and Italy. She and I always lit candles for the family. I still light candles for the people I love when I am in a cathedral.

When my father died, I didn't believe much of anything. I really couldn't, because his death was a complete betrayal to me. It took years for me to even consider the idea of faith again. But then I found I couldn't live without it.

After I met and married Jay, I learned about Judaism. His family members are not big synagogue-goers or observers of Jewish tradition on a daily basis, but retaining their identity is extremely important to them. They observe the High Holy Days. I make great matzoh stuffing for Passover. My secret recipe – if I told you, I'd have to kill you. Sometimes I make it for Thanksgiving too by special request.

What I think restored some of my faith was getting to know the Jewish belief that we have direct communication with God. You don't have to have a pastor or a priest telling you God's will or interceding for you. It's just you and God and your family communing. That made sense to me.

I pray. I haven't decided whether I'm praying to a male or female. Before I go onstage, before the curtain comes up, I ask for help to use my mind and my spirit and my heart to give all I can to that performance. I speak to my actual father and to whatever higher spirit there might be. If there is something greater than us, then that something or someone must be accessible to us.

My grandfather, that wonderful down-to-earth Daddy Russ, who taught me how to persevere, died when he was ninety-five.

Rachel and I went to the funeral. The church they belonged to had a circular sanctuary with the altar in the middle. In front of the altar was his coffin, not open, thank you very much. I had Rachel, who was three years old, on my lap, and she asked, 'Where's Daddy Russ?' I said, 'Well, honey, Daddy Russ is in that coffin. He's in that box.' She said, 'What's he doing?' I said, 'He's sleeping. And he's going to stay asleep now.' She nestled her head on my shoulder and said, 'Good night, Daddy Russ.' And she went to sleep in my arms. That was when I started crying. I was fine up till then.

But I just knew at that moment that she felt the protection he had given me and trusted I would give the same protection to her. I think that sense of continuing protection from generation to generation comes from God, even though I don't believe it's specific to an individual. I thought about how Daddy Russ's words had given me the will I needed when I was at my sickest and I would desperately not want to move, not want to return a phone call, because I couldn't dial the goddamn phone. But I'd hear him saying, 'You just have to, don't you?' So I'd do it, I'd keep believing enough in life to do it.

It was terribly important to Jay and to his mother that Rachel understand her Jewish heritage. The one big confrontation came when my grandmother thought it was terribly important that Rachel be baptized. Now these two ideas about what was terribly important were in direct conflict. It's got to be one or the other. And frankly, as I said, I don't want a religion that condemns other people. So Rachel has been brought up more Jewish than anything. Though she has had a Christian education, too. At the moment, she thinks the whole thing's a bunch of crap. Which at her age is to be expected.

Choose the you that you like best

This will come as no surprise, but I'm not always nice and perfect. For example, I have this ridiculous trait where sometimes I meet someone and I take such an instant antipathy to them that nothing they can ever say or do changes that. I can argue with myself: 'Now come on, that's really stupid, they haven't done anything to offend you.' Forget it. Nothing, nothing cures it. My hackles rise whenever I see this person. And I'm not good at hiding it. I can be patient up to a point, and after that it's like, 'Okay, I told you once, I told you twice, you're a dummy, get out of here.' I can be rather bad that way. I do give the person a couple of chances. I'm a benevolent dictator. But at times, indeed a dictator.

I've also heard my whole life that I'm selfish. The incident with my mother when I was leaving for school in Baltimore and she said I was being selfish made a deeply painful impression on me. And it never made sense to me, because there's so very little I want for myself. I love having a beautiful place to live. I like having nice clothes and I appreciated it when Jay would give me beautiful jewels. But I don't have to have any of that as long as Rachel's taken care of and I'm healthy.

Being selfish, to me, means taking something that someone else needs. I don't believe I've ever done that. So is it my sense of certainty about who I am and what I'm going to do that makes me appear selfish? My need not to admit weakness or appear vulnerable? But I don't know why that should threaten other people, as long as it doesn't take away from them. And that's my fucking credo, to do no harm. So I've always wondered what I'm missing in this message.

I've certainly played plenty of selfish characters. But I've been told that I'm a very generous, supportive actor. Because I believe the whole piece has to be good. Yes, one actor or one character could steal the show. But that doesn't make it a good show. It's not the best for the work. True, I don't waste time with hot air or bullshit. Like the time David Harbour, who played Nick, was annoyed with me about something and bit me – hard – on my neck onstage during a performance of *Virginia Woolf*. It actually made a mark. I just kept going and then dealt with him afterward. I never let any argument or disagreement interfere with my performance. To me that's the priority.

I was pondering my selfishness or lack thereof while I was traveling back to Springfield to help my mother with a fund-raiser recently. At eighty-three, Mom is quite amazing, the chair of the capital campaign for the art museum. I give her myself for one fund-raiser a year of her choice. This one turned out to be a terrific event with the opening of a marvelous exhibit of Andy Warhol's sports paintings that had been on loan from my friend Richard Weisman.

So I asked Mom why she had told me back in my youth that I was going into a selfish, self-promotional career whereas my siblings were all going into public service. She just looked at me blankly and said matter-of-factly, 'Did I? Oh, that's very possible.' Obviously she had no idea why this was so important to me. And when I probed for more, she said, 'Look, there were four of you. There was confusion all the time. I couldn't possibly remember everything I said to any one of you. I didn't mean to hurt you.'

'Okay,' I decided. 'Okay, I can let that one go now.'

I felt the same kind of dissonance at first about my separation from Jay. I don't think either of us was sure we wanted a divorce. We went into the relationship believing it would be forever, with a commitment to the marriage and to each other. I look back and there were wonderful times. I wrote Jay on what would have been our twenty-second anniversary: 'Twenty-two years ago today was one of the most joyous days of my life.' We were there for each other in the most difficult times. I had always thought I could stay in the marriage no matter what.

But over the years, aspects of our personalities became stronger and perhaps imbalanced. I think we each simply became more of what we are. I don't imagine either one of us is a day at the beach to live with. Our friends point out that we are both drama queens. It seems to me that somewhere along the way, we both lost that special ability to put the other person first in our thoughts. My drinking drove a wedge between us, as I have acknowledged. Jay had to protect himself emotionally from me. And I felt that I had to protect myself emotionally from him. His way of protecting himself is to criticize me. That's why I came to feel better about myself outside our home than inside of it, and how I decided I was simply not willing to live that way anymore.

And yes, I do see the pattern that seemed to repeat with my two long-term relationships with men in my life, and yes, I am working on it.

In the end, there wasn't a huge explosion. It wasn't 'I can't stand this anymore' and one of us thundering out of the house. The separation, when it finally came, had the same sense of inevitability that good decisions have. I knew without a doubt that this was not the quality of life I wanted anymore. And I knew the quality of life would be better in different circumstances, for both of us.

I'm choosing to move forward rather than stay in a situation that became untenable for both of us. I am choosing to be the me that I like best.

Appreciate the rewards of necessary losses

Still, the ending of a marriage is a loss, a great loss, even when it is so clearly the right thing to do. Let's face it: there are losses that bring with them great pain and sadness, no matter how positive I want to be in my thoughts.

To be realistic, these middle years are when we start to suffer losses in our lives, whether of people close to us by divorce or death, or our own physical losses, as I've had with RA. Even people with no major illnesses or dependents are likely to find that they have to contend with indignities such as hearing less acutely, having less physical stamina, and so forth. I for one am really ticked at having to wear reading glasses. I seem to spend a lot of time taking them off and putting them on. And they are just one more thing to have to carry around with me all the time.

But these losses are compensated for by the strengths we have gained in experience, knowledge, friendships, and, one might hope, a little wisdom.

And, honey, don't we know so much more about how to use it all now?

In 1988, before RA, before my drinking problem, long before the end of my marriage, I could not have completely understood how we all are buffeted by life. That year, I worked with Bill Hurt and Larry Kasdan on the film version of Ann Tyler's *The Accidental Tourist*, which deals with a terrible loss. It seems worth reflecting upon now. The story is about a couple whose son was killed senselessly, and they try to go on but they can't. She says she can't pretend they have a life anymore. It's called *The Accidental Tourist* because the role Bill plays is a travel writer who writes about traveling but really has no interest in seeing or feeling anything new. His symbol is an armchair with wings. He meets a young woman played by Geena Davis who wants to explore all of life. Then the wife, my character, goes to him having decided that she wants the relationship back, but by this time it is clear that this will not be possible.

The Accidental Tourist, 1988

Travel guide writer Macon Leary's son has died. His way of dealing with it is to go about business as usual, and his wife wants to split up. Macon is then wooed by a quirky, life-loving woman who brings him out of the fog. When his wife decides she wants to give their marriage another try, Macon has to decide who he wants to be.

Directed by Lawrence Kasdan
Produced by Phyllis Carlyle, Michael Grillo, Lawrence Kasdan, John Malkovich, and Charles Okun

William Hurt as Macon Leary
Kathleen Turner as Sarah Leary

Sarah Leary: *There's something so muffled about the way you experience things. It's as if you were trying to slip through life unchanged.*

There is a beautiful scene of acceptance and resignation. It's a great adult film, about relationships and how we do go forward despite our losses. Her characters seem to learn so much that I find it hopeful, even if the learning isn't in the direction they had assumed. And it's about how all of them change in the process.

Bill had stopped drinking by then, and I never saw him clearer. When we started shooting, Larry walked up to the two of us on the set and he said, 'God, I'd forgotten how good you guys are.' It was so sweet of him.

But at the same time, it's disappointing when people forget how moved they were or how impressed they were, how much they enjoyed a performance. Then your name comes back up again and they go, 'Oh, yeah. She's so good.' I don't mind auditioning or showing to someone again that I can do it. But I do get a little tired of hearing, 'Oh, yeah, you're good. I forgot.' Jesus. Honestly.

I suppose this is just another way of saying people do move forward.

As have I. I find it exciting to discover compensating strengths that don't just make up for losses but even feel like unexpected gains. To relate it to the physical, I have the most amazing muscle memory. You tell me, 'Isolate the upper part of your triceps on your right arm.' I can do that. I can tell you almost every muscle in my body and how to trigger it. You want the lower left lat? It's there from all my years of growing up as an athlete, but also my concentration as an actor. Do I need to fire this muscle, to hold this muscle, to sustain this breath? If I close my eyes and concentrate, I can isolate almost every fucking muscle in my body. Which is not usual. But it served me well through coming back from RA, and still helps me compensate, using what I can use for that which I can't. It helps me work around the pain: *All right, I can't use that one because it hurts too badly. So I'll use this one instead.*

The time that Bert, my doctor, told me I'd done everything I set out to do, I felt as though he had kicked me in the stomach. I railed, 'What do you mean? What do you mean, I've done everything? Should I kill myself? What?' And then I thought, *No, he's right. I've done all those things, so now truly is about the quality of my life, what I choose my life to mean, given all my experience and all my power and knowledge and connections and finances. And the legacy I want to leave.* Twenty years ago or even ten years ago I could never have thought like this. I mean, this is the point of getting older.

The ability to apply what I have learned is my most precious rose.

Chapter Fourteen

Take the lead, lady!

A young woman named Jodi in Minneapolis has named her iPod Kathleen Turner Overdrive, writes a blog called 'I Will Dare,' and drives a pickup truck named Ruby.[26] Jodi may or may not know who Kathleen Turner is, but she sounds a lot like Rachel and so many of her young women friends today. They are bold and fearless and they know they can become whatever they choose to be. I find that so exciting, and I encourage them to make good use of their opportunities. I hope the roles I've played in my career and my life have helped embolden some of them.

Taking risks has been a central theme of my life. *Making choices*. A sense of values, sense of morality, never profiting from someone else's harm, is absolutely integral to me, who I am. *Service to other people*, be it in the work, by supporting another actor, or in the world, by volunteering for an organization, is a central theme to me. And *curiosity*. Asking, 'What if I? What if we? What if?' All my life lessons have in some way come out of these basic themes and values.

Risk and choice are about acting, in the sense of taking action. Taking action is taking the lead role in my own life. Acting, in the sense of what I have done in my career onstage and in film, has in the doing taught me so much about taking risks and making choices. I try to pass what I know on to others.

Practical acting: shut up and do it!

That's the name of the course I teach at New York University. I get the students, fifteen or sixteen of them, four hours a week, two hours on Tuesday, two hours on Thursday. They have to audition to take the class. I take only juniors and seniors. I like to work with kids who have had enough experience to appreciate – and put to use – what I'm showing them or asking of them. And I like to have kids who have stuck it out long enough that I believe they have a sincere desire to act.

I tell them to be brave and take risks, not to hedge their bets, and then I give them opportunities to do that in a safe environment. Everybody has to be on his or her feet performing during every class. Nobody gets to sit and watch.

I take them right into stage work for the first half of the course. The biggest performing spaces at NYU hold around 350 people. A Broadway theater or any real commercial theater will usually have a minimum of about one thousand, music houses more like two thousand. These students have rarely tested their voice projection. Perhaps they assumed they would be miked.

But even if they are miked, unless the sound technology person is really brilliant, the audience hears the dialogue coming from a different source than the one it is looking at on the stage. Sound coming from amps set up around the theater, however subtle, creates a lack of reality, a distance between the audience and the play. If you can keep the source of the sound in the same place that the audience's eyes and their interests are, how much closer you can bring them to your character.

So I take my students to a Broadway theater and give each of them time onstage. And all of them spend time in different areas in the theater when they're not onstage, to experience the flow, to find where the inevitable holes are. Jimmy Nederlander Jr. has been very generous in letting me use some of his theaters so that my course can be experiential and practical.

In the stage acting part of the course, we often work on three- and four-person scenes. A duet is not difficult at all. You have two people on the stage and when one stops speaking the audience's attention shifts to the other. But when you have three or four or more people onstage, the audience does not assume where they're going to have to shift their attention next. The actors' job then is throwing the focus like a ball so the audience can follow it as naturally as possible.

Sometimes the kids try to upstage the hell out of one another. So we work on why it is both courteous and better theater for them to pass the line so the actor who is speaking can be seen by the audience. I share my own experiences. For example, if anyone in *Virginia Woolf* could have stolen the show, it would have been Martha. But what does that do to the play? What does that do to the other actors? What does it do to Albee? It's unfair; it's a misinterpretation. So if George needs more support in this scene, if I have to pull myself back a little or do less than I might be able to, then that's what I must do to keep the balance in the work and the focus on the story.

I have no patience with a selfish actor. I'll say, 'At this point you should be passing the ball to her because she has the focus now. And you're holding on to it. So the audience is muddled about whom to focus on. Give it up.'

For the second half of the course, we do on-camera work. It's every actor's job to know where the camera frame is, to know what lens is being used. The higher the number of the lens, the tighter the shot. A 100 lens is on your eyes, a 50 is your head, and so on. You need this information to play to it appropriately. Say we're doing a semitight shot and you are gesturing outside the frame. What the hell good does that do? The camera can't see your gestures. So you have to put all your focus and energy into what you are doing with your face. I try to show them very practical things like that.

At the beginning of my first class, I think the other faculty thought here was this famous actress between jobs needing something to do. But pretty soon some of the teachers would come sit in on the class, and then actors and students would ask to audit. And when the student assessments came in, some said they learned more from me in seven weeks than they had in the three previous years. I thought, *Well, I like this teaching role.*

Acting lessons for life

Most people are not professional actors, but some acting lessons apply to everyone.

Ever wonder why people so enjoy coming together to watch a

show? I know exactly why. It's communion, baby. Before there were documented organized religions, there were festivals. People came together for commerce, for a marketplace, but at the same time they came together to sing, to dance, to share, to create a community.

And this is still true. Certainly in theater, most of the time you are sitting among a set of complete strangers closer than you would stand or sit with people in your own home, violating the space norms around you. You start to breathe in the same rhythms. You start to laugh at the same time. The most fascinating phenomenon is when I hear the laugh the same second from the back of the house as from the front row. It sounds impossible. Sound doesn't travel that fast. So it's a communal understanding. Something's happened that everybody gets it at once.

When you've left that theater or celebration or gathering, you've been part of a greater community. You've been part of something greater than an individual. And you're made stronger by it. I know this in my soul. I feel it at every performance.

Acting lessons also apply to individuals. I know it sounds odd, but I liken good acting to being in the midst of a car crash. If you've been in a car crash, and most people have had some brush with this, just when you realize that it's going to happen, and before you hit, your brain flashes so fast: Is the road wet or is it dry? If I turn to the left and take the impact on the right-hand side, do I have a passenger? Do I have a child in the car? Does the other car have a passenger or a child? Would it be better to take the hit on my side? All these thoughts rush through you in a microsecond – but in that microsecond, you have the time to actually think these things through and make a choice. In fact, you must make a choice.

Good acting is like that – *good* being an important adjective. Time slows down and I have all these choices I can make. What is my hand doing? Where is my voice? Do I want to go up on this word or down on this word? Do I want the pause before? Do I take the drink now? Do I sit or stand? How do I pass the focus to the next person who speaks? Everything is at an incredibly intense level.

It is in some ways addictive, because I feel so incredibly alive when I'm acting. My brain is racing, my body is responding to these instant decisions, and it's a heightened sensibility. It's hard to come down after a great show because I've been living at this level for hours. It makes the rest of life seem very slow and a little dull at times. Living on that racing edge is so thrilling.

I think one should live not necessarily at the intensity of a car crash but in that sort of constant examination. What are the thoughts in my mind? What is my body feeling? Who am I talking to? Am I happy or am I sad? Am I feeling reckless or cautious? It's a question of constantly examining yourself as you go through daily life, and being conscious of making choices.

Acting is, at its essence, the study of human behavior. I grant you, actors are given the words, so part of that study is what the playwright was thinking. How does he want this story told? As an actor, I have to try to understand that. Given the information I have about the character, I have to ask, Why does she react like this? Why does she have this gesture? What's in her background or in her mind, or what's her relationship with this person that makes her answer like this or walk away? Why people behave the way they do is a constant exploration and I think is tremendously interesting.

An audience absorbs things from characters when they watch them, too. And when I'm playing a role night after night after night, month after month, I start to pick up little physical habits and rhythms from the character. My posture was seriously starting to suffer from Martha. She just sprawls everywhere. And she's very breast conscious, so I found myself sticking out my boobs all over the place, and thinking, *Well, this isn't like me*. But she loves those breasts. She carries them high and proud. Audiences often leave plays and movies repeating a phrase or mannerism that has caught them, just as they leave humming a tune after a musical.

I'm constantly analyzing other people. I think anyone can learn from acting how to sharpen those skills. It's observation, basically, and empathy. Look at the other person. Watch the movement, listen to the choice of words, listen to the tone of voice. I can pick up a phone and after the person on the other end says a few words, I'll say, 'Uh-oh, things aren't going well for you today, huh?' You listen, you watch. You try to put yourself in the other person's place: What does she want from you? What do you want from her? You try to be always aware of other people's needs. It's very compassion-based. From acting, you become more tolerant, because you constantly try to examine what the other person is thinking or feeling or needing. Because everybody has needs.

It's what I call the third eye. When I'm working onstage or on film, there's always a part of me that's observing, documenting. It might say, 'Oh, that was perfect, keep that for tomorrow night.' Or, 'That didn't quite work. We're going to have to do some more exploration on that line.' It's like a recorder. After a performance, I can run it back in my mind and see the places that I liked and I want to keep and the places that I feel I have to work more on.

That third eye concept applies to everyone, actor or not. You're not judging; you're just observing, really. And then you can put it together and make sense of it. When I meet someone and want to figure out what's up, these are the skills I use.

There's so much self-exploration in exploring a character. Because what happens is, I'm not pretending to be somebody else; I'm presenting the ideas and the words and the physicality of this other person through myself, from the resources that I have. And those resources are my mind and emotions and body. So when I have to find huge despair or huge joy or whatever the extreme, I explore my own depths, both of capability and personal experience.

There comes a certain point in acting when I reach a depth of understanding of my character that I don't want to put into words. It's what I call my character's secrets. I'm not going to tell anybody else what this deep, dark secret is. If somebody asks me a question, say, about Martha, if it's in the script I can answer it. But if it's in myself, if it's in my understanding of the character, I just say, 'Sorry, that's secret.'

I find some aspects of what I do almost mystical: the inherent understanding, the communication with the audience. And I don't want to know all the nuts and bolts. That would take some of the magic out of it. So I can't reveal all of it even if I wanted to.

Everyone can learn from my practical acting lessons, but a little mystery must remain, for heaven's sake.

The lesson of the labyrinth

Learning from acting represents years and years of training and performing for me. I have been blessed with natural talent. But there has been much struggle, too, and I'm not out of the woods yet.

I still haven't learned sufficiently to refuse to blame myself for everything that happens. I don't mean that I don't want to take responsibility for my actions or choices. I very much want that. But if something doesn't go right or someone else doesn't work out in some way, I blame myself. I don't know why. It's as if I think I could have made it work or should have done a better job or saved somebody from the mistake. Which is unrealistic at best. God knows, Rachel has pointed this out to me over the years by asking where I get off thinking I have the right to take responsibility for other people's behavior. It is rather presumptuous, isn't it, for me to think I have such powers?

But even though now I have the ability to say, 'Wait a minute – maybe this isn't my job,' it's still most often my first instinct to say, 'Oh, it must be something I didn't do – or did do.' I would like to get away from that, because it takes away from my enjoyment of life. It keeps me from feeling totally free to celebrate my accomplishments and who I am. I always feel lacking in some way. I'm not quite sure where this came from, other than perhaps a childhood feeling that I was never quite good enough to measure up to . . . whatever it was I was being compared to. My siblings in the case of my mother, and in the case of my father, his own strong sense of right and wrong – wrong including his disapproval of my acting career.

My current stature on the stage is the source of my greatest satisfaction. It represents the accomplishment of the vision I had when I was twenty years old and starting out in my career. But even at the pinnacle of my career thus far and with great optimism looking forward to roles ahead, I still sometimes feel the jagged edges of yearning for my father's approval.

Oh, I wish so much he would have lived to see the work I've done. I just know that if my father could see me on the stage now, he would appreciate me and what I do. He couldn't conceive of it back then, obviously, because I hadn't done the work to learn what I know now. When I was seventeen, neither of us understood what I would become. But I think he would understand my passion and my work now.

One day when I was at the spa in California with Gloria, we started the morning hike into the hills with the group. I soon realized I couldn't make the whole hike. I so enjoyed being outside, out in the hills. But the hikes got progressively longer and steeper each day. I was pretty sure the rocks that made the trail so challenging to my knees would be my bête noire if I didn't watch it, and I couldn't stand the thought of having to replace the second knee just yet. So I peeled off from the group and went back down the hill alone, feeling rather blue that I couldn't finish what I'd started.

There is a labyrinth at the bottom of the hill. When I came to it, I remembered we'd been told that the idea of the labyrinth is to walk the path of its concentric circles slowly from the outside in. You symbolically walk through your past, and as you come to the center you're at your present. Then, when you go back around the path from the center to the outside, you're in essence walking toward your future. And letting go of your past.

I was all alone with my thoughts in the tranquility of the

labyrinth. I began to walk it. The slow concentric movement mesmerized me. When I got to the center, I stood there, and I started crying. I cried for a good long while, not knowing why. I asked myself, *Why am I crying?* And I thought, *I'm crying because I'm scared, because I just came down from the hill and I'm so afraid of another injury.*

I spend a lot of time saying to people, 'No, I'm fine, I'm fine, I'm fine.' And I *am* fine, to a certain extent. But the fear, the real fear of falling and losing the use of my good knee is much greater than I allow myself to know most of the time. It's the old and constant fear of becoming unable to be self-sufficient and to continue to work at the craft I love.

I stood there alone in the center of the labyrinth with the warm morning sunlight beating down on me, while I beat up on myself for being so scared. When I stopped crying a bit, I started to think, *Now, really, why should I try to hide this even from myself? This is pretty silly. Why don't I just forgive myself for being afraid? It's all right.* I stayed with that and let it sink in for a good while.

And then my self-forgiveness let me think about getting to a certain point where I could let my parents go. That whatever issues I have, I'm the one responsible for them, and it's about time.

I kept coming back to thoughts about my father.

A few years ago, Mother read an interview in which I talked about the argument Dad and I had just before he died, when I stormed out and went to Stratford against his wishes. In the interview, I disclosed the guilt I'd carried with me for all those years, thinking he had died angry with me, and how I harbored a fear that my behavior might have added to whatever physical stresses led to his heart attack.

Mother said to me, 'You must stop saying that. Your father wasn't angry at you. He was laughing about it when I arrived home and he told me about your disagreement. He said, "Oh yeah, she's in Stratford. She'll be home tomorrow. She's doing her thing."'

Well, my God. Here I'd been holding this inside me all these years. I was so sure he had died mad at me. And that haunted me, absolutely haunted me. But he didn't die angry with me! My mother said he wasn't angry at all. And that he was looking forward to my coming home and helping him with the garden.

I had not been stretching to make those assumptions, taking into account his upbringing and his rigid moral sense. But no, it turned out he was proud of my rebelliousness in some ways. He actually appreciated the ways I was so unlike my siblings in the same way he appreciated their academic achievements and talents. I was blazing new ground. And he wasn't angry about that; he loved me for it.

Damn.

I really hadn't processed that till now. Walking the labyrinth, I felt I could finally give up all those feelings of fear and guilt that had festered because I'd never had any closure with my father; because there wasn't time for him to be with me as an adult or for me to grow up enough so there could be mutual forgiveness, because there couldn't even be the acceptance that allows forgiveness to exist. Now I can stop beating up on myself. I am free to continue my own growth. I am truly free to go forward to the rest of my life.

It's funny, but the more I let go of those things about my relationship with my father that had been holding me back emotionally, the more I appreciate the ties that bind me to him.

I feel very strongly about many of the same things he felt strongly about. First among those is service. I hope that I honor him by continuing to act on that.

I had to share these insights right away, so at the spa that night at dinner, I couldn't resist reading an essay by Maya Angelou to the whole group. Maya talks about how people grow older but growing up is more challenging. One has to assume responsibility for the time one takes up and the space one occupies. I really believe that. And she says you should try to see yourself with power: not power so that you can get even with anyone else, but power so you can become even with your vision.[27]

And that was the very lesson my walk to the center of the labyrinth and back out gave me in the solitude of the early morning. I recognized that I have been becoming my vision of myself. And that is very satisfying.

Stepping forward into the rest of my life

I feel *actively* happy right now. It's not as if everything is perfect and there is nothing wrong. But I do feel absolutely, positively walk-around-with-a-smile-on-my-face happy. Which is such a wonderful thing. I don't know if I've ever truly spent much of my life feeling that way.

It feels like a new beginning. With the many responsibilities of the last twenty-one years being over, essentially, that load has become so much lighter. And then to couple that with the greater access to my choice of work is a pleasure. I think if I called up a producer, any theatrical producer, now and said, 'I want to play a certain role, I have to do this role,' he or she is certainly going to think about it. That's a nice feeling. And I have fewer financial responsibilities. So I feel buoyant. Yes, I have responsibilities that I still must meet and want to meet, but I feel so free. I love where I am now. I have the excitement of visualizing a whole new life ahead of me.

I was in my gynecologist's office, where I observed a woman obviously due to give birth that day. Her husband came rushing in and the two of them sat there talking about what had happened that day, anticipating this birth, and everything he said was so positive, as compared to my years of living with someone who looked for what was wrong or what might go wrong. Who I don't think ever allowed himself and by extension me to say, 'Let's just be happy.' I know that's some of my doing too because I'm a little superstitious, thinking that if I say, 'Oh, I'm so happy,' something bad will come and bang me on the head. But somehow I've passed out of that, or am passing out of it at least. I can feel it is actually possible just to enjoy being alive. I love the feeling. God!

And it seems that when I approach life with that attitude, life responds to me more positively, too.

For many years, I've had lovely responses from people on the street, people I meet at some event, a crew I'm just starting to work with or whatever. But I walk around now with a smile on my face and people grin at me. It seems as if everybody knows who I am again. I don't think my work is more visible, unless it's that my old movies are on TV every single day. But I get a very positive sense that something good is happening.

I went to have lunch the other day at a nice restaurant after I'd done a Citymeals-on-Wheels delivery. It was late and I really needed something to eat. I sat down at the bar with my book, as

I often do. The bartender got me my water and menu, and took my order. Then he came back and said, 'You're Kathleen Turner!' I said, 'Yeah, I am.' And he said, 'But you're so nice.' I laughed because I thought that was so funny. I don't know what he was expecting, but he said, 'You're so nice.'

Now, don't get me wrong. It's not that everything is perfect. I miss not having to worry about my weight. Every year I kind of get thicker no matter what I do. I have a friend who said that the year she hit menopause she went from a twenty-nine-inch to a thirty-four-inch waist without gaining a pound. Oh, yeah, I miss my waistline.

And I get tired more easily. That's just the way it is. While I'd like to attribute all of that to RA, let's face it, some of it is the normal aging process. By Saturday night after two shows that cap my eight *Virginia Woolf* performances in a week, I'm pooped. There's a line at the very end of the play when George says to Martha, 'Are you tired?' and she goes, 'Yes.' And he says, 'Well, it's Sunday tomorrow, all day.' She says, 'Yes,' in a way that means 'Oh, God, yes, please yes.' I know that feeling. I certainly can't keep the hours that I used to. Going out at midnight after a show is inconceivable to me now. But I look forward to what's next with a new optimism because it is a new and good stage of life that I am entering. Every step is still forward.

So I am looking forward to traveling around to do a five-city sweep of *Who's Afraid of Virginia Woolf?* in the first half of 2007. Martha came right back when we started rehearsing. It's almost scary how fast. Martha and I are just having a ball, and George and I are taking the third act to even deeper places than we've ever been before. Meanwhile, the British awards I have received for my Martha – the Evening Standard Award and the London

Critics Award, not to mention the Olivier nomination – more than make up for that missing Tony.

But once we finish this production, I will be done with Martha and ready to move on. Time for Martha to go upstairs to bed.

I would like to get some more film work, either in Europe or here. I'd like to set aside a month to live in Italy to really get a sense of whether it is the right place for me to buy a home. I'd rent a place and do my own shopping and laundry – well, maybe not my laundry – but see how I can function there. I plan to spend my time searching in the hills behind Rome. I want some countryside that's very accessible to Rome. I love the language, I love the people, I love the friendliness. I love the climate. I love the architecture. I love that there are so many objects of beauty present that they are almost taken for granted. I want to surround myself with such comfort and colors. And I'd like to have a garden. But I want good access to Rome because I'm a city girl. Or maybe it'll be Spain . . .

And besides, I don't plan to go there just to sit in a nice house. I plan to create another life there, to teach, to work in films. I think there are excellent opportunities for me to direct in Europe. I'll take some low-budget films and prove what I can do. And so I'll have such a different tempo, such a different rhythm, such a different attitude toward life. I'll have a couple extra bedrooms, have people come to visit, and find good work for myself that doesn't interfere with my living. I can't imagine ever giving up New York entirely. Or Broadway. It will be a balance. Half and half would be lovely, but I'll have to await some inevitable choices on that.

Five years from now, I'd like to have more stage directing

under my belt. I'll direct a play again at Williamstown in the summer of 2007, which I will enjoy very much.

I want to continue teaching. I'm much more directed than when I first began teaching and am learning well how to handle the job. While I am touring, I'll teach master classes at universities where we are performing, and I'll do events for my service organizations too. I can teach anywhere, under almost any circumstances. When I do have more time in Europe, why don't I just teach there also? I certainly don't have any desire to sit around. That would be very boring. I want to build my real chops, my credentials with teaching. This is how I feel about directing too. I need to take it in steps so I have a résumé that's absolutely demonstrable.

I think the idea of taking those steps forward into the next roles in life is to explore offshoots of one's central passion or central ability. Almost any field or talent must have different avenues open for exploration.

There are some plays I would especially like to do. *Sweet Bird of Youth. Happy Days*, the Beckett piece. There are so many great classic ladies of a certain age created by Shaw or similarly wonderful writers.

Since I knew at twenty that I wanted to play Martha when I was fifty, I suppose I should think about what I want to play when I am eighty. That would be *The Royal Family*, obviously, the one about three generations of actors. I'd play the Eva Le Gallienne role. And for some reason, Lady Macbeth has been on my mind lately. I haven't done Shakespeare in years. I'm going to go back and read *Hamlet* again. Wouldn't I be scary?

By this time, I'll have legendary status and then I can go on to my ultimate dream job, which would be playing the West End at night while serving as U.S. ambassador to Great Britain by day, ambassador to Great Britain being preferable to me than my eighth grade classmates' prediction of ambassador to the moon. Perhaps I will do this in the administration of our first female president.

The smell of a man and other future facts of my life

My mother never had another relationship with a man after my father died. For a while, she was the head of the Girl Scouts in Midland, Texas, where she worked primarily with women. Then she moved back to Missouri when my younger brother finished high school. At that time, she decided to become a paralegal. Well, it was an extraordinary thing for her to do. It meant going back to university in her late fifties. And I think she was the first woman in Missouri to pass the test on her first try.

I asked her, 'Why did you want to do all of this?' She said it was partly because she was interested in the job, but also that she wanted to work in a law office because she so missed the smell of men. That struck me as quite a poignant observation. Which I now understand.

Yeah, I miss the smell of a man now, too. I imagine that I will come to feel that sense of wanting a masculine smell and presence around.

I would enjoy interesting company. There's a problem – well, there are two problems with my dating again. One is that so many of the men my age have worked very hard to achieve their position in their careers. But in the process they often get narrow in their interests. Other interests such as literature that don't apply to their field, or simply add to enjoying life, are not in their makeup anymore. I would find it a little stifling not to have a person with well-rounded interests to enjoy. The other issue is that men seem to be simultaneously attracted to and put off by my success, my position, my intelligence – they're wary of me. So that might make it difficult for me to find that enjoyable companion.

But I think I'd like to fall in love again. Jesus, I'd like to have sex again, you know? Oh, wouldn't that be nice. Good sex. Really good sex. I'd love to have really good sex. But I'm not at the point yet at which I'm that hungry for the smell of a man. I'm just fine right now without it. I imagine I will get there, but not yet.

And meanwhile, I would like to do many other things that are fun and interesting. I discovered that I like to jump out of planes when Rachel persuaded me to go skydiving with her. How thrilling that was – to think I had gone from being unable to even pick my child up when she was small to skydiving side by side with her as she reached adulthood.

I like to have things happen on the spur of the moment with friends, like when we had the beach house and someone would say, 'Okay, why doesn't everybody go and grab a ton of food from the market?' We'd start cooking and whoever showed up was great and whoever didn't, didn't. I just loved that. Want to go to the theater tonight? It's six-thirty. Yeah, okay, let's go. Things like that.

I like to laugh. I like to laugh a lot. A lot, a lot, a lot. And I like anybody with good jokes. I can jump around, acting stupid when nobody can see me – the clue being when no one can see me.

I like to try weird things to eat. And honest to God, if I get to choose my last meal, it's going to be steamed crabs and black truffle pasta. That's my last meal, baby.

If I were a character in my own play, I would be funny, smart, irreverent, silly, stubborn, demanding. Fifty-two years old. I don't want to go backwards. On the whole, pretty good qualities, but with some real flaws. I don't mind admitting when I'm wrong, as long as I'm sure I'm wrong. Which takes a lot of convincing. I have my own moral stance and moral consistency. I'm compassionate. Impatient. Seriously impatient. I just don't fucking suffer fools.

I didn't trust myself enough when I first became a professional actress. I am confident now that I am a lot better than my fears and doubts let me think at that time. I was actually a lot better than almost everybody else then, but I didn't know that yet. I would have liked to know that and save myself a lot of angst, but I don't think you can have that perspective at twenty-two. The wisdom of age, experience, and the hard knocks of life has given me the view that we should always go ahead with the assumption that we are good, because, you know, it might very well be true.

I still need to learn to value myself more. I still need to stop second-guessing, or stop immediately saying 'It must be my fault' when something didn't work out right, somebody isn't happy, or something didn't happen the way I hoped it would. I have to get past that and go toward keeping my focus on simply making things better.

The thing about lessons learned is that the lessons change. When you start out, you think you learn something, and then it evolves and you find out that there's more to it and there will always be more to learn as long as you are alive. So the lesson you thought you learned then isn't what you know now.

Years ago, I also had different goals from the ones I have now.

My idea of success used to be becoming an international name and an international actor, to wield power in my profession. My view has completely changed. Now what I want is on a much more personal level. Not to wield my power as an actress so much as to be effective and contribute as a person. I want to lie down at the end thinking that I helped make the world better. It sounds terribly pretentious, but I really do mean that. And the older I get, the more I mean it.

I never thought of wanting to be like anyone else. I would see other actors' performances and think how wonderfully they did it, how their body echoed the words, echoed the thought, echoed the momentum of the character. That they were just right, they were in the right zone doing the right thing with the right choices. That's my appreciation more than inspiration. I have learned a great deal from other people, but I have typically had an unerring sense of what is really, authentically me. I'll do a small head toss, the head toss that defines my claim to be able to make any audience love me. It's a small movement, but the people immediately react with delight. And I delight with them.

So that's me, my life and the lessons I have to offer so far. I might be wrong – not often – but there's just no other way I could act. Or do. Or be.

I suppose you could say I'm just drawn that way.

Filmography and stage roles

Filmography

1981 *Body Heat*
1983 *The Man with Two Brains*
1984 *Romancing the Stone*
1984 *A Breed Apart*
1984 *Crimes of Passion*
1985 *Prizzi's Honor*
1985 *The Jewel of the Nile*
1986 *Peggy Sue Got Married*
1987 *Giulia e Giulia*
1987 *Switching Channels*
1988 *Who Framed Roger Rabbit*
1988 *The Accidental Tourist*
1989 *The War of the Roses*
1991 *V.I. Warshawski*

1993   *Naked in New York*
1993   *House of Cards*
1993   *Undercover Blues*
1994   *Serial Mom*
1995   *Moonlight and Valentino*
1997   *A Simple Wish*
1997   *The Real Blonde*
1999   *Baby Geniuses*
1999   *The Virgin Suicides*
2000   *Beautiful*
2000   *Prince of Central Park*
2006   *Monster House*

Stage Roles

1977   *Mr. T.*
1978   *Gemini*
1980   *Travesties*
1980   *The Seagull*
1985   *A Midsummer Night's Dream*
1989   *Love Letters*
1990   *Cat on a Hot Tin Roof*
1995   *Indiscretions*
1997   *Our Betters*
1997   *Tallulah!* (West Sussex, England)
2000   *Tallulah!* (U.S. Tour)
2000   *The Graduate* (London)
2001   *The Graduate* (Toronto)
2002   *The Graduate* (New York)
2003   *The Exonerated*
2005   *Who's Afraid of Virginia Woolf?* (New York)
2006   *Who's Afraid of Virginia Woolf?* (London)
2007   *Who's Afraid of Virginia Woolf?* (U.S. Tour)

Acknowledgments and Afterword

Kathleen: The book was your fault, Gloria. Absolutely. People have approached me about this idea before. I think there's some unauthorized biography in airport bookstores. Before you talked me into it, and you did talk me into it, I wasn't sure at first. And then I said I'd learned a lot of lessons. I find as I get older that it's more and more important to me the kind of person I am, the quality of my life's meaning. Someone said the object of our lives is not what we achieve materially . . . it's the growth of our soul that matters. And I suppose I felt – well, I did feel – that my soul was finally in a place that I could contribute.

Gloria: Nothing could have been further from my mind than this book when we started the conversation. I was at a vulnerable place in my life. I'd left a long career that had defined me and had not yet decided what my next phase of life was going to be. I'm at the age when most people are thinking about retirement and I'm thinking about my new career! I intended – still intend – to write a book about America's difficult relationship with sex. So I got a new book agent, Karen Gantz Zahler. We have her to thank for the whole idea, because she suggested I write your biography.

K: I worried it would seem self-promoting. And that's never been my credo. My publicists are told to protect me, not promote me. And they do. Thank you, Alan Nierob of Rogers and Cowan for that, and also Alan's colleague Nicole Perez.

We left that day very unresolved. I said, 'I'll think about it.'

G: Then you had more foot surgery, right, after that?

K: Ha, honey, every year.

G: So you were out of commission for a little while.

K: I had some thinking time. It's terribly distressful to me to be incapacitated and not be able to move around and do what I want. This morning I took boxing lessons. But when I was laid up, I had time to think about what I could say in a book.

G: Then we had lunch again. Lunch is a theme here.

K: That's when I said, 'Yeah, okay.' And I said no gossip.

G: Our editor, Karen Murgolo at Springboard Press – whom we thank profusely for her belief in this book, her sound advice, and her gentle persuasion – by this time had persuaded us to turn the book into a memoir. People asked me, 'Why would Kathleen be writing her memoir now? She's only in her fifties. Why didn't she wait until she was eighty to write it?'

K: And the answer is that it's a great place in life to be thinking about where I have come from and what I want to do with the rest of my life. The other half of it. I'm not at the end of my life looking back, I'm at the middle of my life looking forward. And because there are so many women now my age who really, truly are in kind of the same place: starting careers again, changing careers. Being done with the responsibilities they have carried for many years. There are a lot of us. There's a lot to look forward to.

G: When we started, I knew I liked you a lot. But the more I learned about you, the more I loved you and respected you. And the more I feel truly honored to have had an opportunity – not that your voice needs to be amplified – to help put this book out there to the world.

K: Well, thank you. I will confess that it's more exposure than I ever planned on giving about myself. On many levels. I don't share my problems with the world. It was tough to go into the gorier depths of some of my troubles. But at the same time, I'm not a liar. I lie really badly. As I said, the better an actress I've become, the worse a liar I am. I hope it's because I'm a more honest actor. I was pretty scared, telling so much.

G: We had many people supporting us.

K: I want to thank Cristiana Sadigianis for all her help on this book and always. Cristiana started out as my assistant a few years ago without a lot of experience and is now learning how to design and produce photo shoots. I am very proud of her.

G: I want to acknowledge Jean Brown, who transcribed all the tapes. She was remarkable. She did not miss a word; she got everyone's voices and inflections.

K: She also tried to show emphasis. The pauses or the sounds. I just talked. You organized my thoughts and put them into perspective and tried to find the correlations and make sense of it, to sort it out when one thing I've said runs into another. Honestly, total, total credit to you, Gloria.

G: No, I thank Onnesha Tao Roychoudhuri profusely, because never in a million years could I have been able to sift through all that information and content without her expert help, her crackerjack research, photo gathering, and fact checking. Also, she taught me how to use the 'find' function on the computer, which has changed my life.

K: Double that! She had fifty years of my life in her hands, baby.

G: She did the most amazing job of going through it, putting pieces together, finding stuff when I couldn't find it, offering suggestions, answering my weird, stupid questions.

K: Keeping you on track.

G: All that. Also, thanks to Aiden Amos, my intern when we started this project, who did some of the initial research, and Iliza Bershad, my intern who helped organize the photos.

K: I want to thank my family, my mother and siblings, all of them. And my daughter, Rachel, especially. Because she makes life such a blessing. The best thing about having a child is, it bumps you out of the center of attention. There's something more important than you. And that's a nice thing, to be pushed out of the middle. Honestly, it's such a relief. People who continue on and on through the years being the center of attention must go nuts.

G: I appreciate that your mother, Pat Turner, went through all your family photos for us. She told me that she was very nervous about the book. I said, 'Don't worry about it. You've come out looking wonderful and you'll love the book.' And she said, 'Well, my older son has promised me that he will read it first.'

K: I thank Sam Cohn, my agent, because he has been most

stalwart, wise, loving, and amazing. And I love him. Oh, dear, the list of thank-yous is very long.

G: We must thank your friends Sandi Kaufman, Kathy Dougherty, and Margo MacNabb, who went to City Crab and spilled the beans about you.

K: My girlfriends. They're great women.

G: They didn't really spill very many beans. But just hearing how they talked to each other and to you and how you all interacted with each other was great.

Two of my friends read the manuscript and critiqued it. Nadia Berenstein suggested wonderful edits that greatly improved the writing. She's one of the smartest young women and one of the best writers I have ever known. Carol Jennings, a dear friend who helped me write my first book, looked at the big picture of it all and said, 'Okay, this is where I couldn't figure out why you were saying this. This is where I couldn't quite follow.'

K: Oh, excellent. Specific. Thank you.

G: And thanks to my darling husband, Alex Barbanell, who has a penchant for breaking into conversations with totally irrelevant questions.

K: Here we are working in your dining room and he interrupts and tells about the Natural History Museum: 'We've got a great exhibit.' Yes, thank you. I know you do.

* * *

K: I think one reason that this book is special is not just because of what I say. I think it's because you and I working on the book collaboratively is a reflection of the way women are together. And that's important. I think it is most important that it was two women writing together.

G: It's easy somehow for two women to work without egos getting involved. It was so straightforward.

K: There was certainly pressure to do it in a more regimented, contractual way. Neither of us is going to screw with the other.

* * *

I do want to thank some important men. Edward Albee first. Edward is brilliant. Thank you, Edward, for this incredible play, this incredible role.

I tried at the beginning to go up against him, to match him quip for quip. I got slammed every time. You cannot top Edward. I'll never forget, closing night on Broadway, we had a small cast party. And as a joke, I said, 'Look, why don't we put on each other's costumes or attitudes and I'll be George, he'll be Martha, Nick will be Honey, and Honey will be Nick, and all this stuff.' And it was extremely funny, bumping about the other's persona that we'd observed for ten months. And at the end, Edward stood up to give a toast and said, 'I'm so glad to see that you remember so well your performances from Boston.' Forget it! You can't top this guy! You cannot top him. He's got this killer instinct. Just say, yes, Mr. Albee, thank you, Mr. Albee, thank you.

And also thanks to the great George, Bill Irwin, and Anthony Page, our director. It'll be two years now that I've worked on Martha, and one of the neatest things is that I'm free as a bird. Every time we do it, I'm more comfortable and more confident. I feel like I can't go off track. So, Martha and I are just having a ball. It's such fun. The second act is really a tough sell, a really tough piece, when she gets to be her most disreputable . . . most coarse. She loses control. And I just felt great. Watch what I can do . . .

[Exit laughing.]

Notes

1. Virginia Woolf, *A Room of One's Own* (Harcourt, 1929), 38.
2. Ben Brantley, 'In a Costumer Designed by Nature,' *New York Times*, April 5, 2002 (available online).
3. Ben Brantley, 'Marriage as Blood Sport: A No-Win Game,' *New York Times*, March 21, 2005 (available online).
4. Gail Sheehy, *Sex and the Seasoned Woman* (Random House, 2006), 22.
5. Suzanne Braun Levine, *Inventing the Rest of Our Lives* (Viking Penguin, 2005).
6. Janet Maslin, 'Body Heat,' *New York Times*, August 28, 1981 (available online).
7. Vincent Canby, 'The Pleasures of "Body Heat," ' *New York Times*, October 25, 1981 (available online).
8. *Enron: The Smartest Guys in the Room*, DVD. Alex Gibney,

director; Bethany McLean and Peter Elkind, writers. (Magnolia Pictures, 2005).

9. Suzie Mackenzie, 'Drama Queen,' *Guardian*, March 18, 2000.

10. Andy Barker, 'Heard the One About . . . ?' *Guardian*, March 12, 2006 (available online).

11. Maureen Dowd, 'Kathleen Turner: Inside an 80's Woman There Smolders a 30's Star,' *New York Times*, January 5, 1986 (available online).

12. Fred Schruers, *Premier*, August 1991.

13. Kitty Donaldson, 'Women Lower Tone for Some Vocal Equality with Men,' *New York Times*, June 4, 2006 (available online).

14. Tennessee Williams, *Cat on a Hot Tin Roof* (Penguin Books, 1955).

15. 'Kathleen: Heading North,' *New York Post*, April 19, 1990.

16. Mark Gado, 'A River of Tears: Happy Land,' Court TV Crime Library, October 15, 2006 (available at www.crimelibrary. com/notorious_murders/mass/happyland/fuego_3.html).

17. John Berger, *Here Is Where We Meet* (Pantheon, 2005).

18. Steve Schneider, 'A Day at the Beach, but Without the Burn,' *Orlando Weekly*, May 22, 1997 (available at www.orlando weekly.com/artsculture/story.asp?id=153).

19. Jesse Green, 'Kathleen Turner Gets Her "Virginia Woolf,"' *New York Times*, March 22, 2005 (available at www.iht.com/ articles/2005/03/21/features/turner.php).

20. William A. Sadler, *The Third Age* (Perseus Books, 2000), 193.

21. Gail Sheehy, *Sex and the Seasoned Woman* (Random House, 2006), 16–17.

22. Sharon O'Brien, 'How Baby Boomers Will Change Retirement,' About.com: Senior Living, October 15, 2006

(available at seniorliving.about.com/od/retirement/a/new boomerretire.htm).

23. Stephen Macmillan Moser, 'After a Fashion,' *Austin Chronicle*, February 1, 2002 (available at www.austinchronicle.com/gyrobase/Issue/column?oid=oid%3A84503).

24. Virginia Woolf, *A Room of One's Own* (Harcourt, 1929), 58.

25. *New York Times*, May 31, 2002.

26. Corey Anderson, '9/27 Morning Communiqué,' Minneapolis City Pages, September 27, 2006 (available at blogs.citypages.com/blotter/2006/09/927_morning_com.asp).

27. Willa Shalit, *Becoming Myself* (Hyperion, 2006), 1–5.